DATE DUE

PRINTED IN U.S.A.

Home, School and Leisure in the Soviet Union

This volume is dedicated to the memory of
Geoffrey Russell Barker, 1923–1977

Home, School and Leisure in the Soviet Union

Edited by

JENNY BRINE
MAUREEN PERRIE
ANDREW SUTTON
University of Birmingham

London
GEORGE ALLEN & UNWIN
Boston   Sydney

First published in 1980

GEORGE ALLEN & UNWIN LTD
40 Museum Street, London WC1A 1LU

© The University of Birmingham 1980

British Library Cataloguing in Publication Data

Home, school and leisure in the Soviet Union.
1. Russia – Social conditions – 1970–
I. Brine, J J   II. Perrie, Maureen
III. Sutton, Andrew
309.1'47'085   HN   80-40382

ISBN 0-04-335040-2

Set in 10 on 11 point Plantin by Northampton Phototypesetters and printed in Great Britain
by Billing & Sons Ltd, Guildford, London and Worcester

Contents

Editors' Introduction

All the contributors to this volume were colleagues or postgraduate students of Geoffrey Barker, working in areas close to his own teaching and research interests. In inviting contributions for the book, we were concerned first and foremost that it should have thematic coherence, and the phrase 'daily life' encapsulates the essence of our theme. Recent trends in social history, such as the 'History Workshop' publications, influenced to some extent by the development of the women's movement, have begun to focus attention on topics which are of intrinsic interest and importance in people's everyday lives. Themes such as work and leisure, home and family, education and popular culture, can now be regarded as appropriate issues for serious academic study. Geoffrey Barker was very much in sympathy with these developments, and in the field of Soviet studies he pioneered work on aspects of daily life, both in his own writings and by his encouragement of research students. The topics indicated in the title of this memorial volume reflect the range of Geoff's academic interests in the last ten years or so of his life.

The first part of the volume is concerned with aspects of family life. Greg Andrusz's chapter examines the material basis of domestic life, the provision of housing, and shows how the contradiction between the collectivist aspirations of Soviet society and the privatisation of housing provision affects the role of women in particular. Alix Holt describes women's domestic labour and analyses the problems which exist for the typical Soviet woman who works both inside and outside the home. Barbara Holland discusses the role of abortion in controlling the fertility of Soviet women.

The second part begins with a chapter by Elisabeth Koutaissoff which provides an overview of the problems facing Soviet educationists in the present and the future. Felicity O'Dell's chapter examines an aspect of the broader role of Soviet education – child socialisation and the inculcation of moral values through the study of literature. The following chapters by John Dunstan on boarding schools, Madeline Drake on child care, and Andrew Sutton on backwardness describe Soviet provision for special categories of children.

The third part is concerned with aspects of leisure in the USSR. Denis Shaw examines Soviet recreational planning, with emphasis on the physical environment. Jim Riordan's chapter traces the development of Soviet sport, and Jenny Brine looks at patterns of recreational reading in the USSR.

The chapters focus on the contemporary USSR, although most contributors have placed recent developments in their broader historical context. As is to be expected when people of one culture study life in a society different from their own, a comparative element is present in many of the chapters. The authors have utilised a wide range of Soviet and Western published sources. Several contributors have made use of Soviet sociological surveys and 'time-budget' studies. Alix Holt and Madeline Drake have supplemented their printed sources with interview data which they themselves collected in the USSR.

The contributors represent a wide range of academic backgrounds, including education, geography, librarianship, psychology, social history and sociology. Geoff would have approved of this, since he believed strongly in the value of the multi-disciplinary approach to Soviet studies which developed in Birmingham. One advantage of an interdisciplinary environment is that it inhibits excessive use of technical terminology and specialist jargon. The contributions to this volume, while firmly rooted in the authors' own disciplines, are also accessible to the general reader and of interest to the non-specialist.

Most of our contributors share a sympathy for the socialist ideals of Soviet society, but they are not uncritical of the way in which these aspirations have been translated into reality. The optimism and humanism of many of the contributions is very much in line with Geoff's own approach to the USSR.

And finally, the sex of the authors. Geoffrey Barker did much to encourage greater participation by women in academic life. We are sure that he would be pleased by the number of female contributors to his memorial volume.

JENNY BRINE
MAUREEN PERRIE
ANDREW SUTTON
June 1979

The Contributors

G. D. ANDRUSZ is Senior Lecturer in Sociology at Middlesex Polytechnic. He spent a year in the USSR studying at the Kiev Civil Engineering Institute and finished his PhD in 1979. He has published articles on urban sociology and his book *Housing and Urban Development in the USSR* is to be published by Macmillan in 1980.

JENNY BRINE is Librarian of the Centre for Russian and East European Studies, University of Birmingham. She is working on a thesis on reading and libraries in the USSR. Her previous publications are on Soviet libraries and bibliography.

R. W. DAVIES is Professor of Soviet Economic Studies and former Director of the Centre for Russian and East European Studies, University of Birmingham. He is the author of several books and articles on Soviet economic history.

MADELINE DRAKE is a Principal Research Officer at the Centre for Environmental Studies, London. She is a former research student of the Centre for Russian and East European Studies, University of Birmingham, and is working on a thesis about child care in the USSR. Her previous publications are on housing in Britain.

JOHN DUNSTAN is Lecturer in Soviet Education in the Centre for Russian and East European Studies and Faculty of Education, University of Birmingham. He also taught for five years in a British boarding school. His PhD was on problems of provision for high-ability children in the USSR and he has published a book, *Paths to Excellence and the Soviet School* (Windsor, Berks: NFER, 1978) and several articles about Soviet education.

BARBARA HOLLAND is a postgraduate student at the Centre for Russian and East European Studies, University of Birmingham, and is working on a thesis entitled 'Medicine as an agent of social control in the USSR with special reference to reproduction'. She has also worked in Moscow as a translator.

ALIX HOLT is a postgraduate student at the Centre for Russian and East European Studies, University of Birmingham. She is writing a PhD thesis on 'Women and the family in the USSR, 1917–30', and is also working on a book about the international communist women's movement. She has published a number of articles, mainly about women and the family in the USSR, and edited and translated *Alexandra Kollontai: Selected Writings* (London: Allison & Busby, 1978). She spent a year in Moscow as an exchange student and worked there as a translator for several years.

ELISABETH KOUTAISSOFF was Lecturer (later Senior Lecturer) in the Centre for Russian and East European Studies, University of Birmingham, for over twenty years and was then Professor of Russian, Victoria University, Wellington, New Zealand. She is now retired. She has published a book, *The Soviet Union* (London: Benn, 1971), and many articles about Soviet education and Russian literature.

FELICITY O'DELL is a former research student at the Centre for Russian and East European Studies, University of Birmingham, now teaching English as a foreign language in Cambridge. She finished her PhD in 1975, and an adapted version of it was published as *Socialisation through Children's Literature: The Soviet Example* (Cambridge: Cambridge University Press, 1978). She has also published (with David Lane) *The Soviet Industrial Worker: Social Class, Education and Control* (London: Martin Robertson, 1978), and articles on Soviet education.

MAUREEN PERRIE is Lecturer in the Centre for Russian and East European Studies and the Department of Modern History, University of Birmingham. She has written a book and several articles on pre-revolutionary Russian history.

JAMES RIORDAN is Senior Lecturer in Russian Studies at Bradford University. He finished his PhD in 1975 and an adapted version of it was published as *Sport in Soviet Society* (Cambridge: Cambridge University Press, 1977). He also edited *Sport under Communism* (London: Hurst, 1978) and his book *Soviet Sport: Background to the Olympics* is to be published by Blackwell in 1980. He has also published many articles on Soviet sport and leisure, and written several children's books. He worked in the USSR for five years as a translator and played for Moscow Spartak.

DENIS J. B. SHAW is Lecturer in the Department of Geography, University of Birmingham. He studied at Voronezh State University for a year and has travelled extensively in the USSR. He finished his PhD in 1973. He has published articles on Russian historical settlement and on Soviet spatial planning and problems of settlement. He has written a book (with J. Pallot) on *Planning in the USSR*, which is to be published by Croom Helm in 1980.

ANDREW SUTTON works as a developmental psychologist in Birmingham Area Health Authority (Teaching) and Birmingham Local Education Authority, and is also an Honorary Lecturer in the Faculty of Education, University of Birmingham. His MPhil degree involved the use of Soviet diagnostic techniques on English educationally subnormal children, and his publications include work on child development, child abuse, mental retardation and children's rights.

Acknowledgements

The editors would like to thank John Dunstan, Nick Lampert and other members of the Centre for Russian and East European Studies for their help and advice in the preparation of the typescript. Mrs Olga Griffin typed the manuscript promptly and accurately, and Mrs Nancy Moore provided secretarial assistance.

A Note on Prices and Transliteration

In certain chapters of this book, prices of goods and services have been given in roubles and kopecks, so as to give readers some indication of relative prices within the USSR. Readers should beware of converting these prices into sterling or dollars by either the official exchange rate or any of the various black market rates, since these do not give a reliable measure of the 'purchasing power parity' of the rouble against Western currencies when comparing the real income and expenditure of typical households. The official rate gives an unrealistically low value; on the other hand black market rates are likely to be on the high side. The contributors have avoided comparisons in terms of monthly wages, as the structure of family income and expenditure is very different from that in all Western countries.

The transliteration system used in this book is British Standard 2979–1958, without diacritical marks.

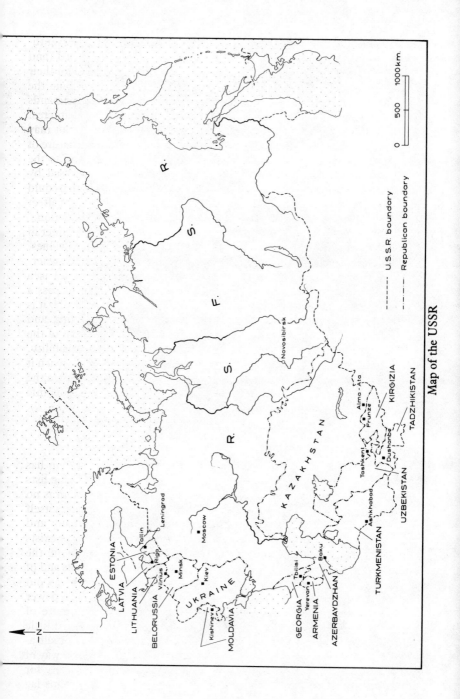

Map of the USSR

Part One

Housing, the Family and the Role of Women

1
Housing Ideals, Structural Constraints and the Emancipation of Women

G. D. ANDRUSZ

EARLY ASPIRATIONS AND THEIR DEMISE

As early as 1919 the Programme of the 8th Congress of the Russian Communist Party (Bolsheviks) adopted a resolution to the effect that the emancipation of women should not be limited to the achievement of formal (i.e. political and economic) equality with men. Emancipation was taken to mean much more than this, in particular their being freed from the burden of domestic work, including child-minding, by the setting up of communal blocks of flats (*doma-kommuny*) with public dining rooms, laundries and crèches, and by the establishment of a system of pre-school facilities ('Programma . . .', 1919, pp. 43, 48). Female emancipation had two very closely related goals: one was liberating the woman from household drudgery and the other drawing her into productive labour and so giving her economic independence (Lenin, 1919, p. 201). Translating intent into reality required changes in the physical and cultural environments.

Both metaphorically and literally the architects of the Revolution were the architects and town-planners who in their designs of dwellings and juxtapositioning of kindergartens, schools, social and cultural facilities and workplaces would provide a setting for a cultural revolution.

The years immediately after the October Revolution saw the working out of some of the theoretical and practical difficulties of constructing *doma-kommuny* as an altogether new form of settlement with its emphasis on a collectivised way of life. But it was not until the mid-1920s that these ideas found a concrete expression when, towards the end of 1925, the Moscow Soviet arranged a competition for a communal block of flats. The three- to four-storey building was to house a maximum of 800 people – single persons, couples (married or 'comrades') and families with three to five members. The dining hall could cater for 250 people at one sitting. Each floor had a room with a supply of boiling water and two gas rings for preparing or warming up food for sick residents and children at odd times; another room was set aside for ironing and washing children's clothes; there were separate wash rooms for men and women (one tap per ten persons). Other facilities included a fully mechanised laundry, a library-reading room and club each with sufficient space for 100 people; a kindergarten for 120 children and a crèche for 30 (*Iz istorii* . . ., 1963, pp. 63–4).

There is little in this or many of the other blue-prints for the communal blocks which appears to us today as in any way 'revolutionary'. For instance the communal block built for the Commissariat of Finance (*Narkomfin*) between 1928 and 1929, consisting of one- and three-roomed flats each with its own bathroom and kitchenette, connected to another building that provided a variety of communal services, had limited influence on the creation of a collectivised way of life. On the other hand, plans of a more radical flavour were being advanced. In 1930, a complex of flats designed to accommodate 2,000 people was to consist of eight main blocks, a social centre and children's sector. In each five-storey block the first floor was reserved for services. The remaining floors were given over to living and sleeping quarters, each unit of which had a living area of 6·3 square metres and was intended solely for sleeping and relaxing. Each of these eight blocks was to be connected to the social centre where there were to be facilities for education and training, leisure and recreation (*Perspektivy* . . ., 1975, appendix A).

Lunacharskii, too, was an advocate of the *doma-kommuny* recommending that they should form the basic city unit, accommodating from 1,000 to 3,000 people. Children were to be brought up mainly outside the nuclear family, the younger ones in crèches and kindergartens near the block itself, the older ones in boarding schools where they would be given technical education and practical training (Lunacharskii, 1930). S. G. Strumilin (1930, p. 13) proposed the combination of towns and villages into agro-industrial complexes of 10,000 to 20,000 people. Once again, individuals were to be housed in communal blocks: he explained the necessity for socialising traditional household activities and sought to demonstrate the economic advantages of 'factory kitchens'.

In contrast, N. A. Milyutin (1930), though sharing the views expressed by Strumilin on the ways that social life ought to be organised, considered that it would be premature and unrealistic to try to put them into practice at the time; it was necessary, first of all, to create appropriate conditions for the public upbringing of children and only gradually to supplant the individual domestic households with a system of social institutions. Four years earlier a housing specialist and staunch supporter of the housing co-operative had made a similar observation:

> The separate kitchen will continue to occupy a place in each flat for a long time. The collectivisation of domestic work is a long process and it will only be completed through a series of intermediate forms; therefore, at present, it is necessary to provide a separate kitchen in small flats . . . The transformation of domestic life will take decades and will be no easy matter. (Belousov, 1926, p. 25)

This interpretation was based on, and revealed an awareness of, the backwardness of the population and the paramount importance of raising their general level of culture. One way of doing this, and simultaneously inculcating a sense of responsibility towards property was through encouraging the housing co-operative movement (Kozorenko, 1928, p. 262)–which, of course, has only the most tenuous connection with a 'collectivised way of life'. But if there were those like Milyutin who argued for the transition from capitalist individualism to socialist collectivism to be carried out 'at a snail's pace', there were others who wanted the new way of life to begin immediately. L. Sabsovich (1929*a*), for instance, wanted child-rearing to be completely socialised; there were to be no kitchens or shops selling food products; adults would live in communal blocks consisting of 2,000 to 3,000 people, each individual having 5 square metres 'of his own' for sleeping and relaxing, the remainder of his time being spent in common rooms. Elsewhere Sabsovich was to argue the need for a cultural revolution to accompany the political and economic changes taking place:

> The material and social preconditions (in the form of a very high level of development of the productive forces, the elimination of classes and the socialisation of all instruments and means of production) are still not sufficient for the construction of a socialist society. There is a need for a cultural revolution – it is necessary completely to re-educate the individual, and to do this, it is imperative to alter totally his living conditions and forms of existence. (Sabsovich, 1929*b*, p. 128)

The new property relations established by the political revolution of October 1917 gave rise at the objective level to new social relations; but, at the level of individual consciousness, the Revolution could no more than create the conditions for new social relations. Almost a century and a half earlier, the overseer of the French Revolution, the Committee of Public Safety, had noted in a similar vein that: 'You must entirely refashion a people whom you wish to make free, destroy its prejudices, alter its habits, limit its necessities, root up its vices, purify its desires' (cited by Nisbet, 1970, p. 40). It was in the faith that people may be refashioned in a historically short period that the 'leaders' of the French and Russian Revolutions built their hopes, and it was on this faith in part that they foundered.

This debate initially mirrored those taking place on the rate and nature of economic development and on the path which urban development should assume. In this broader arena the views of Sabsovich confronted those of the town-planner Okhitovich (1930) who, caught up with the revolution ushered in with the development of the private car, recommended that in some cases each person should possess his own house and car. The advocates of the individual detached house rested their arguments on one solid foundation: the mass of the population was in fact living in one-storey houses under private ownership. But the manner in which reality was presenting itself, low-rise, low-density housing development, was no ground for encouraging it further, for the whole concept of small settlements composed of owner-occupiers had strong Proudhonist overtones with a tendency to espouse the virtues of decentralised authority and a property-owning democracy. There certainly could be no capitulation on this ideological front: the compromise made during the New Economic Policy (1921–8) to private builders had been accepted on purely practical grounds, but in the long term they could not and would not be allowed to shape the physical pattern of the new socialist society. In 1934, the government defined its position on the owner-occupied, single-storey house when it declared that 'Since the existing practice of house-construction does not, in many cases, correspond to the growth of the cultural level and needs of the broad mass of the population . . . houses in towns and workers' settlements must be four and five storeys and more' ('Ob uluchshenii . . .', 1934). As a result, by the mid-1930s, the government had effectively turned its back on the Anglo-American tradition in town-planning (Ebeneezer Howard, Clarence Stein, Frank Lloyd Wright) in favour of the European tradition, whose most celebrated exponent was Le Corbusier. With judicious exceptions the 'cottage-type' of dwelling was to give way permanently, at least in town-planning theory, to high-rise, high-density living.

Writing in 1929, Lissitzky (1970, p. 35) summed up the feeling of the architect-planners of this period. In the West, he wrote, it was simply a matter of resuming construction activities where they had left off before the First World War, though under changed economic and technological conditions. In Russia this became a question of solving a new social problem of fundamental cultural significance. The Soviet architect was given the task of establishing a new standard of housing by devising a new type of housing unit, not intended for single individuals in conflict with one another, as in the West, but for the masses. Just two years later it was denounced as ultraradical, on the grounds that it espoused 'gigantism' in the forms of costly and grandiose projects ('O vypolnenii . . .', 1931). In June 1931 a plenary session of the Central Committee of the All-Union Communist Party (Bolsheviks) couched its argument against Lissitzky in a more strongly worded and more ideological form. It stated that in matters of organising the new socialist way of life, a decisive struggle was required, directed against both the 'right opportunists' who were acting against the Bolsheviks' decision on the appropriate rate of development for the economy, and the 'left opportunists' who were operating with all sorts of 'harebrained proposals' such as the need to eliminate individual kitchens, etc. ('O moskovskom . . .', 1931, p. 333).

Overall, these experiments and their designers, both of which came under attack with the onset of the five-year plans, made an impact little greater than such utopian designs for living as those of Robert Owen, Fourier and Campanello in the previous century. Nevertheless, this was a remarkable period in the history of socialist architecture and town-planning, which one Soviet writer, looking back, depicted in the following manner:

> In the first years after the October Revolution, we did very little building but we did a lot of designing (leaving most of it, it is true, on paper) and even more talking. Whatever was old was swept out as having outlived itself. A new system, a new regime also means a new style. Recall the poster of those years; a half-naked worker in an apron, hammer in hand, standing against a background of some sort of construction site. This was the concept of architecture of the new – if not a factory, if not a fly wheel, at least something industrial. (Nekrasov, 1960)

It was precisely this search for 'newness' under a new social formation and a pervading spirit of adventurousness amongst Soviet architects that attracted Le Corbusier to the USSR and led him to comment on his return from Moscow in 1928, in a letter to the Soviet architect Alexander Vesnin, that 'at the present moment, Moscow is the most vibrant architectural centre' (Shvidovskii, 1970, p. 22).

A characteristic of the 1920s was the open discussion taking place between individuals putting forward different ideas and offering divergent interpretations and policies in all spheres of cultural, social and economic development. Those involved in the debates and discussions were neither consciously nor unconsciously in favour of policies inimical to the interests of the working class. On the positive side, an abundance of expressed views reflects and generates creative energy; on the negative side, at specific historical conjunctures, its potentially anarchic quality can eventuate in a cardiac arrest in the body politic. Ideas, for example, about art, aesthetics, architecture, city layouts, city size, relationships between men and women, though not the prime movers in the social process, are important. As Engels (1890, p. 443) explained: 'The economic situation is the basis, but the various elements of the superstructure . . . also exercise their influence upon the course of historical struggle and in many cases preponderate in determining their form.' And, of course, men can choose between different sets of ideas or values, albeit, as Schumpeter (1970, p. 12) remarks, 'from standpoints, views and propensities that do not form another set of independent data'. Moreover, these ideas are themselves not only moulded by the objective economic conditions, but the choice between them is also moulded by these conditions.

For Kautsky and those others who held that a socialist revolution was only possible in the most advanced industrial countries, it seemed that, since the objective economic premises for socialism did not exist in Russia, there could be no political or cultural revolution in that country. Lenin, however, viewed the situation differently. He admitted that the development of the productive forces in Russia had not attained the level that made socialism possible, but then added:

> What if the complete hopelessness of the situation, by stimulating the efforts of the workers and peasants tenfold, offered us the opportunity to create the fundamental requisites of civilisation in a different way from that of the West European countries? . . . If a definite level of culture is required for the building of socialism . . . why cannot we begin by first achieving the pre-requisites for that definite level of culture in a revolutionary way and then, with the aid of the workers' and peasants' government and the Soviet system, proceed to overtake the other nations? (Lenin, 1923, p. 381)

For Lenin, the visionaries, those who viewed the cultural transformation of Russia not just as a possibility but as a necessity, were not fantasists but important agents in the construction of socialism. Their conception, in focusing on social relationships and on providing the institutional forms, especially those propitious to the breaking down of traditional patterns of division of labour between the sexes, could be instrumental in releasing the creative potential of the masses, which in turn would have a positive effect on the pace of economic development.

Yet the death-knell of the 'building for the new way of life' (*dom novogo byta*) had been rung; research was channelled into seeking solutions to more easily realisable (and, arguably, more important) issues, principally methods of supplying accommodation as quickly and cheaply as possible. This meant, above all, research into the development of industrialised building techniques. This emphasis was prompted by the acute and deteriorating housing situation.

It was against a background of squalid living conditions and the dominance of a private housing sector that one has to assess the judgement that the schemes put forward to create a more collectivised way of life by erecting *doma-kommuny* were 'harebrained proposals'. An expansion in housing and municipal services was acknowledged by Kuibyshev in the Report on the Second Five-Year Plan as 'a precondition for safeguarding the health of workers, raising labour-productivity and freeing female workers from the slavery of the domestic economy' (cited in Veselovskii, 1945, p. 154). Although it would be wrong to regard the aims of 'safeguarding the health of workers' and the 'emancipation of women' as being solely concerned with increasing the size of the workforce and ensuring its fitness for the labour process, there was a clear tendency for policy speeches throughout the 1920s and 1930s to lay stress on the social engineering aspects of housing in the state's strategy for raising labour productivity. In either case, the notion of housing as a consciously created, built environment designed to help bring about a change in cultural values was replaced by a cost-efficiency concept of housing which postulated a simple linear relationship between any improvement in the standard of accommodation and industrial output.

THE *MIKRORAION*

It was not until the 1950s that architectural design and town-planning reached a new turning point with the resuscitation of the concept of the *mikroraion* (neighbourhood unit) – 'a complex of residential buildings combined with a variety of services and retail outlets meeting the population's daily needs' – which has become 'unquestionably accepted as the primary structural planning unit' (Sazonov, 1973, p. 172). Each *mikroraion* is essentially a pedestrian precinct with only access roads, and with its boundaries normally drawn by main traffic thoroughfares. It embraces within its boundaries crèches, kindergartens and primary schools; shops to meet the residents' daily requirements, library and club facilities and space for garaging cars. The essence of the *mikroraion* as a planning concept is that it combines housing and a diverse range of services to form a systemic whole within a much larger hierarchically arranged 'stepped system' (*stupenchataya sistema*). The concept of the 'stepped system' of social services is found not only in the theoretical articles and handbooks for planners but also in government-approved documents which determine town-planning in the Soviet Union. Over the past twenty years, during the period of ascendancy of the stepped system concept, a series of ordinances has been issued by the government seeking to deal with the need to improve the standard of services (public dining rooms, laundries, pre-school facilities, etc.), the providing of which 'not only leads to economies in material and labour resources but also radically alters the way of life of the family in the process of freeing the woman from domestic slavery' ('O dal'neishem . . .', 1959).

However, the stepped system, and the *mikroraion* (neighbourhood) in particular, is more than an organisational device for providing a variety of services conveniently. It also carries a strong normative element. It was – and remains – a construct directed at achieving specific social objectives, though this is now being questioned. If the *mikroraion* forms a closely knit social whole, then the system of services must be spatially distributed in such a fashion that each member of the community will spend less time outside its boundaries, for to step outside these boundaries to satisfy daily needs only serves to damage the integrity and harmony of the whole (Sazonov, 1973, p. 174).

In a very real sense, the *mikroraion* is an extension of the idea of the communal block (*dom-kommuna*) as described by Strumilin (1964) in his book *Our World in Twenty Years*. In the section on 'What is the Commune?' he asks how the collectivisation of the workers' way of life can be brought about and how women can be freed from domestic slavery. His answer is that communes with populations of 2,000 to 3,000 persons should be organised along the lines of the modern sanatorium or hotel, with public catering facilities and a complete range of services (for example, laundries, clothing and shoe-repair workshops) for the residents. Complexes of communes in large cities would form *mikroraiony* whose population could meet its daily, basic needs without going beyond the confines of such a '*mikroraion* of communes' (Strumilin, 1964, p. 424).

More recently, Gradov has put forward a design proposal for a 'productive-residential district' (*proizvodstvennozhiloi raion*) accommodating 40,000 people, covering an area of 156 hectares. The population is housed in four tower blocks of 100 to 200 storeys, which he calls 'housing-neighbourhoods' (*dom-mikroraion*). Each tower block provides a range of services on the ground and first floor and then at 20-storey intervals, including crèches and schools. The central area in this district, with an area of 30 hectares, is the main shopping and cultural centre where industry is located. According to Gradov, 65 per cent of all industrial enterprises cannot be classified as 'harmful' and so may be situated in residential areas. His plans are quite consistent with the basic goals laid down by the government towards which the society is supposed to be moving: (1) a reduction in distance between place of work and residence (in Gradov's schema, the journey to work takes only five minutes); (2) automation of the productive process which 'eliminates the difference between mental and manual labour'. This principle is incorporated into Gradov's system by designing schools which provide practical training (*trudovoe obuchenie*) and by continuing to improve 'the architectural, artistic form of industrial complexes so that they are comparable to the standards achieved in residential construction' (*Rekomendatsii . . .*, 1974; *Perspektivy . . .*, 1975, table 20).

Visions such as those held by Strumilin and Gradov are unlikely to leave the architect's drawing board or the intellectual's drawing room for a very long time. Even the far less dramatically envisaged collectivisation of social life – the formation of associations (*kollektivy*), which were to unite residents in the task of self-government and the organisation of social life in the *mikroraion* – has never materialised (Sazonov, 1973, p. 174). This 'failure' alone might be sufficient reason for questioning the 'community' aspect of the *mikroraion*; but there is, from a Marxist perspective, an even more important reason. The central focus of an individual's life activity is his place of work. Consequently, the locus of his community or collective is to be found in the factory or organisation where he works rather than where he lives. Since a goal of socialism is the elimination of differences between mental and manual labour, furnishing man with the opportunities to cultivate his inherent creative capabilities, it is at the workplace that he can realise himself as an innovator, it is there that he is part of a 'natural' collective – one formed out of interaction and interest. Furthermore, as barriers between mental and manual labour are reduced, interaction becomes less restricted to those in the same occupation or engaged in analogous tasks and comes to embrace individuals fulfilling other functions within a given productive or administrative unit. In this view, social clubs and recreational activities are best organised around the place of work rather than the place of residence. Similarly, pre-school facilities (which continue to be financed mainly through the workplace) are better associated spatially and socially with the factory or office rather than with the home.

This corporate structure, where the whole life-process revolves around the place of work (which not only provides social clubs, pre-school places for workers' children and access to rest homes, but also meets the medical needs of its employees and supplies them with accommodation) tends to involve the individual in a widely embracing microsystem such as is to be found in some Western corporations. Yet, this Durkheimian corporation, itself a twentieth-century (or industrial) equivalent of the mediaeval guild, may be seen to stand in contradiction to the high level of geographical mobility which is increasingly a feature of advanced industrial societies. Neither the work- nor home-based community (*kollektiv* or *mikroraion*) seems adequately to take into account the fact that individuals are members of social networks which transcend arbitrarily drawn socio-spatial boundaries. In socially mixed residential units – as the *mikroraiony* normally are – individuals belonging to different (or the same) social groups will have no greater motivation or tendency to interact with their neighbours than residents in an English neighbourhood unit. Population mobility is constantly increasing, especially where leisure activities are concerned. Individuals are not finding their source of entertainment 'localised in some sort of rigidly drawn territorial boundary' but more and more on a city-wide basis. This tendency had been commented upon in 1964, when two sociologists noted that social contacts in towns were widely dispersed, with less than half of all friendships arising out of a common place of residence or workplace, or even of education. They concluded that the grouping of people together on the basis of ensuring the satisfaction of their basic living needs had no real significance in the establishment of social contacts (Kogan and Loktev, 1964). Greater mobility occasions a greater demand for private car ownership, and is, in turn, further stimulated and intensified by it.

THE RISE OF THE PRIVATE CAR

In 1960, two contributors to an All-Union conference on urban planning noted that a widespread assumption that the use of the private car – particularly in the USA – has been the most important variable in influencing settlement patterns, was not entirely correct. After pointing out that land rent does not determine settlement patterns in the Soviet Union they listed a series of reasons why private car ownership would not develop to the same degree in the USSR (Kamenskii and Vasilevskii, 1961, pp. 74–5). A few years later, after Khrushchev's fall from power, the government concluded a contract with Fiat to set up a car assembly plant with an eventual annual output capacity of 700,000 cars. Between 1970 and 1975 car production rose from 344,200 to 1,201,000, an increase of 249 per cent (*Narodnoe . . .*, 1976, p. 265). The Tenth Five-Year Plan envisages an annual output of about 1,300,000 cars at the end of the plan period (1980). In a detailed study of the growth of car traffic and road construction for three time periods (10 to 15 years; 25 to 30 years and 100 years) based on 1970, Yakshin (1975, p. 34) estimated that car output will increase by 1·5 per cent per annum for the next 70 years (i.e. doubling during that period) and thereafter remain constant.

At present, there are about twelve cars per 1,000 people in the Soviet Union, 71·8 per cent of which are privately owned, 23·2 per cent reserved for officials and 5 per cent are taxis. By 1985, 91·6 per cent of cars on the road will be driven by private motorists, 4·6 per cent will be reserved for officials and 3·8 per cent will be taxis (Efimov and Mikerin, 1976).

The debate in the Soviet Union on the spread of private motoring – the implications that the advent of 'mass motorisation' has for the society, the desirability of this development and the ultimate ratio of the number of cars to the population to be aimed for – reveals the persistence (as in Western Europe) of contrasting views on private car ownership. A conference held under the auspices of the section of the presidium of the Soviet Sociological Association concerned with the social problems of motorisation, set up in March 1975, reflected the differing opinions that exist on the extension of private car ownership. On the one hand, there were those who questioned whether it is necessary for every citizen to own his own car when public transport, especially in large cities, is improving all the time. Cars ought to be used mainly for recreation and the state should operate a car rental service which would eventually lead to the curtailing or total banning of private car usage in cities. One reason for adopting this stance was stated to be that private motoring has serious effects on various spheres of people's lives, including personality formation. The growing number of private cars could awaken individualistic tendencies that are incompatible with the moral standards and principles of Soviet society; the car could become a prestige symbol, as it has in Western countries; car ownership often leads to individualistic, antisocial tendencies ('my' parking place, etc.) and aggravates interpersonal conflicts. On the other hand, Yu. E. Volkov, a member of the presidium, thought that privately owned cars, despite their as yet limited number, had become a permanent feature of Soviet life. They do not contradict the moral goals of the society; a passenger car can have no greater negative moral-psychological influence on its owner than does anything else that he owns (Efimov and Mikerin, 1976).

Those expressing fears about the spread of car ownership – based on current experience in the Soviet Union (where the car is a prestige symbol), on observations of the negative consequences of mass car ownership in Western countries, and on a consideration of the benefits of a highly developed public transport system – are unlikely to have a very much greater impact on transportation policy than their counterparts in Western countries. Volkov was almost certainly voicing the government's opinion when he spoke of the private car as 'a permanent feature of our life'. According to Yakshin (1975, p. 34), by 1995–2000 there will be 140 cars per 1,000 people, an increase from 12 per 1,000 in 1970.

It is inaccurate to focus solely on élites as generators of change, for change is often brought about by a concatenation of forces, some of which are the unintended consequences of actions and policies aimed initially at achieving goals quite unrelated to the results they eventually produce. People are rewarded with cars for saving hard (and sacrificing the consumption of other goods and services), and for their 'contribution to society'. Often these individuals will combine the qualities of parsimony, productivity and party loyalty. The demands made by this broad social group of car owners, as a latent interest group, may not have been anticipated by the government, but may have to be met, at least in part. It is not possible to state the nature of these demands beyond saying that (1) they could correspond to the 'awakened individualistic and anti-social tendencies' expressed by some Soviet commentators mentioned above, tendencies which could 'lead to aggravated interpersonal conflicts', and (2) they might affect people's choices on where to live and in what type of accommodation.

The internal combustion engine is, in itself, neutral; the manner in which it is utilised will reflect and reinforce a particular set of values. The privatisation of the internal combustion engine, like the ownership of certain consumer durables (say a washing-machine) is a concomitant of privatised family life. To state this is not to pass a moral judgement on private car ownership or the nuclear family: it is rather to suggest the universality of certain forms of living and possession corresponding to a particular level of development of the forces of production. A highly developed sense of responsibility, which would permit a more rational use of the car than occurs when it belongs to one person, is only possible (not necessarily realised) in the absence of scarcity, that is at a much higher stage of economic development than has been reached to date in the Soviet Union.

WOMEN AND HOUSING POLICY IN THE USSR TODAY

As the rise of the private car indicates, the standard of living has improved considerably. Furthermore, however long the waiting lists and however cramped living conditions, the housing problem is no longer regarded as acute. As a result, the government considers itself in a position to devote more attention to the issue of quality and comfort. The changed economic and political climate that now exists has led to a freer rein being offered to those with new ideas, in the sphere both of the architectural design of individual buildings and of the systems of buildings at the city and sub-city levels. Ideas put forward and tentatively tested in the first decade of Soviet power began to appear again in the 1960s. The visions of the nature of socialist society, notably its collective character, have changed little (Gradov, 1968). Paradoxically, half a century ago these conceptualisations of the environment most conducive for producing a 'new way of life' ran too far ahead of the level of development of the society for them to be implemented; today, these revamped ideas perhaps lag behind, or have been largely rendered redundant by the development of Soviet society which has created new social structures and new demands amongst its population. Can it be said that a new socialist way of life has been created (or is being created) in the Soviet Union? One measure of this is the existence of equality between the sexes.

The emancipation of women, in the political rhetoric of the Communist Party, has meant far more than the achievement of political and economic equality with men; in the main, equality in the sense of access to job opportunities has been achieved (see Lane, 1976, ch. 7). The construction of a socialist society, however, is not completed with the 'expropriation of the expropriators' and the transformation of social relationships in the workplace: this revolutionary action should be seen (as it normally is) as the first step in the creation of socialism. Thereafter, 'the march towards socialism' presumes and demands a cultural revolution in people's norms and mores expressed in their relationship to one another in all spheres of social activity. A certain faction of the intelligentsia has tended to believe that such a cultural revolution will be associated with particular architectural forms and spatial usages. Yet, there are also factors which act as obstacles to social and cultural transformation and which are also partly responsible for the cultivation or maintenance of an individualistic ethos.

The Influence of Rural Mores on Urban Behaviour: the Dual Role of Women

According to one view, familiar to Western students of urbanisation, the urban way of life has been so diffused throughout society, that in the USSR today one can no longer properly speak of a rural way of life at all, except perhaps in rural areas in Central Asia (where in any case, its characteristic features are scarcely separable from ethnic influences) (Perevedentsev, 1975, p. 45). But just as the urban way of life has in many ways been transported into the countryside, rural mores still find expression in the town, simply because the overwhelming majority of adult urban residents have had their origins in the countryside. It is possible that the role of rural social relationships in the dynamic interchange between the spheres of industrial and agricultural production has been underestimated. This is especially true in a country in which, even in 1976, 98·9 million people lived in rural areas. The 1970 census recorded 105·6 million people as rural; they were living in 469,253 settlements, 94,296 of which had under five inhabitants. A further 131,532 settlements had populations of between six and fifty persons. The impact which the countryside has on the culture and social and political consciousness of the society at large makes itself felt directly through the continuing migration from the countryside to the towns: between 1959 and 1970, 16·4 million people migrated to the towns (*Naselenie SSSR*, 1974, p. 54).

The way of life of the peasant population and of other social classes living in the countryside has altered considerably over the last seventy years. The October Revolution and subsequent economic policies transformed social relations on the land, whilst the growth in the Gross Domestic Product has brought an array of material benefits to the population. Despite general improvements in the standard of living which have taken place, 'the difference between town and village is recognised by all Marxists who are conducting research into social processes under socialism as remaining a social difference and, moreover, one of the main social differences continuing to exist at the present level of development of Soviet society' (Rutkevich, 1970, p. 3). The main factor responsible for this difference was and remains the unequal levels of development of the productive forces in manufacturing and agriculture. In spite of this gap, it is not the case that the village merely exists in the shadow of the town, trailing behind the latter in the degree of economic development and in the level of provision of social and cultural services, for its comparative backwardness has a series of consequences for the society as a whole. One of the more important consequences derives from the role of women in the rural economy.

Western and Soviet sociologists generally assume that peasant migrants to the city will take with them many of the norms, mores and traditions of their former way of life, one of the most important of these being the preservation within the urban environment of the unequal division of labour between the sexes found in the villages. This particular cultural norm is reflected, as Table 1.1 shows, in the fact that women of all social groups spend twice as much time on housework as men.

Another study conducted by a research institute attached to the USSR State Planning Commission found that 'working women with children spend, on average, four to five hours per day on housework – a figure which rises to eight to nine on their "days off"'' (*Demograficheskie problemy* . . ., 1969, p. 108). An earlier study carried out on a sample of 8,468 women in Gor'kii in 1962 revealed that women workers spent the same number of hours on housework as on their full-time jobs (Sogesarev, 1965, p. 106). Most urban women, then, have two working days – one spent in production and the other in the home. Gordon and Klopov note that the inequality between the sexes in carrying out housework is 'one of the most important social problems in the modern city' and suggest that there are two ways of lightening the burden borne by the woman: (1) by 'creating the conditions' for involving men in domestic work; (2) cutting down on the overall amount of housework. Whilst the latter is almost entirely a product of better accommodation and domestic equipment and improved services, the former requires changes in 'the cultural

Table 1.1 Daily time-budgets by sex and occupation in 1966

	Sex	Working Time		Non-working Time connected with 'productive work'		Types of Time Expenditure Housework		Satisfaction of Natural Physiological Functions		Free Time	
		Mins	%	Mins	%	Mins	%	Mins	%	Mins	%
Unskilled manual	M	433·7	30·1	82·6	5·7	147·9	10·3	576·6	35·9	259·2	18·0
	F	424·7	29·5	88·9	6·2	291·0	20·2	490·5	34·0	144·9	10·1
Semi-skilled non-manual	M	435·0	30·2	103·0	7·1	130·3	9·1	488·5	33·9	283·2	19·7
	F	439·4	30·5	87·5	6·1	252·3	17·5	497·7	34·6	163·1	11·3
Skilled manual working with machinery	M	429·6	29·8	109·1	7·6	112·8	7·8	506·2	35·2	282·3	19·6
	F	428·3	29·7	85·9	6·0	218·5	15·2	502·0	34·9	205·3	14·2
Skilled mainly manual	M	438·4	30·4	88·5	6·1	141·9	9·9	484·6	33·6	286·6	20·0
	F	453·5	31·5	78·8	5·5	218·4	15·2	489·1	33·9	200·2	13·9
Highly skilled workers combining mental and manual labour	M	475·2	33·0	101·6	7·1	114·1	7·9	503·5	34·9	245·6	17·1
	F	424·4	29·5	108·5	7·5	234·9	16·3	505·7	35·1	166·5	11·6
Skilled white-collar workers	M	445·6	30·9	92·3	6·4	110·6	7·7	495·0	34·4	296·5	20·6
	F	426·1	29·6	97·3	6·8	236·7	16·4	510·3	35·4	169·6	11·8
Highly qualified white-collar workers	M	454·6	31·5	126·2	8·8	122·1	8·6	503·6	34·9	233·6	16·2
	F	430·9	29·9	109·9	7·6	233·3	15·2	485·6	33·8	180·3	12·5
Heads of 'productive collectives'	M	509·0	35·3	103·8	7·2	102·5	7·1	494·1	34·4	230·6	16·0
	F	487·4	33·8	77·8	5·4	212·3	14·7	476·7	33·2	185·8	12·9

Source: Trufanov, 1973, p. 106.

climate' – the overcoming of traditions and customs which 'forbid' the male to take part in the cleaning of the flat, washing and food preparation (Gordon and Klopov, 1972, p. 126). Observation and correspondence and commentary in the press provide little ground for believing that any major reorientation in values is imminent. For instance, three letters, all from men, written in response to a letter in which a woman had proclaimed her belief that a woman's behaviour and manners should be feminine, agreed whole-heartedly with her. They went further in advocating a special upbringing (*vospitanie*) for girls so that they develop all the desirable attributes of femininity, such as modesty, timidity and homeliness, while boys should be brought up to be courageous, hard, principled and responsible ('O mode . . .', 1976). Whilst it can be safely asserted that there are many Soviet women who would concur with this view, there are other women who reject the idea that the most important task of a woman's life is to bear and bring up children, and that 'all else is a mere addition'. Another contributor to *Literaturnaya gazeta*, a woman, pointed out that 'work is psychologically no less important for most of today's women than it is for men'. She added that if girls should be prepared and trained for their function as wives and mothers, then boys should be trained for being husbands and fathers. Best of all, both should be brought up to be 'a real person' (*nastoyashchii chelovek*). Housework must be shared equally by both partners. At present, all too frequently the situation is one where the woman works 'a second shift' at home while her husband watches the television. A boy brought up in such a family grows up with an idea that 'he is a tender hot-house plant which ought to be cherished and protected by a woman' (Drunina, 1977).

Thus, it would seem that rather than work on creating a social and cultural climate conducive to fostering an alternative pattern of role relationships between men and women within a nuclear family setting or within new social arrangements, the government has focused on changing the 'concrete', physical environment.

Women, Domestic Work and Manpower Shortages

Although Lenin and some of his contemporaries were probably genuinely concerned about the unequal nature of the relationship between the sexes, the main motive force behind statements and legislation aimed at 'freeing the woman from domestic slavery' has largely been a pragmatic one. The large amount of time spent by women on domestic duties has two important consequences for the economy. First, it has a negative effect on the contribution which they make to the public sector, that is to say, the heavy demand which housework and child-minding makes on their time means that they cannot undertake full-time occupations, or that when they do, their productivity is lowered. The changing structure of the family, with young couples increasingly living apart from the grandparents (who formerly looked after the children, shopped and performed a variety of domestic tasks) and the shortfall in pre-school places, means that there is no alternative for women (who may also be mothers) but to take responsibility for exercising these functions (Novikov, 1977; 'Detskim . . .', 1978). Secondly, a married couple find it financially difficult to survive, if they wish to clothe themselves in the fashion and stock their home with domestic furnishings, a television set, etc., when the woman is not the recipient of a full-time wage. In an acquisitive society in which real incomes remain relatively low, an opportunity cost of material goods is children. That this is, indeed, the opportunity cost is shown in the declining urban birth rate which has fallen from 30·5 births per 1,000 in 1940 to 26·0 in 1950, reaching a low of 15·3 in 1968 from which date it has risen steadily to 17·0 in 1975 (*Narodnoe . . .*, 1976, p. 41). The extent of the decline had certainly not been anticipated. (*Voprosy . . .*, 1966, p. 254).

Although the birth rate for the Soviet Union as a whole remains high in comparison with most other industrialised countries (United Nations, 1977, pp. 82–3), the overall rate of population growth has been declining (Urlanis, 1974, pp. 117–19). Of the two factors commonly cited as responsible for this decline – the estimated loss of 15 million males in the Second World War and the increasing number of women restricting family size – it is the latter which is of decisive importance.

According to one Soviet sociologist (Perevedentsev, 1975, pp. 57–9), the 'most common cause' for the declining birth rate is the changing economic role of children. In the traditional rural society, children were regarded as a guarantee against old age and were, in any case, by the age of 10 valuable contributors to the household. In the towns, on the other hand, there is a sharp rise in the family's expenditure on children, who are, on average, consumers until they are 20. Not only do they consume the parents' income, but also their time: 'in towns children require constant attention. Child neglect (*beznadzornost'*) is a purely city problem'. This demand on the parents' time comes into conflict with the demand for a full-time occupation, and Perevedentsev asserts that women's demand for full-time employment is not dictated solely by economic necessity: it is also a social demand, that is women prefer to go out to work rather than to remain at home with children. Given prevailing attitudes on the dual role of women as workers in both the public and domestic sectors, the need for a second family income, and the far from universal acceptance by women themselves that the separation of mother and child for most of the day during the child's early years is desirable or not harmful, then work outside the home is, in many cases, a choice forced by domestic economic necessity.

These changes in the demographic and social structure will have an increasingly greater impact on the economy. By 1970, there were 1·7 million fewer workers than the planners had projected as necessary in that year. Although the manpower situation may not deteriorate too rapidly during the 1970s, by the next decade the decline in the rate of growth of the population of working age could create a serious constraint on the fulfilment of economic plans (Feshbach and Rapawy, 1973). Kosygin, in his speech at the 25th Party Congress, stressed the need for a more efficient use of manpower since 'it is necessary to bear in mind that in the 1980s there will be a decline in the natural increase in labour resources' (*Materialy* . . ., 1976, p. 126).

The 'Programme for Social Development and Raising the Standards of Living' contained in the Party document for the 25th Party Congress specified a package of measures designed to 'improve the conditions of work and domestic life (*byt*) of working women' which has, as its unstated objective, the raising of the birth rate:

> Introduce for working women partly-paid leave so that they can take care of their child until it is one year old. Create for women with children broader opportunities to work at home. Expand the network of pre-school and school establishments and all-day nurseries. To build 2·5–2·8 million places in crèches and kindergartens. Special attention to be paid to improving the running of children's institutions. Create conditions for shortening the time spent on housework by developing the network of domestic services, public eating places and increase the output and sale of semi-prepared meals (*polufabrikanty*) and kitchen equipment. (*Osnovnye* . . ., 1976, p. 70)

These proposals represent one side of what Soviet authors (*Perspektivy* . . ., 1975, p. 14) refer to as a 'dialectical contradiction' in housing policy – between the expansion and extension of public services, on the one hand, and the provision of a high standard of comfort in the home, on the other. Soviet Marxism identifies three general categories of 'life-style' corresponding to three broad historical epochs. First, in primitive society, a collectivised way of life predominated – individualised demands existed only in a rudimentary form. Secondly, the development of private ownership and a class-antagonistic social formation gave rise to an individualistic ethos. Thirdly, under communism, the tendency to collective life is accompanied by the development of individual elements and aspects of life-style. Since at present the Soviet Union maintains that it is in the process of building a communist society, the actual working out of this contradiction is of the greatest significance and Soviet writers are right to discuss housing and town-planning strategies in terms of it.

A key premise underlying their housing designs (and social policy in general) is that:

> the family is the primary cell (*pervichnaya yacheika*) of society, whose functions under socialism are: the strengthening of conjugal relationships based on equal rights, friendship and common interests; propagating the species and child-rearing; recreation and relaxation providing basic services for day-to-day living in a common household. (*Perspektivy* . . ., 1975, pp. 22–3; Kharchev, 1964)

These functions are to be carried out mainly in the 'residential cell' (*zhilaya yacheika*) – the flat – which has to satisfy *inter alia* the individual's physiological needs (sleep, 'personal hygiene'), provide an environment for social interaction between family members and between a close circle of friends and other kin, and for the pursuit of professional interests and hobbies. One Soviet sociologist, speaking at a symposium on 'Problems of Urbanisation,' commented that 'one of the most important trends in contemporary life is an expansion in the functions of the family and home'. He went on to say that under conditions of rigid, formalised, mainly impersonal contacts in large cities, the home is the most important sphere where the individual not only sheds the psychological load of the urban environment, but also where he can engage in free, personal intercourse with people who are psychologically close to him (Yanitskii, 1969, p. 143).

So, as far as the foreseeable future is concerned, the role of the home and the nuclear family will not alter much. It is probable that with improvements both in living-space standards (which, ultimately, will mean ensuring that each household has one room more than the number of members in the family) and in the range of domestic appliances available, social life will become more and more privatised, with individuals spending more time with the family at home. Of the two alternative methods of liberating people from the 'burden of unproductive domestic work', the socialisation of essential services (eating out regularly, taking clothes to laundries, having the flat cleaned by specialist agencies, etc.), and the provision of semi-manufactured products and domestic gadgetry, it is the latter which will persist. (On consumer goods, see 'Industriya . . .', 1977.)

CONCLUSIONS

In all societies, housing is more than a physical structure of bricks and mortar. It reflects and reinforces social relationships and contributes to structuring patterns of interaction. Although there is still a serious housing shortage in the Soviet Union, the government's vast house-building programme has meant that millions of families are annually moving into new self-contained flats, at last leaving behind them the communal flat, with its shared kitchen and bathroom. Until 1958, the most common type of urban dwelling was the 'communal flat' (*kommunal'naya kvartira*) which housed several families (Dmitriev, 1973, p. 150). Normally, this meant that there was a common entrance to the flat with a single room (or at the most two) leading off the hallway into the family's private accommodation. The kitchen and bathroom leading off the hall were shared by all the families in the flat.

As in the 1930s, the Soviet government is faced with a choice: to provide traditional single-family dwelling units in blocks of flats, or to experiment by constructing housing complexes which would express the goals and ideals of a socialist society. Over the past fifteen years, designs have been drawn up and submitted by research institutes for 'houses with collectivised services'. One such proposal, for Moscow, the 'House of the New Way of Life' (*dom novogo byta*) actually materialised. Its construction, however, has been the subject of a controversy which revealed the polarity of attitudes towards such residential complexes. Critics pointed to the high costs involved in providing the extensive range of services and facilities (including swimming pool, cinema and theatre), and asserted that it was élitist and more suited to certain social groups than others. In fact, one of the blocks was transferred to Moscow State University as it would better meet the needs of students, some of whom were married with small children, than of workers (Zhuchok, 1969). Experiments will continue, but housing policy is now firmly geared to building self-contained family dwellings with increasing amounts of living space, which have to be furnished and equipped. The 22nd Party Congress, held in 1961, effectively turned its back on the 'alternative' of the *dom novogo byta* when it passed a resolution unequivocally stating that: 'Each family, including young couples, will have a well-appointed flat corresponding to the demands of hygiene and the cultural way of life' (*Materialy* . . ., 1962, p. 390). The adoption of the slogan 'to each family its own flat' is of historical significance. It represents not only an acknowledgement of the public demand for self-contained dwelling units to house the small nuclear family, but also the government's commitment to the nuclear family.

A combination of propaganda, exhorting women to engage in public production, and economic need has resulted in a high proportion of women being employed full-time in the public sector. The persistence of a set of attitudes towards domestic work has meant that the burden of cooking and child-rearing rests with women. This disadvantageous status is a contributory factor to the declining birth rate. The government's reaction is to improve the provision of public services and to increase the output of consumer durables. In so far as the central concern of the government is not the domestic burden that is disproportionately borne by women but the low birth rate, the most important innovation introduced at the 25th Party Congress was the extended maternity leave. This measure, taken in conjunction with the building of more nurseries and kindergartens, may have the desired effect of more children being born, but it will not affect the male–female role segregation that exists at present. The concession allowing working mothers to 'work less than a full working day or less than a full working week and to work at home' will only legitimise and accentuate the existing role segregation. Indeed, the proposal need not have specified 'women with children' and could have instead referred to 'a parent'. It is a measure of the strength of feeling that child-rearing and looking after the home is 'woman's work' that the statement was worded in this sex-specific way (*Osnovnye* . . ., 1976, p. 70).

The present trend suggests that the working out of the contradiction between individualistic tendencies inherent in the growing home-centredness and collectivist ideals embodied in the widespread use of public services is likely to intensify. Furthermore, it is possible that the set of norms and values which may be imputed to the more privatised, consumer-oriented, home-centred, car-ownership-seeking nuclear family with segregated role playing that is emerging in the Soviet Union, will articulate with certain tendencies towards individualism in the sphere of production.

BIBLIOGRAPHY

Belousov, V. Ya., *Kul'turnye zadachi zhilishchnoi kooperatsii* (Moscow, 1926).
Demograficheskie problemy zanyatnosti (Moscow, 1969).
'Detskim sadam – zabotu i vnimanie', *Izvestiya*, 7 February 1978.
Dmitriev, N., *Zhilishchnyi vopros* (Moscow, 1973).
Drunina, Y., 'Muzhshchina i zhenshchina', *Literaturnaya gazeta*, 9 March 1977.
Efimov, V. T. and Mikerin, G. I., 'Avtomobilizatsiya v razvitom sotsialisticheskom obshchestve', *Sotsiologicheskie issledovaniya*, 1976, no. 1, pp. 128–38.
Engels, F., 'Letter to J. Bloch (1890)', in K. Marx and F. Engels, *Selected Works*, Vol. 2 (Moscow: Foreign Languages Publishing House, 1949), pp. 443–4.
Feshbach, M. and Rapawy, S., 'Labour constraints in the USSR', in *Soviet Economic Prospects for the Seventies: a Compendium of Papers presented to the Joint Economic Committee, Congress of the United States* (Washington: GPO, 1973), pp. 485–563.
Gordon, L. A. and Klopov, E. V., *Chelovek posle raboty: sotsial'nye problemy byta i vnerabochego vremeni* (Moscow, 1972).

Gradov, V. A., *Gorod i byt* (Moscow, 1968).

'Industriya – narodnomu potrebleniyu', *Ekonomicheskaya gazeta*, 1977, no. 37.

Iz istorii sovetskoi arkhitektury, 1917–1925 gg.: dokumenty i materialy (Moscow, 1963).

Kamenskii, V. A. and Vasilevskii, V. I., 'Puti resheniya problemy rasseleniya krupnogo goroda; na primere Leningrada', in *Trudy VI sessii Akademii stroitel'stva i arkhitektury po voprosam gradostroitel'stva* (Moscow, 1961), pp. 58–81.

Kharchev, A. G., *Brak i sem'ya v SSSR: opyt sotsiologicheskogo issledovaniya* (Moscow, 1964).

Kogan, L. B. and Loktev, V. I., 'Nekotorye sotsiologicheskie aspekty modelirovaniya gorodov', *Voprosy filosofii*, 1964, no. 9, pp. 131–9.

Kozorenko, N. I., *Zhilishchnyi krizis i bor'ba s nim* (Moscow, 1928).

Lane, D., *The Socialist Industrial State: towards a Political Sociology of State Socialism* (London: Allen & Unwin, 1976).

Lenin, V. I., 'O nashei revolyutsii (1923)', in his *Polnoe sobranie sochinenii*, 5th edn, Vol. 45 (Moscow, 1964), pp. 378–82.

Lenin, V. I., 'O zadachakh zhenskogo rabochego dvizheniya v sovetskoi respublike; rech' na IV moskovskoi obshchegorodskoi bespartiinoi konferentsii rabotnits, 23 sentyabrya 1919', in his *Polnoe sobranie sochinenii*, 5th edn, Vol. 39 (Moscow, 1963), pp. 198–205.

Lissitzky, E., *Russia: an Architecture for World Revolution* (London: Lund Humphries, 1970).

Lunacharskii, A. V., 'Arkhitekturnoe oformlenie gorodov: kul'tura v sotsialisticheskikh gorodakh', *Revolyutsiya i kul'tura*, 1930, no. 1, pp. 54–61.

Materialy XXII s''ezda KPSS (Moscow, 1962).

Materialy XXV s''ezda KPSS (Moscow, 1976).

Milyutin, N. A., *Problema stroitel'stva sotsialisticheskikh gorodov* (Moscow, 1930).

Narodnoe khozyaistvo SSSR v 1975 g.: statisticheskii ezhegodnik (Moscow, 1976).

Naselenie SSSR: spravochnik (Moscow, 1974).

Nekrasov, V., 'O proshlom, nastoyashchem i chut'-chut' o budushchem', *Literaturnaya gazeta*, 20 February 1960.

Nisbet, R. A., *The Sociological Tradition* (London: Heinemann, 1970).

Novikov, V., 'Nesostoyavshchiesya novosel'ya', *Izvestiya*, 4 January 1977.

'O dal'neishem razvitii i uluchshenii obshchestvennogo pitaniya; postanovlenie TsK KPSS i SM SSSR, 20 fevralya 1959', *Resheniya partii i pravitel'stva po khozyaistvennym voprosam*, Vol. 4 (Moscow, 1968), pp. 552–8.

'O mode i staromodnosti', *Literaturnaya gazeta*, 24 November 1976.

'O moskovskom gorodskom khozyaistve i o razvitii gorodskogo khozyaistva SSSR; rezolyutsiya plenuma TsK VKP(b), 15 iyunya 1931 g.', *Resheniya partii i pravitel'stva po khozyaistvennym voprosam*, Vol. 2 (Moscow, 1967), pp. 320–33.

'O vypolnenii direktiva SNK SSSR i TsK VKP(b) ob uluchshenii i udeshevlenii rabochego zhilishchnogo stroitel'stva', *Sobranie zakonov i rasporyazhenii pravitel'stva SSSR*, 1931, no. 4, art. 143.

'Ob uluchshenii zhilishchnogo stroitel'stva; postanovlenie SNK SSSR, 23 aprelya 1934 g.', *Resheniya partii i pravitel'stva po khozyaistvennym voprosam*, Vol. 2 (Moscow, 1967), pp. 471–3.

Okhitovich, M. A., 'Ne gorod – a novyi tip rasseleniya', in *Goroda sotsializma: sotsialisticheskaya rekonstruktsiya byta* (Moscow, 1930) pp. 153–5.

Osnovnye napravleniya razvitiya narodnogo khozyaistva SSSR za 1976–1980 gg. (Moscow, 1976).

Perevedentsev, V. I., *Goroda i vremya* (Moscow, 1975).

Perspektivy razvitiya zhilishcha v SSSR (Moscow, 1975).

'Programma Rossiiskoi Kommunisticheskoi partii (bol'shevikov) (1919)', *Kommunisticheskaya partiya Sovetskogo Soyuza v rezolyutsiyakh i resheniyakh s"ezdov, konferentsii i plenumov TsK*, Vol. 2 (Moscow, 1970), pp. 37–59.

Rekomendatsii po proektirovaniyu obshchestvennykh tsentrov mikroraionov (Moscow, 1974).

Rutkevich, M., 'O sotsial'nom razlichii mezhdu gorodom i derevnei v sovremennyi period', in *Problemy razvitiya sotsialisticheskikh obshchestvennykh otnoshenii; materialy gorodskoi nauchnoi konferentsii obshchestvennykh nauk* (Sverdlovsk, 1970), pp. 3–11.

Sabsovich, L. M., *Goroda budushchego i organizatsiya sotsialisticheskogo byta* (Moscow, 1929*a*).

Sabsovich, L. M., *SSSR cherez 10 let: gipoteza general'nogo plana kak plana postroeniya sotsializma v SSSR* (Moscow, 1929*b*).

Sazonov, B. V., 'Sotsial'nyi smysl gradostroitel'nykh kontseptsii obshchestvennogo obsluzhivaniya gorodskogo naseleniya', in *Planirovanie sotsial'nogo razvitiya gorodov*, ed. O. I. Shkaratan and A. N. Alekseev (Moscow, 1973), pp. 166–87.

Schumpeter, J., *Capitalism, Socialism and Democracy* (London: Allen & Unwin, 1970).

Shvidovskii, O., *Le Korbyusier: tvorcheskii put'* (Moscow, 1970).

Sogesarev, G. A., *Metodologiya sotsiologicheskogo obsledovaniya problem narodonaseleniya SSSR* (Moscow, 1965).

Strumilin, S. G., 'Problemy sotsialisticheskikh gorodov (1930)', in his *Izbrannye proizvedeniya*, Vol. 4 (Moscow, 1964), pp. 7–43.

Strumilin, S. G., 'Nash mir cherez 20 let (1964)', in his *Izbrannye proizvedeniya*, Vol. 5 (Moscow, 1965), pp. 386–456.

Trufanov, I. P., *Problemy byta gorodskogo naseleniya* (Leningrad, 1973).

United Nations Department of Economic and Social Affairs, *Statistical Yearbook, 1976* (New York: UN, 1977).

Urlanis, B. Ts., *Problemy dinamiki naseleniya SSSR* (Moscow, 1974).

Veselovskii, B. B., *Kurs ekonomiki i planirovaniya kommunal'nogo khozyaistva* (Moscow, 1945).

Voprosy narodonaseleniya i demograficheskoi statistiki (Moscow, 1966).

Yakshin, A. M., *Perspektivy razvitiya seti gorodskikh magistralei* (Moscow, 1975).

Yanitskii, O. N., 'Simpozium po problemam urbanizatsii', *Voprosy filosofii*, 1969, no. 10, pp. 141–5.

Zhuchok, Ya., 'Dom s privilegiyami?', *Literaturnaya gazeta*, 8 January 1969.

2
Domestic Labour and Soviet Society

ALIX HOLT

> Things change but they stay the same – they stay the
> same but they change.

INTRODUCTION

Until recently housework was considered to be outside the realm of scientific inquiry. It was something that needed doing and someone did it; there was nothing more to be said. With the development of the women's movement in the West this silence has been broken. Over the last decade housework has been discussed and analysed from every angle. Early articles exposed housework as monotonous, tiring and time-consuming, and this attention to the subjective experience of women working in the home has continued. Much recent writing, though, has sought to explain why housework exists in the first place and what role it plays in the political organisation of society. Most of these contributions have taken a Marxist analytical framework as their starting point and have attempted to understand housework in terms of the Marxist categories of value, surplus value, productive and unproductive work (Seccombe, 1974; Coulson, Magas and Wainwright, 1975; Gardiner, 1975). Under this influence, housework is now usually referred to as 'domestic labour' and housewives as 'domestic labourers'. The main concern of the discussion has been to explore the nature and purpose of domestic labour under capitalism. Some historical observations on pre-capitalist societies have been made, but no one has considered the issues raised by post-capitalist societies. By examining domestic labour as it exists today in the Soviet Union I hope to begin this inquiry and extend the scope of the present debate.

Alexandra Kollontai, writing in 1922 of how she thought society would be organised by 1970, envisaged the complete equality of the sexes, communal life-styles and the absence of a domestic economy

(Kollontai, 1922). She was not alone. Lenin (1972, pp. 63–4) was of the opinion that housework 'crushes, strangles and degrades [woman], chains her to the kitchen and the nursery; she wastes her labour on barbarously unproductive, petty, nerve-racking, stultifying and crushing drudgery', and in the early years after the Revolution there was a general assumption among the Bolsheviks that domestic labour would be socialised, that canteens, nurseries and other communal facilities would take over the work women had traditionally done in the home. The visions of Kollontai and the other hopeful transformers of daily life have not so far materialised; Lenin's words have gone unheeded. The liberation of women, which Frederick Engels (1970, pp. 501–3) saw as a two-fold process – the entry of women into the national economy, on the one hand, and the socialisation of the domestic economy on the other – has been only half accomplished. Though Soviet women work outside the home, constituting at present 51 per cent of the labour force, domestic labour shows no sign of withering away, absorbing a staggering total of 180,000 million hours of labour annually (Yankova, 1975, p. 46). Because between 75 and 85 per cent of the work is the responsibility of the female members of the family this total divides out as three to four hours per woman per day (Andryushkyaviche, 1970, p. 82; Kharchev and Golod, 1971, p. 70; Lapidus, 1978, pp. 70–4).

Soviet political and economic theorists do not see this state of affairs as problematical. A statement to the effect that domestic labour will disappear under communism is usually considered a sufficient answer to the question of why it continues, even under 'mature socialism'. Sociologists, on the other hand, recognise housework as a problem and over the last ten to twenty years have conducted a number of studies dealing with the 'leisure' and 'free time' of working people (see, for example, Petrosyan, 1965; Gordon and Klopov, 1972). A few of these studies have focused specifically on the distribution of a woman's time between her job and domestic responsibilities (Yankova, 1970; Kharchev and Golod, 1971). They detail the hours and minutes that people spend washing clothes or watching television and show how factors such as social background, gender and marital status affect the way individuals use their time. The most obvious problem is that housework is not easily quantifiable and does not lend itself to such analysis. This is illustrated by the fact that Soviet sociologists sometimes reach diametrically opposite conclusions! B. A. Grushin (1967, p. 51), for example, has maintained that the volume of domestic labour is progressively decreasing, Z. Yankova that it is increasing (1970, p. 77). Natal'ya Baranskaya's short story, 'A week like any other', a diary of seven days in the life of a Soviet working mother, captures accurately the reality of the woman's daily round and draws attention to the amorphous character of domestic

labour. The women in the story have difficulty filling in the questionnaires handed round at work

> 'Time spent looking after children?' – that's something none of us
> can separate out. We 'look after' them in between other jobs. As
> Shura says: 'Serezha spends the whole evening in the kitchen with
> me. During the day he misses me very much, so in the evenings he
> doesn't leave my side.' (Baranskaya, 1969, p. 47)

They decide the question is absurd: ' "How can you give an account
of the time spent on domestic tasks, even if you walked about the
whole week with a stopwatch in your hands?"' (Baranskaya, 1969,
p. 48).

Nevertheless, time-budget studies can be useful as a rough guide in
building up a picture of who does the housework and how long it takes
and, by comparing surveys done at different times, in distinguishing
patterns of change. But the data have to be put in a context and
interpreted. Without a detailed knowledge of everyday life in the
Soviet Union the significance of tables and percentages remains
elusive, and meaningful comparisons with Western societies are
impossible. The information that Soviet women spend nearly an hour
a day shopping may both surprise and shock, but only if we are
familiar with the nature of the Soviet distribution system and the
standards of its service sector can we appreciate the emotional and
physical strains that these sixty minutes entail.

The sociologists themselves give few clues to this social reality
behind the statistics, and recent Western writing (Sacks, 1976;
Lapidus, 1978), while providing a careful survey of Soviet findings,
has been less successful in conveying the texture of Soviet life.
Sociology in the USSR is at its weakest when it comes to explaining
what changes people want and why, and it is obviously extremely
difficult for Westerners to conduct surveys or interviews. With the
aim of filling these two gaps I intend to look in some detail at the
various aspects of Soviet woman's domestic labour and to quote at
length from conversations I was lucky enough to have with a number
of women in the spring of 1978 (see Appendix at the end of the
chapter). These accounts of what housework is like and what Soviet
women think about it can become the starting point for understanding
why the domestic economy has been retained in the USSR and what
its function is in present Soviet society. The role of domestic labour
cannot be understood in isolation from the economic, political and
social structures of society and it is important to examine the way the
oppression of women is connected with the inequalities and shortcomings of the social system as a whole. At the same time, society is the
sum of its parts and domestic labour contributes to the preservation of

the present social system. Consideration of the work that Soviet women do in the home can not only extend the scope of the 'domestic labour debate', but also contribute to a more rounded appreciation of Soviet society and politics.

DOMESTIC LABOUR

Cleaning and Washing

Though housing has improved considerably over the last fifteen years or so people still count their space in square metres rather than by the number of rooms. The Soviet woman does not have a large area to keep clean and tidy. She is not likely, however, to have much technology to help her. In the countryside many women do not have gas, electricity or running water; they can still sometimes be seen washing their clothes in the river. Even in Moscow not all homes have hot running water. Some urban women use a tub and a flat iron to do their weekly washing. Basic items like soap are cheap at 21 to 55 kopecks a bar and plentiful, but even washing powder is sometimes hard to find. Washing-up liquid is not manufactured at all and possible substitutes such as *Domaks*, which advertises itself as 'a universal concentrated washing substance that does not harm the hands' is expensive (it is one of a number of imported East German chemical products) and on sale only in the major cities.

Some electric cleaning appliances have become more widely available over the last decade. Annual production of vacuum cleaners, for example, more than trebled in the period 1965 to 1976 and now stands at over 2 million (*Narodnoe . . .*, 1977, p. 510). Prices were reduced by 10 per cent in February 1977 and now range from 20 to 60 roubles, depending on size and quality. The models come with impressive names: for 42 and 58 roubles respectively you can purchase a 'Whirlwind' (*Vikhr'*), a 'Cyclone' (*Tsiklon*) or 'Electric Strength' (*Elektrosila*). The vacuum cleaner, though, is not the invaluable cleaning instrument it is in the West because wall-to-wall carpeting is unknown, very few families have any carpets whatsoever, and those that do often hang them on the wall. The Soviet Union manufactures vacuum cleaners of the non-upright type, and women use them mainly for cleaning upholstered furniture; they sweep the floor with the traditional rush broom (*venik*) which they buy from the peasants down at the local market.

A washing-machine is of more use to the Soviet household, and it, too, is not the luxury item it once was. Soviet statistics claim that 72 per cent of families own a washing-machine (*Materialy . . .*, 1977, p. 179). Personal observation suggests that this figure is much exaggerated. Probably it assumes that all machines ever produced are in full working order! A survey of the families of women workers carried out in the provincial town of Kostroma between 1965–8 found that just under 17 per cent had washing-machines (Kharchev and Golod, 1971, p. 76) and though the percentage has undoubtedly risen since, this seems to be a more realistic figure. The problem is not only that insufficient machines are manufactured and that their quality leaves much to be desired but that they have to be made small to fit into Soviet kitchens and bathrooms, and with a capacity of only about three kilos (compared to the four to five kilos of the average Western model) they are often more trouble than they are worth. As Natal'ya Nikolaevna, a middle-aged woman living in Moscow explained:

> Yes, I have a washing-machine. You can see it standing there, in the corner of the bathroom. It's such a bother to get it out and fit it up, I don't use it any more. It doesn't take much at a time so you have to do so many loads. I've gone back to doing my laundry in the bath and in my enamel basins.

Zhenya, a 25-year-old woman from a working-class family in a provincial Russian town has chosen another solution to her laundry problems:

> I personally don't like washing-machines. I don't like to wash all the linen and things at home. After all, washing and hanging out laundry is very, very hard work. We've got a big bath and there is somewhere to hang the washing out, but it's hard work. It's as hard as the work of a blacksmith in his smithy. The number of calories of energy expended is the same. So I use the laundry and I am averagely satisfied with the results. Because I save an awful lot of time and it costs me very little to have the washed, starched and ironed linen waiting for me.

Prices are certainly moderate. It can cost 11 kopecks to have a shirt laundered and 20 kopecks for a sheet. Even so, not all women think public laundries are a good idea. An elderly Ukrainian woman I asked, Tat'yana Vladimirovna, shook her head: 'Public laundries?, I never go near the places. How do I know they boil and wash things properly?' Natal'ya Nikolaevna's response was the same. A younger woman, Ira, married with one small child, said she would prefer to use a laundry, but the nearest was some distance from her house and there was always quite a queue. The public laundries, like the washing-machines, are deficient in both quality and quantity. Laundrettes suffer from the same shortcomings and are also fairly expensive, a load of 5 kilos costing 74 kopecks. Fewer than 15 per cent of urban families take advantage of either facility (Kharchev and Golod, 1971, p. 82).

The choices women can and do make about how to do their washing and cleaning are influenced by education, income and social background. As one would expect, the educated professional woman whose family has a relatively high income is more likely to have a washing-machine or use a laundry. Probably the single most important factor determining the nature of a woman's domestic labour is whether she comes from town or country. Rural women are likely to have more space to keep clean and tidy and larger families to cook for and look after, but, as already indicated, they are less likely to own labour-saving gadgets and also less likely to be in easy reach of public facilities. The other distinction to be made, apart from that between rural and urban women, is between privileged and non-privileged. Privileged families have priority access to consumer goods (ownership of a refrigerator or washing-machine was for a long time a sign of social status). Though these perks may have a high social value, however, the difference they make to domestic labour is not fundamental. Some privileges – an extra room, a carpet – create more work, while none of the household appliances marketed in the Soviet Union significantly reduces the time or effort involved in housework. Only the highest echelons of the Soviet élite can command the services of a domestic help (*dom-rabotnitsa*). Other women, even if they could afford to pay, cannot find one. Since nearly all Soviet women work in the national economy they are not available to be hired to do other people's housework.

Shopping

Shopping takes time. It takes a long time. One reason is the shortages in the shops which provide the butt for many Soviet jokes. For example:

> Under communism, according to the claims of the Communist Party, there will be no queuing for sausage.
> 'What is a queue?', the American citizen asks.
> 'What is sausage?', the Soviet citizen asks.

Meat has never been in abundant supply, but since the serious shortages began in 1976 this particular joke has become almost too true to be funny any more. The assortment and quality of boiled sausage, the staple protein intake of the Soviet workers, have been steadily decreasing and the sought-after smoked sausage (*kopchennaya*), or even the half-smoked (*polu-kopchennaya*) are almost unobtainable either through official or unofficial channels. During 1977, boiled sausage was still on sale in the larger towns, though it was not freely available. In Yaroslavl', for example, there was some sausage on sale every day, but always in a different shop and never very much of it. In the summer of 1978, a friend wrote from the Black Sea, 'We decided we might go vegetarian this holiday, but as it turns out we have no choice. There's no meat in the shops.' At the moment the problem is meat. Not so long ago it was onions and a few years before that, potatoes and mustard. Consumer goods can disappear from the shelves for months in the same way. Both Soviet industry and Soviet agriculture have proved consistently unable to produce enough of everything on a regular basis. Washing powder, pillows and mascara are just some of the goods that are usually available somewhere but have gone completely missing for long periods.

There is even a shortage of shops; and this shortage is permanent. Between 1960 and 1973, the number of retail outlets rose slightly, from 567,300 to 690,200 and the number of persons served by each outlet fell from 381 to 363 (Barker, n.d., p. 20). Given that the volume of consumer goods on sale has gone up over this period these figures represent only a tiny improvement in standards of service, and if they are compared with the UK ratio of 89 persons served by each retail outlet (ibid.) it is not difficult to understand how this shortage increases the length of the Soviet queue. To overcome the lack of shops, assistants are often sent to trade in fruit and vegetables on the street, where they create more queues, only this time exposed to the rain, wind and freezing temperatures. Another reason for the queues is the inefficiency and red-tape of the Soviet distribution system. Vegetables lie rotting in warehouses; a double consignment of children's shoes is delivered to one shop and none to another. In large towns food shops are usually stocked with cheese, milk, butter and bread, flour grains and tinned fish; but supplies of fresh fish, meat, fresh fruit and vegetables are irregular. Shops selling clothes, furniture and hardware always have something for sale, though not necessarily the particular item, size or design that the buyer has in mind. The line between shortage and inefficient distribution is finely drawn and for the shopper the consequences are the same.

The Soviet woman, unlike the Western woman, cannot plan her weekly meals, make out a shopping list and set forth, confident that provided her money does not run out she will return with what she wants. Apart from taking a long time, Soviet-style shopping is both physically and emotionally tiring.

Q: Do you shop every day?
Lena: Yes, the shops are not very far away. But sometimes they are very crowded. The queues are very long. If you ask for something without waiting in the queue, saying that you have a child in a pram outside in the cold, they won't let you jump your turn. They grumble and shout and get really angry.

Shopping in the rural areas is not the same as in the towns. Village shops are fewer and farther between and less well stocked. On the other hand, collective farmers grow some of their own produce, so purchasing food-stuffs is not such an urgent problem. Despite differences, the basic problems remain the same. This is also true for women of the privileged élite. The special rations (*paiki*) reserved for high-ranking officials usually contain only luxury items such as caviare, coffee and oranges, so that the women in the family must still go shopping. A few have cars to fetch and carry and an even smaller number have the right to use the special government shops, but only the wives of the very top officials are saved from the queues altogether. The problems which Baranskaya's heroine, Olya, has getting her shopping home on the crowded public transport have been experienced by every Soviet woman:

At last the tube train arrives at the end stop. Everyone jumps up and rushes to the narrow stairs. But I can't, I'm carrying parcels of eggs and milk. I trail along at the back. When I get to the bus stop there are queues for six buses. Shall I try to get into one that is filling up? But the bags! All the same I try to climb into the third bus. But because of the bags in both hands I can't get a grip on the handrail, my foot slips off the high step, I hit my knees very painfully, and at this moment the bus starts moving. Everyone's yelling and I scream. The bus stops, some guy by the door grabs me and pushes me in. I fall onto my shopping bags. My knee hurts and there's probably scrambled egg in my bag. But I'm offered a seat. Now I can have a look at my knee, at the hole in my stocking covered in blood and mud, and I can open my bag and satisfy myself that only a few eggs are broken, and one cardboard container with milk is squashed. I'm terribly upset about the stocking – 4 roubles a pair! (Baranskaya, 1969, p. 48)

The whole approach to shopping in the Soviet Union is different from that in the West. Thoughts of shopping intrude into every corner of a woman's existence. There is so much planning involved, especially if she has arranged for friends to come round or is preparing for some family or national celebration (New Year, May Day, etc.).

Ira: I make a point of shopping towards the end of every quarter for getting ready for birthdays and things. Because I know that shops are trying to meet their plan targets and so you can sometimes find red fish, salami, or even a bit of caviare. And I store these things in the fridge until I need them.
Q: Do you have any other way you can obtain delicatessen foods for special occasions?

Ira: Yes, a friend of my aunt's is something to do with a food store and we can ask her if we need things. Also, my father-in-law can sometimes get things through the economic institute where he works. At the moment I'm in the process of getting a suit for my husband. He's very tall and big and the government shops don't seem to recognise his size. The only ones I've found that might fit him are in such dreadful old-fashioned styles. So I'm ringing this friend of a friend who is supposed to be able to get hold of a foreign-made, imported suit. Oleg refuses to do it himself, so I'm having to make the phone calls and be polite and ask favours. I really don't like doing it at all. It's very unpleasant. But, after all, he does need a suit.

Because of the shortages, the *defitsit* as it is known in Russian, a lot of shopping is done outside the shops through a complicated network of 'bribery', negotiation and mutual favours between friends and friends of friends. The variety and quality of goods the woman can obtain in this way depends on her contacts (*znakomstvo, svyazi*) which in turn depend on the social circle in which she moves. Tat'yana Vladimirovna has a friend who sells fruit and vegetables outside the local tube station; Natal'ya Nikolaevna has an acquaintance who is a director of the large Moscow department store, GUM. All women, though, have some unofficial source of goods. All women maintain 'useful' friendships, ring round and scheme in search of medicine for an elderly relative, or a summer holiday for the family.

Shopping in the Soviet Union is a way of life. It requires an almost impossible combination of imagination, initiative, endurance and public-relations skill. Like cleaning and washing, shopping is women's work. Though men may sometimes stand in queues and help carry the bags, it is the women who plan and direct the operation and they who usually carry it out. It is the woman's responsibility to convert the family's wages into its standard of living.

Cooking
Cooking is, if possible, even more exclusively women's work. In the towns the 'communal kitchen' is still by no means a thing of the past, but new housing does mean that most women have a kitchen of their own. Kitchen equipment is in better supply. Enamel saucepans, until recently searched and queued for by women, now line the shelves. Refrigerators, too, can be purchased easily, without a long wait or large bribe. One Moscow shop I visited in the spring of 1978 had no less than ten different models in stock, ranging in capacity from 120 to 240 litres and in price from 120 to 345 roubles. A number of other, mainly electrical, goods have appeared in the large towns. Electric mincers are in the shops for 25 roubles, and coffee jugs for between 15

and 17 roubles. With the meat shortage, and coffee currently selling at 18 roubles a kilo, however, neither is of much help in the Soviet kitchen. Electric kettles (no automatic models) and frying pans, both at 7 roubles, and juice-makers at 27 roubles are of more immediate use, but most women are suspicious of their quality and have insufficient space to store them anyway. Though the kitchen is gradually changing, compared with the West its mechanisation has only just begun. All vegetables have to be sliced and diced by hand and, given that elaborate soups and salads are the basis of Ukrainian and Russian cooking and root vegetables a vital ingredient in the main dishes of the other Soviet nationalities, this means women spend a good deal of time in the kitchen. Convenience foods have yet to be mass produced. The few packet soups so far marketed are too tasteless to be taken seriously, and the frozen food from Bulgaria and the jars of vegetables from Hungary, though of better quality, are in short supply.

Most factories provide a canteen, and smaller enterprises a snack-bar (*bufet*), where cheap meals are sold. Zhenya has a low opinion of the quality of the public catering system:

> It is impossible to eat in the canteens; other people do eat there. In Russia a lot of people do, but both my husband and I grew up in families which paid a great deal of attention to food. At work there is a *bufet* and, of course, it is possible to eat things there, natural things – a piece of cheese, for example, a piece of sausage, tea, yoghurt (*kefir*). But we don't eat things like cooked meat.

Zhenya's family is not as unusual as she thinks. Though the vast majority of the population finds the canteens adequate for midday meals they prefer to eat breakfast and supper at home (Kharchev and Golod, 1971, p. 82).

Women in town and country, regardless of age, education or social position cook supper and weekend meals for their families. Rural kitchens are often more spacious, though less well equipped, than urban ones; wives of party officials, for example, may have smarter kitchens, a greater range of appliances and easier access to convenience foods. Nevertheless all women, regardless of age, education or social position, cook supper and weekend meals for their families. The number of restaurants is too small, the queues too long and the prices too high to make eating out a viable alternative. Only a tiny handful of women have other women to do their cooking for them.

Child Care
Cooking is one of the most widespread of women's activities, and its practice is similar for Soviet and Western women. Child care is the

most universal of women's experiences, but differences in its practice
are greater. In some respects, because of the low level of technology
and the shortages, child care in the USSR is more demanding. It
involves women in a considerable amount of extra, routine housework. Zhenya, for example, said that though she used the public
laundry she washes the baby's things at home, boiling them carefully
to safeguard against infection. Baby foods are only available in the big
towns and are not always popular, even with urban women, because of
both their quality and their price. Lena prefers to prepare her
children's food herself:

> I prepare cereal (*kasha*), yoghurt (*kefir*), curd cheese (*tvorog*) and
> vegetable purée myself. I don't trust what they sell in the shops. I
> prepare everything myself. And I stop all the other women who live
> round here that I'm friendly with from buying them. Well, I advise
> them not to. These baby-food mixtures are very harmful. The
> children can get ill. I tell them they are lazy, that they could easily
> make something from rice or flour or grain. The shop stuff is bad.
> It's got sugar in it and the flour is not right. If you do it yourself you
> can see the products you're using. I never buy anything ready
> made. Well, I buy the milk products, of course. I haven't got a cow!
> I can't make milk!
> Q: Is it easy to buy the mixtures?
> Lena: Yes, they can be bought everywhere.
> Q: What about the countryside?
> Lena: No, not in the country. They don't sell anything like that
> there. I think that's better. All country people are healthy. They
> never get ill.
> Q: Is it cheaper if you make things yourself?
> Lena: Yes, the mixtures are very expensive; baby food is expen-
> sive. *Malysh*, for example is expensive. A box costs 1 rouble 50
> kopecks. That's very expensive.

Then, because prams, push-chairs, baby clothes and toys are all in
short supply their purchase adds to shopping time. Buying clothes
and toys for the children is often the main aim of a family trip to one of
the big urban centres. Dzerzhinskaya Square in Moscow is more
famous within the USSR for its big children's shop, *Detskii mir*
(Children's World), than for the KGB headquarters, and its underground station is always a constant bustle of women with large paper
packages. A national television programme on consumer goods,
screened in August 1978, interviewed a number of women shopping
there. One woman, standing in a long queue for children's winter
tights, explained that where she came from tights were sometimes on
sale, but never the right size. She came from Tbilisi, the capital of

Georgia, 2,000 kilometres from Moscow. Another woman in the same queue came from the Urals.

The provision of day-care facilities for children, on the other hand, compares favourably with that of any other country and does save women many of the problems which working mothers face in the West. Accommodation is cheap: the charge is calculated according to the family income and is always very low; 5 or 6 roubles per month is an average fee. It is also provided on a large scale: between 1960 and 1976 the number of children attending crèches and nurseries rose from 4·4 million to 12 million, representing an increase from 23 to 37 per cent of all children under school age (Lapidus, 1978, pp. 131–2). Because the number of crèches (which take children under 3) is relatively small, this means that the vast majority of pre-school urban children over the age of 3 do go to day nursery. Nevertheless, the facilities are still insufficient. Since all women work the demand for day-care is very high. And since all women work in the national economy the private monetary baby-minding arrangements between women, so common in the West, are very rare. Some women (particularly in the country) may rely on relatives to look after their children, but the vast majority of working women rely on the state. Mothers have to put their names down for nursery places and wait their turn. Lena managed to get her son into a crèche straight away, despite a waiting list, because, as the director put it: 'I know you're a trained dressmaker and I can always do with someone who sews well'. Day-care accommodation, like anything else in short supply, is subject to the laws of the black-market:

Q: Was it easy to get your child into a crèche?
Zhenya: No, there are a lot of nurseries, but still not enough and you usually need contacts to get your child into one that's near where you live. Our grandmother works in the government department where the allocation of places is done, so we were OK. But for others it is very difficult.
Q: Are there any crèches that are open twenty-four hours a day, five days a week?
Zhenya: Yes, I could get our child a place in one if I wanted, but I don't. I wouldn't see her that way for a whole week. It's mostly single mothers or those with unhappy families who place their children there, families where the father drinks.

Not only is the number of nurseries insufficient, the service offered is inflexible and institutionalised. Either the state looks after the children only for the period while parents work, or it does not let them see them for a week. People have no control over the organisation of facilities and no way of demanding that their different and changing needs be met. Child care is designed primarily to meet the needs of the national economy, freeing women to work in the labour force. The task of looking after children in the evenings and at weekends belongs to the family, in effect to the mother. 'In the view of the well-known American scholar B. Spock', wrote the Soviet economist Perevedentsev recently, 'a mother's caresses are as necessary to an infant's spiritual health as milk is to his physical health' (Perevedentsev, 1975). Children now take longer to reach independence and mothers are now expected to supervise children's intellectual and moral education, not just their physical development. Though government child-care facilities have improved over the years, time spent looking after children has increased. Women 'look after' their children 'between other jobs'. Child care expands to fill the available time.

THE ROLE OF DOMESTIC LABOUR

This survey has brought out some of the differences between domestic labour in the USSR and the West. The Soviet state has intervened in some areas and accepted a certain responsibility for some aspects of domestic labour, notably through its provision of public laundries, canteens and child-care facilities. In every case, though, either the price, the quantity or the quality of the services provided has severely limited their liberational effect. None of the government measures has socialised domestic labour in the way envisaged by early Bolshevik theory. In fact, because of the low level of its mechanisation, housework is in many ways more arduous than in Western societies. But the similarities are more striking than these differences. A definite domestic economy continues to exist and, as in the West, is associated with a clearly marked sexual division of labour. Housework is women's work. Under capitalism it is 'precisely the dual and contradictory role of women as both domestic and modern industrial workers that imparts the specific dynamic to [their] oppression' (Coulson, Magas and Wainwright, 1975, p. 60), and this remains true in the USSR: it is the Soviet woman's dual role in the national and domestic economy that shapes her life. Since almost all Soviet women work outside the house this 'double shift' is for them an even more universal and continuous experience. There are important differences in the pattern of paid work, particularly with regard to the number of women in professional jobs. The high percentage of women in the Soviet medical service is well known. While in Great Britain only 0·4 per cent of engineers are women, in the Soviet Union the figure is 40 per cent (Lapidus, 1978, p. 182). But on the whole, the sexual division of labour within the home determines the jobs women do outside it. Women predominate in the textile, clothing and food industries, in teaching and healing and the service sector – all areas which have traditionally been regarded as 'suitable' for women. Secondly, women's 'second shift' keeps them segregated in the unskilled and low-paid jobs, partly because domestic responsibilities drain women's energy and also because they maintain the coherence of an ideology that presents women as home-oriented and lacking in leadership qualities.

The debate on the role of domestic labour in Western countries has focused on the fact that as capitalism developed it adapted the feudal organisation of domestic tasks to its needs. Because the domestic economy is privatised, the nature of the work involved and its performance on the basis of the sexual division of labour have remained unaffected by changes in other economic structures. Nevertheless, as the debate has pointed out, capitalism has moulded the domestic economy to its needs. In Western Europe, housework has changed over the last two centuries and the level of mechanisation and socialisation varies today from country to country, but in every country and at every time it has ultimately served the interests of profit (Adamson, 1976; 'Women's domestic labour', 1976).

The driving force of the post-capitalist economy is no longer the search for profit, and thus the organisation of the domestic economy must be determined differently. Cultural traditions and the level of economic development continue to influence the content and performance of housework, but it is now the degree of control over social life that individuals and in particular women are able to exercise that is the most important factor. The low level of socialisation of domestic labour in the Soviet Union is thus directly related to the lack of control which Soviet citizens have over political and economic institutions. It should not be understood, though, as merely a mechanical reflection of the country's political and economic system. In order to maintain itself in power, the Soviet government has to be responsive to pressure from below and for this reason individuals are able to have some indirect influence on social development. The rate of the economic development of housework has been much lower than that of other areas of the economy. This suggests that the pressure that women are able to bring to bear on the government is less than that of other social groups. The organisation of domestic labour in the Soviet Union today must therefore be understood as the result of the particular historical experience of Soviet women as a social group. In the 1920s all forms of popular self-organisation were crushed, but because of women's isolation in the home and the family they were able to salvage least. In the 1930s, millions of women entered production, but these were peasant women, used to working hard and accepting male authority. They did not challenge their dual role and this fact gave the Soviet government more room for manœuvre. The hard work which women did in the home allowed the government to postpone the development of light industry and it reduced the social tension created by the continual failures of Soviet agricultural policies. Recent feminist writing has pointed out how the economic recession in Western Europe has affected women in particular. The cuts in government spending mean that the amount of domestic labour increases. Women 'absorb' the crisis (*Women Under Attack*, 1976; Adamson, 1976, p. 3). Soviet women have been 'absorbing' the crises of their government for decades. The problems of the Soviet economy – the inconsistencies of the plan, the inefficiency and inflexibility of management, the underdevelopment of the service sector – all are well known to Western specialists, who frequently discuss these problems, but not the effect they have on the lives of women. A recent article in *Pravda* (Orlov, 1978) revealed that a certain plant was manufacturing only small sizes of shoes, because in this way they could reach their planned targets more easily. Since this decision did not stop some people having large feet it must have sent women searching, queuing and bribing in order to keep their families suitably shod. Another article ('Zaprosam . . .', 1977), criticised the general low level of services and admitted that since public laundries had been allowed to take in washing from institutions such as hospitals, service to the public had deteriorated. The bulk orders, which were much quicker to handle and more profitable, now accounted for 75 per cent of their turnover. The plan was fulfilled at the expense of women. All working people suffer from the economic shortcomings, but women, as the main consumers, are the most directly hit.

Women have not acted as a social pressure group, neither have they been represented in the decision-making process. The male planners have not been under pressure from below and they themselves have not seen the socialising of domestic labour as a priority. One result of the male bias of the governing élite has been that it has done little to improve the position of its own women. In the West, where socialised services are usually commodities provided by private enterprise, professional and middle-class women have a distinct advantage over working-class women. Professional women can afford to buy appliances, nursery accommodation, and often the services of the working-class women whose power to perform domestic labour becomes a commodity on the market. In the USSR, this buying and selling of domestic labour is almost non-existent and though easier access to consumer goods and services is one of the perks of the privileged, this gives the privileged woman few advantages over other women.

WOMEN'S CHANGING ATTITUDES

A precondition for changes in the organisation of domestic labour and women's dual role is the emergence of women as a social force. The monolithic face the Soviet Union presents to the outside world makes it difficult to tell whether there is any shift in women's attitudes. There are no trade unions, political parties or women's organisations which can be studied as a barometer of public opinion. An examination of statistical evidence, however, does indicate that many of the changes that have caused or reflected increasing conflict and contradiction in the lives of Western women are under way in the Soviet Union. Soviet society has become increasingly urbanised. Marriage is a far less stable institution. Divorce rates have risen most steeply in the towns, but the increase has been substantial everywhere (Chuiko, 1973, ch. 3). The birth rate is falling (*SSSR* . . ., 1977, p. 22) and the extended family is on the decline (Volkov, 1976, p. 26). Finally, while women's educational opportunities have increased over the last two decades and women now constitute over 50 per cent of the student body (*Zhenshchiny* . . ., 1975, pp. 55–70), their status in the work-force has not greatly improved (Sacks, 1976; Lapidus, 1978, ch. 5).

In the West, the press is an important indicator of social development and Soviet newspapers and journals, read carefully, can also provide vital though less direct evidence of change. The Soviet press is selective in the way it represents reality and usually gives the impression that there is unanimity on every issue and universal satisfaction with the *status quo*. It almost always takes woman's dual role for granted and assumes that everyone else does as well. Every year on 8 March, International Women's Day, the papers print their ritual eulogies to women. In 1976 *Pravda* wrote that:

> The warmth of the female soul, the solicitude of wives and mothers, makes the Soviet family strong. Loving and attentive women raise their children – the future builders of communism – to be healthy of body and ideologically firm of mind, to be worthy citizens of the socialist fatherland. The nation is grateful to you, women, for your great and noble work. ('Sovetskim . . .', 1976)

But recently there has been a good deal of debate in both the specialised and the popular press about family life and its discontents which contradicts the bland image of happy families projected by the media at large. Divorce has been a favourite topic of discussion, and also more significantly the question of the family's internal organisation. When a mother of ten children wrote to *Literaturnaya Gazeta* in 1974, complaining that the public did not have sufficient respect for mothers of large families and the government gave insufficient support (Kuchina, 1974), another paper, *Komsomol'skaya Pravda*, entered the discussion from a different angle, arguing that the social problems women faced could only be solved if men did 'at least half the housework' (Strelyanyi, 1976). The question of family equality has been raised again recently in a series of articles in *Literaturnaya Gazeta* on love and marriage. The two women poets, Tamara Zhirminskaya (1977) and Yuliya Drunina (1977), who contributed to the series, both expressed the opinion that men should play a more visible role in the family and do their fair share of the housework. Other women agreed, but not the editors. This became clear when shortly afterwards the paper printed a letter from a male reader complaining that his wife did not work hard enough in the home:

> As the time passes I begin to worry more and more that fewer years are left to me to make my contribution to science; after all, I am the man in the family and my duty is to work and not to slave away in the kitchen or over the washing – when I have a wife for that.

A number of the numerous indignant replies were published in a subsequent issue, together with a note from the editors expressing their surprise at women's response and admitting that the first letter they opened and read, which seemed to them 'extreme' and 'warped', turned out to be the rule and not the exception. 'The man in the family', according to one letter, 'is a capricious child never satisfied with anything, or a roaring lion who nags his wife over petty things. I'm not generalising from my own experience. You only have to listen to what women talk about when they're together.' Another pointed out that if a woman had written in complaining that, though her husband did not drink or smoke and was not unfaithful to her, he refused to do her washing and cooking, the editors would have thought her crazy and certainly would not have published her letter, 'which only goes to show that it isn't a problem of girls not being prepared for family life, but of husbands being their wives' dependants' ('Otkuda . . .', 1977).

Soviet ideology has always done more than mirror social roles. It has offered a model of perfect womanhood for women to aspire to and has ignored the tensions to which the Soviet family has always been subject. But the new interest which the press is showing in the question of who should do the housework suggests that the social changes traced by the statistics have influenced women's attitudes and expectations. The popular health journal, *Zdorov'e*, with a circulation of over 11 million, introduced articles on husbands and housework six or seven years ago and their number has steadily increased. Even the cartoons in *Krokodil* have recognised the new concern for equality in the home. One entitled 'A present from the wife' shows a man trying on what he thinks is a tie, but it is in fact an apron shaped as a tie. 'The tie is fine', he is saying, 'but what are the strings for?' ('Podarok zheny', 1978).

The conversations I had with young Soviet women also suggest that dissatisfaction with the dual role is growing. None of the women I spoke to romanticised their role in the home. They stated quite unequivocally that they found housework exhausting, both physically and mentally. Describing how she felt in the period after the birth of her child, Zhenya said, 'I was not so much lonely as simply very tired. I was so busy all the day.' All the women recognised that the way household tasks were arranged was unfair. They considered that men could and should help and they had tried actively to involve their husbands. In every family the housework was a source of conflict.

Q: Have you tried to teach Viktor to cook?
Zhenya: He categorically refuses even to make cereal for the baby. He says he'd rather take the baby out for walks and things.

She said she was lucky her husband liked spending time with the baby, as most men did not. Lena was less lucky.

Q: Do you think that men can look after young children as well as women?
Lena: Yes, they can. They can but they don't want to. They can. They can. I'm convinced they can. They just don't want to.
  When our first child was born my husband did not want to have anything to do with him. He said, 'Let the child grow up a bit then I might help. When the child is physically developed I will develop him mentally.' You understand, he wants the child made ready. He doesn't, of course, want to have to look after the child from birth. He hid under the pillow so as not to hear the child crying. You understand?
Q: Does he help with other things around the house?
Lena: He goes out all the time. You have to force him to do anything. Sometimes I feel guilty, as if it's my fault. That I've been mean to him. I don't know if I'm right but sometimes when he makes a face or says something cutting I feel that I've done something unforgivable.
Q: Does he change the nappies?
Lena: No, God, no. He does wash them sometimes and then he feels very pleased with himself. How come you've dirtied so many nappies today, he says to me as if it were I who had dirtied them and not the child [laughter].
Q: So you quarrel about housework?
Lena: Yes, yes. That's all we quarrel about. Up until the birth of the first child everything was fine: we love each other, we go everywhere together, we wash our own clothes, take turns with the cooking, share the shopping – all without quarrelling. But when the

child arrives, then we start digging at each other. Why, I don't know. Of course, I don't say to him: 'You must do this', or 'You must do that'. I simply ask him. I say: 'Please wash the nappies', or 'Please do that.' Maybe that's the wrong way to go about it. Some men get spoiled when you treat them well [laughter]. They take advantage of you and do just what they want [sigh]. I'm not just talking about one individual man but about them all. They're all like that. Mine at least does something. But it's only because I insist. I hate all the long conversations persuading him. If only he would offer to do something, if only he would say, 'Let me do this', or, 'Shall I do that?' But it never happens. When he does offer to do something it's in such a way that you don't want to accept [laughter]. You understand?

Though neither woman was very successful at persuading her husband to help and the division of labour in the household remained along traditional lines, their attitudes on child upbringing were far from traditional and very different from those of most Soviet child psychologists, who stress the importance of teaching a 'correct sexual orientation' even in the very earliest years of childhood.

Q: Do you bring Tamara up any special way because she is a girl?
Zhenya: No. I don't think you should make any difference between a girl and a boy. I don't bring her up any differently. Probably later on, though.
Q: If you had a son would you teach him how to cook?
Zhenya: Yes. Children should be brought up the same. Boys should learn to cook and girls should be taught boys' games – like cycling, etc.

When I asked whether they saw the socialisation of housework as a viable alternative to its mechanisation, they said that they did and that it was preferable. When I asked Lena what would be her ideal life-style, and what she thought was the best solution to the problem of child care, her answer came without a moment's hesitation.

Lena: Of course it would be best to improve nurseries, etc. A young woman would then have time to herself and time for her own work . . .
Q: So you think it is possible theoretically to have laundries that can clean linen properly and can cope with all types of clothes as well?
Lena: Heavens, yes. Why not?

Even if Soviet women would theoretically welcome socialisation, the government is not about to pursue such a policy, which leaves women a number of difficult choices to make, particularly with regard to the care of their children. While pre-school institutions have always been considered to have a positive influence on a child's development and even in recent years have not come under attack in the way they have in other East European countries (Scott, 1976, ch. 8), women know that children, particularly in the crèches, are always falling ill and that they have to take time off work to look after them. Also, now that women know more about child psychology and are more aware of the importance of childhood, they are more critical of the quality of pre-school child-care provisions. Women are suspicious of facilities over which they have no control.

Q: Do you think that the staff at the nursery do a good job?
Zhenya: No. When I went to the crèche I noticed these huge steps and I thought: 'Oh, God, will my child have to climb up those steps. She could easily fall down and hit her head or break a limb.' When I saw those steps I really didn't want to put my child in the crèche.

If women go out to work when they have young children they feel a certain amount of guilt about it. They are influenced by the psychologist's talk of the importance of 'maternal love' and, anyway, they want to do the best for their children. With the increasing concern for the quality of upbringing, Soviet women are torn between their desire to work and their desire to be good mothers. When Olya, the heroine of *A Week Like Any Other*, breaks under the strain of her round-the-clock responsibilities and her husband suggests that an answer to the problem would be to give up work and stay at home with the children, she replies:

Dima, do you really think that I wouldn't like to do what's best for the children? Of course I would. But what you suggest is just . . . it would destroy me. And my five years studying? My degree? My working record? My job? It's easy for you to chuck all that overboard. And what'll I be like, sitting at home? As cross as hell; I'll nag at all of you the whole time. (Baranskaya, 1969, p. 53)

Sociological surveys show that the vast majority of Soviet women, particularly those with skills, do not want to solve their child care problems by giving up their work outside the home (Yankova, 1975, p. 43). It seems unlikely that large numbers of women will choose to leave their jobs in the national economy, but the decision to stay is not easy. The way Zhenya describes her decision to return to full-time work illustrates this.

Q: So at the moment you are at home a lot doing the housework. You say that most of your time is spent on the cooking and that's the bit of housework that you like doing most of all?

Zhenya: Yes, but finally I get very tired of doing it. So we have got the child a place in a crèche. And I am very glad that I shall be working from first thing in the morning to three in the afternoon, for seven hours instead of three like I am at the moment. And we don't have to collect the child till 6 or 7 o'clock. I shall have a couple of hours to go round the shops alone, taking it calmly. Or I can rest for an hour and then spend an hour preparing the meal.

Q: Why did you decide to send Tamara to the crèche?

Zhenya: You can't go on living on half a wage.

Q: Do you think it's good for the child to go to a crèche at that age?

Zhenya: No, not really. Tamara's only just 2. It's good for the child from the age of 3. But it's already easier by the time the child is 2. It would be better to wait a year till nursery age and not send her to the crèche at all. There are too many children there and not enough staff. It's hard work so people don't want to work there [sigh]. Mostly it's women who have small children themselves who work there. You can look after your child and get a wage at the same time.

In the course of conversation, Zhenya says she has sent the child to a crèche because she is tired of doing housework, even the cooking which she enjoys, but when the question is put directly she says it is the financial pressures. Women avoid explaining their decisions, even to themselves, in terms of their own 'selfish' motives, preferring the acceptable motive of sacrifice for the good of the family. This probably explains the apparently contradictory findings of surveys investigating women's motives in taking up paid employment. When asked 'Would you work even if your husband earned the equivalent of both present wages?', the vast majority of women answer 'yes' (Yankova, 1975, p. 43). But when asked why they work most women say, 'Because the family needs the money'.

One way that women can and do protect their own interests is by limiting their families. All the women I spoke to had strong views on this subject. Lena said two children were plenty and there was no way she was going to have any more. Zhenya said she might possibly have a second, but only if she and her husband managed to move to another town and get a good flat, and not for a few years anyway because she wanted to study. Ira was under pressure from her husband who wanted a second child: 'He says it would be good for our son not to be the only child in the family. Well, I agree but I can't face the prospect of going through everything again [sigh].'

Between 1950 and 1974, the birth rate dropped from 26·7 births per 1,000 of the population to 18·2 (*SSSR* . . ., 1977, p. 22). The official reaction to this has not been sympathetic. Families should be larger, the economists and demographers agree, women should have at least three or four children. Demographers have calculated that otherwise only 30 million babies will be born in the last quarter of the century, which is too few, in view of the country's need for labour resources (Cohn, 1973; Perevedentsev, 1975). The problems of the Soviet economy are of long standing and all efforts to solve them by improving technology and productivity have had little success. Other East European countries finding themselves in a similar situation – low productivity and slow growth – have sought to boost their economic performance by increasing the birth rate and thus ultimately the labour resources at their disposal. Several countries have restricted abortion rights and have introduced a system of maternity benefits whereby women are paid to stay at home with their children for a number of years (Scott, 1976, chs 6–7). The Soviet government, too, has already introduced a number of measures to encourage larger families (Acharkan, 1975). Also the current Five-Year Plan has promised women more opportunities to work part-time or take work home and have longer maternity leave (*Osnovnye* . . ., 1976, p. 70). So far, though, the measures have been limited and the promises have not been kept, but since the economic situation has not improved the government will be under pressure in the coming period to find ways to increase the birth rate.

Western analysts have noted the serious shortage of labour in the USSR and the consequent concern of the authorities over family size, but they have shown little interest in the significance of this for the social position of Soviet women. They forget that statistics of average family size are more than just figures on a page for the women who have to bear and raise the children, and that it was women's conscious choice to limit their families that led to the falling birth rate in the first place. The dilemma which the Soviet government faces in determining an effective economic strategy cannot be fully understood unless the changing attitudes and expectations of Soviet women are taken into consideration. Similarly, welfare measures need to be seen in the context of the country's economic difficulties, as designed primarily to provide labour and not as a disinterested attempt to promote the liberation of women. Whilst in the short term, benefits of the type introduced in other East European countries and envisaged by the Five-Year Plan offer working mothers some relief, they reinforce the sexual division of labour and provide no long-term solution.

What emerges clearly, when the changes in women's lives are considered against the background of the general economic and social developments in Soviet society, is that the interests of women and the state are in conflict. The state wants more children; women want to control their fertility. In Western Europe the falling birth rate coincided with a period of recession and unemployment; in the USSR it comes at a time of acute labour shortage. On the one hand, this raises the possibility of women's rights being withdrawn; on the other, it gives women a strong position from which to press the government for concessions. The question of the social role of women has become one of the important areas of bargaining and struggle between the population and the state.

The development of Soviet family policy is another illustration of this. As living standards and expectations have risen over the last decade, the Soviet government has stressed the role of the family as the unit of consumption and leisure. This accentuates the division between work and home and encourages individuals to see the latter as the main focus of thought and energy, and thus the family acts as a stabilising social influence. In this sense, the present strategy of 'strengthening the family' is a continuation of Stalinist policies. But there are important differences. Under Stalin, 'strengthening the family' meant a tightening of marriage, divorce and abortion laws, and also of ideology. The government has had to respect the popular distaste for repressive legal regulation of family affairs and the desire for a more meaningful private life – which is understood by women as more companionship and equality in the marriage relationship. Now the emphasis is on the internal cohesion of the family and the content and quality of relationships, particularly the new and extended role of the father. The current changes are splitting the individual's existence into 'public' and 'personal', creating a family distanced and separate from the other areas of social life, atomising individuals and limiting their capacity for collective action. At the same time, they are a concession to the demands of both sexes for more control over at least some part of their lives, and of women for more equality. At present the situation is fluid. Whether the present policy is continued or whether steps are taken to replace it by the more traditional approach – of which there are still plenty of advocates – will depend in no small way on the ability of the Soviet women to defend their interests.

Women today are more confident of themselves and take more initiative in individual situations to establish their rights. Though this has affected and restricted government action, the state still has immense power to shape women's life-styles and decisions. In the absence of democratic political structures, and specifically of women's organisations, it is difficult for women to exert any collective pressure on the state or even develop a sense of collective identity. Their responsibilities for domestic labour set women against each other. In queues, for example, women see themselves as competing against each other rather than as battling together against an inefficient system. Cramped living conditions can add fuel to the flames.

Q: Do you think that your housing situation makes life more difficult?

Lena: [who lives in one room with her husband and two children, sharing a kitchen and bathroom with the six inhabitants of the two other rooms in the flat] Yes . . . the living conditions, of course. The shared bathroom [sigh]. The neighbours. Never mind. One gets used to it and our neighbours are good. So we don't feel the lack of space so much. It would be different if we had different kinds of neighbours: old, or young and bad-tempered. I know the types. There's a situation in our block. This young woman has two children; the woman who shares the flat is religious, she goes to church. But she is always going on at the young woman. Sometimes she even catches her in the corridor in the evenings – she's a really huge woman – and she says 'If you get in my way while I'm doing my washing I'll do you in'.

In the circumstances, it is difficult for women to be sensitive and understanding about the burdens the dual role places on the other women. Lena, recounting her bad experiences in maternity hospital – the lack of staff and their rudeness, and the casual standards of care – concluded that women should not be allowed into the medical profession.

Without a collective identity, it is hard for women, despite their dissatisfaction and their search for a new image, to identify a suitable alternative. Soviet culture has no models to offer and so, like young people who are turning to Western music and fashion, often borrowing indiscriminately, Soviet women are beginning to appropriate the Western ideal of femininity. At one time they prized platform shoes, then denim dresses became fashionable. Women are prepared to skimp and save in order to pay the high prices of the black market, to make trips to the big cities in search of mascara and lipstick, preferably Czech, Yugoslav or Western. A notice stuck to a mirror in the women's room of a Moscow academic institution read 'English lipstick for sale. 5 roubles. Contact X in philosophy department.' In the West, fashion and the feminine image have been used to persuade women to accept their inequality. There is the possibility that in accepting femininity Soviet women will be reconciled with their domestic role and that their protest against the drabness and inefficiency of the Soviet system will lead them to act in accordance with, rather than against, the state's interests. Lena, however, linked her femininity not with domesticity but with her approval of domestic labour's socialisation. Her concern that her hands had suffered from laundering her child's nappies came in the same breath as her advocation of public laundries. Femininity did not blunt her dissatisfaction with her dual role; it was linked to it, as her answer to the question on the best solution to the problem of child-care indicates:

> Lena: Oh, of course it would be best to improve nurseries, etc. A young woman would then have time to herself and time for her own work. You begin to forget the last time you had a manicure. You don't have time to think about cosmetics.

Femininity for her is part of her search for self-determination.

A survey carried out on the qualities teenage schoolgirls in Moscow considered most important in men and women, showed them to be unconcerned about femininity, but very concerned about self-determination. In men they rated 'respect for women' as most important, and put 'bravery' in tenth or eleventh place. Of thirteen female characteristics given they placed 'dignity' and 'strength of character' at the top of the list and 'housewifery' and 'domestic efficiency' at the bottom (Bel'skaya, 1977).

CONCLUSIONS

The lives Soviet women lead are not identical in every respect with those of women in Western countries. But the domestic economy continues to exist and domestic labour is still their work. As in the West, it is woman's dual role as labourer both in the domestic and national economy that shapes her existence. In fact, because almost all Soviet women work outside the home, the impact of the dual role on their lives is even greater; despite differences between urban and rural, privileged and unprivileged, all Soviet women share a very similar experience.

Various factors have been put forward to explain the role of the domestic economy in capitalist society. The ideological importance of the family – around which domestic labour is organised – has frequently been noted. The family acts to brake the fight of working people against exploitation and oppression, and teaches its members to accept hierarchical relationships and the virtue of obedience to authority (Mitchell, 1971, ch. 8). More recently, the strictly economic advantages of the family have been underlined. Through her day-to-day servicing of the working members of the family and her long-term care and education of children – the future workers – the woman reproduces labour power (Beechey, 1977). Capitalism has never shouldered more than minimal responsibility for these tasks, partly because there has been no pressure from below, and more importantly because of the expense involved. It has been suggested that this high cost is one of the main reasons why capitalism has not up till now pursued a policy of socialisation, but that in the future both this and the ideological objections may lose their significance, in which case there is no theoretical reason why capitalism should not socialise domestic labour (Gardiner, 1975; 'Women's domestic labour', 1976, p. 14.) It has been argued elsewhere, however, that capitalism spontaneously generates the family and the domestic economy – that an economic system based on the search for profit constantly reproduces the elements of the oppression of women (Coulson, Magas and Wainwright, 1975, pp. 68–9).

The survey of the organisation of domestic labour in the USSR shows clearly that the family continues to be used as an ideological instrument of stabilisation. Similarly, it can be seen that the woman in the home bears most responsibility for the care of the present and future workforce and provides free-of-charge services which it would be expensive for the state to provide. The question of whether domestic labour can be said to be spontaneously generated by the Soviet system is more difficult to answer. The problem is that while it can be demonstrated that the search for profit – the dynamic behind a capitalist economy – has disappeared, it is difficult to determine what has replaced it. The Soviet Union does not have a clearly defined mode of production in the way Western societies do. Thus while the nature of domestic labour, even under capitalism, is not mechanistically determined by the main economy – the domestic economy because of its privatised nature is to a certain extent separate and is also subject to social and ideological influences – the same is even more true in the Soviet Union. It is not the economy, as such, that reproduces domestic labour but the social formation as a whole. Because the law of value does not operate and economic relations are much less clear-cut and established than under capitalism, social groups, despite their lack of formal organisation, have a more direct relationship with state power. The nature of domestic labour is less dependent on purely economic forms and more on the balance of power between women as a social group and the government.

The description of the domestic labour which Soviet women do has highlighted its backwardness, even by Soviet economic standards. This suggests that the organisation of the domestic economy has to be understood historically as a result of the distance of women from the decision-making process and the difficulty they have had in developing as a cohesive social group. The changes in postwar Soviet society, most importantly the educational improvements and the increasing number of women entering the industrial labour force, have, on the one hand, increased women's expectations and self-confidence and, on the other, aggravated the problems experienced in combining their domestic and social roles. Women have begun to recognise the contradictions in their position and to press for changes.

If the present organisation of domestic labour is to be understood in the context of the weakness of women as a pressure group, it follows that their development of a collective identity could lead to changes. And it is not ruled out that the government will introduce measures that further socialise domestic labour. Because of the government's economic difficulties, women's desire to limit their families has come into conflict with the interests of the government in an increased birth rate, and thus the struggle of women against their dual role has assumed a central political importance.

An examination of domestic labour in the Soviet Union shows how the patterns of living and behaving associated with the existence of a domestic economy have over the centuries become firmly embedded in social practice. It also shows the extent to which they can withstand the pressures of large-scale economic and social transformation. This reinforces the argument underlying the domestic labour debate: socialist change requires that the forms of domestic labour be consciously understood and challenged. This examination also emphasises the importance for any social formation of the manner in which its labour force is reproduced. Without an analysis of domestic labour we cannot make sense of Soviet politics and society.

APPENDIX: INTERVIEW DATA

The five women interviewed were chosen because I knew them well enough to ask them to answer my questions. The interviews were taped. I made some cuts in the excerpts I selected, but otherwise kept faithfully to the transcribed material. From my contact with Soviet women I should say that these five are fairly typical of urban women. In the absence of large-scale surveys of social attitudes the material in these interviews fills some gaps; but more importantly this method of interviewing can reveal things that would usually be left unsaid – in a one-to-one, supportive atmosphere women feel freer to speak for themselves.

Some Background Data on the Five Women
Zhenya: 25 years old with an 18-month-old daughter. She has secondary medical education and has recently returned to full-time employment as a keep-fit instructor in an institute. Her husband teaches literature at a provincial university. They live in one room in a communal flat.

Lena: 23 years old with a 2-year-old son and a 6-month-old baby. The daughter of peasants who moved to the city after the war. Trained as a tailoress. Presently at home looking after her children, but taking in sewing on a private basis. Her husband is an unskilled worker. They live in one room in a communal flat.

Ira: 30 years old. Her one child is 8. Went to university and now works as a teacher. Both her parents work in academic institutions and her husband is doing research. She lives in a three-roomed flat.

Natal'ya Nikolaevna: Of working-class background. Finished secondary school and has worked all her life as a clerk. Has grown-up children. Her husband is in management. They have a one-room flat.

Tat'yana Vladimirovna: A pensioner in her 60s. A widow with no children. Previously worked in a nursery. Lives in a one-room flat.

BIBLIOGRAPHY

Acharkan, V. A., 'Sotsial' 'no-pravovaya priroda posobiya na detei maloobespechennym sem'yam', *Sovetskoe gosudarstvo i pravo*, 1975, no. 11, pp. 34–41.

Adamson, O., *et al.*, 'Women's oppression under capitalism', *Revolutionary Communist*, no. 5 (1976), pp. 2–48.

Andryushkyaviche, Ya., 'Zhenskii trud i problema svobodnogo vremeni', in *Problemy byta, braka i sem'i*, ed. N. Solov'ev, Yu. Lazauskas and Z. Yankova (Vilnius, 1970), pp. 78–86.

Baranskaya, N., 'Nedelya kak nedelya', *Novyi mir*, 1969, no. 11, pp. 23–55. (An English translation, called 'A week like any other', was published in *Spare Rib*, 1977, nos 53–60.)

Barker, G., 'Men and Women, Marriage and the Family in the USSR', unpublished notes for students (Birmingham: University of Birmingham, Centre for Russian and East European Studies, [n.d.]).

Beechey, V., 'Some notes on female wage labour in capitalist production', *Capital and Class*, no. 3 (1977), pp. 45–66.

Bel'skaya, G., 'Otkuda berutsya plokhie zheny', *Literaturnaya gazeta*, 7 September 1977.

Chuiko, L. V., *Braki i razvody* (Moscow, 1973).

Cohn, H. D., 'Soviet population policy', *Problems of Communism*, vol. 22, no. 4 (1973), pp. 41–55.

Coulson, M., Magas, B. and Wainwright, H., 'Women and the class struggle', *New Left Review*, no. 89 (1975), pp. 59–72.

Drunina, Yu., 'Muzhshchina i zhenshchina', *Literaturnaya gazeta*, 9 March 1977.

Engels, F., 'Origin of the family, private property and the state', in K. Marx and F. Engels, *Selected Works* (Moscow: Progress, 1970), pp. 461–583.

Gardiner, J., 'The role of domestic labour', *New Left Review*, no. 89 (1975), pp. 47–58.

Gordon, L. A. and Klopov, E. V., *Chelovek posle raboty: sotsial'nye problemy byta* (Moscow, 1972).

Grushin, B. A., *Svobodnoe vremya: aktual'nye problemy* (Moscow, 1967).

Kharchev, A. G., and Golod, S. I., *Professional'naya rabota zhenshchin i sem'ya* (Leningrad, 1971).

Kollontai, A. M., *Skoro – ili cherez 48 let* (Omsk, 1922).

Kuchina, V., 'Moya gordost', moya obida', *Literaturnaya gazeta*, 20 November 1974.

Lapidus, G., *Women in Soviet Society* (Berkeley, Cal.: University of California Press, 1978).

Lenin, V. I., *On the Emancipation of Women* (Moscow: Progress, 1972).

Materialy XXIV s"ezda KPSS (Moscow, 1977).

Mitchell, J., *Women's Estate* (Harmondsworth: Penguin, 1971).

Narodnoe khozyaistvo SSSR za 60 let: yubileinyi statisticheskii ezhegodnik (Moscow, 1977).

Orlov, Ya., 'Eshche raz o nekhodovykh tovarakh', *Pravda*, 25 March 1978.

Osnovnye napravleniya razvitiya narodnogo khozyaistva SSSR na 1976–1980 gg. (Moscow, 1976).

'Otkuda berutsya plokhie muzh'ya: obzor pisem', *Literaturnaya gazeta*, 30 November 1977.

Perevedentsev, V., 'The family: yesterday, today and tomorrow' (*Nash sovremennik*, 1975, no. 6), *Current Digest of the Soviet Press*, vol. 27, no. 32 (1975), pp. 1–5.

Petrosyan, G. S., *Vnerabochee vremya trudyashchikhsya v SSSR* (Moscow, 1965).

'Podarok zheny' (cartoon), *Krokodil*, 1978, no. 21.

Sacks, M. P., *Women's Work in Soviet Russia* (New York: Praeger, 1976).

Scott, H., *Women and Socialism* (London: Allison & Busby, 1976).

Seccombe, W., 'The housewife and her labour under capitalism', *New Left Review*, no. 83 (1974), pp. 3–24.

'Sovetskim zhenshchinam', *Pravda*, 7 March 1976.

SSSR v tsifrakh v 1976 g. (Moscow, 1977).

Strelyani, A., 'Ogon' na sebya', *Komsomol'skaya pravda*, 8 February 1976.

Volkov, A., 'Izmenenie velichiny i sostava semei v SSSR', in *Demograficheskaya situatsiya v SSSR* (Moscow, 1976), pp. 17–33.

Women under Attack, Counter Information Services Anti-Report no. 15 (London: CIS, 1976).

'Women's domestic labour', in *On the Political Economy of Women* (Conference of Socialist Economists Pamphlet no. 2) (London: stage 1, 1976), pp. 3–16.

Yankova, Z. A., 'O semeino-bytovykh rolyakh porabotayushchei zhenshchiny', *Sotsial'nye issledovaniya*, vol. 4, 1970, pp. 76–87.

Yankova, Z. A., 'Razvitie lichnosti zhenshchiny v sovetskom obshchestve', *Sotsiologicheskie issledovaniya*, 1975, no. 4, pp. 42–51.

'Zaprosam vopreki', *Pravda*, 15 November 1977.

Zhenshchiny v SSSR: statisticheskii sbornik (Moscow, 1975).

Zhirminskaya, T., 'Kuda devalas' zhenstvennost' moya', *Literaturnaya gazeta*, 11 May 1977.

3

'A Woman's Right to Choose' in the Soviet Union

BARBARA HOLLAND

There is a Soviet joke that runs:

Q: Under socialism is it possible to plan the birth rate?
A: No. In this matter the means of production are always in private hands.

It gets to the heart of what is currently becoming one of the most difficult issues facing the Soviet government. On the one hand, the birth rate, the indicator of the extent to which existing labour power is being reproduced, is a factor of major importance to the planned economy. It is, however, one that is exceedingly hard to regulate precisely because 'the means of production' are women's bodies – as child-bearers, and as domestic workers caring for children.

Throughout history, women have attempted to regulate their fertility to suit themselves, regardless of whether their efforts have been considered legal or illegal, moral or immoral, and regardless of the needs of the state. Obviously the moral code or the population policy prevailing at a given time, whether it be punitive abortion laws, financial incentives to have children, or mass birth-control programmes, have had an influence. But within such limitations, women have always tried to exercise choice and with the recent revival of feminism, demands have been raised in many parts of the world for women to have the *right* to choose freely, to take control of their own bodies.

The International Campaign for Abortion Rights, in its manifesto calling for an international day of action in March 1979, declared that:

Nowhere do women have the absolute right to control their fertility, the absolute right to decide whether or not to have children or the facilities to make their choice a real one . . . The issues of women's right to reproductive control – contraception, abortion and freedom from compulsory sterilisation have become interna-

tional political issues forcing debate and confrontation around the
world . . .
   Women demand:
* the right to control their own bodies
* the right to contraception
* the right to abortion
* the right to refuse forced sterilisation. (International Campaign
  for Abortion Rights, 1979)

This recognises the two aspects of 'the right to choose'; first, the
right to terminate an unwanted pregnancy by easy access to safe, legal
abortions, and secondly the right to have children. In practical terms,
the latter means more than just the absence of forced sterilisation
(though this initial step is crucial for many Third World women). It
means creating the optimum social conditions for child-rearing,
involving financial assistance, child-care facilities, flexible living
arrangements, and, most importantly, the political involvement of
women themselves in making the crucial decisions about resources
and priorities.
   This chapter will look in detail at the first aspect of 'the right to
choose' in the Soviet Union – the functioning of the abortion law. The
current situation cannot be understood, however, without some
discussion of the second aspect – the position of motherhood in Soviet
society.

SOVIET PRO-NATALISM

The Soviet Union claims to have created the necessary conditions in
which women can make a genuine choice about having children. As
Professor Yu. P. Lisitsyn says, on the one hand there are medical and
social measures that provide an incentive to motherhood, and on the
other the final decision about whether to continue a pregnancy rests
with the family; thus 'in this way a policy of conscious motherhood
has been created' (Lisitsyn, 1973, p. 175).
   The substance of this claim rests on the provision of a network of
subsidised crèches and nurseries; on women's right to claim 112 days'
paid maternity leave and up to one year's unpaid leave; and on the
financial assistance given to families with a low income or with many
children. These provisions are not especially generous, however.
Child care is not available to all; with more and more grandmothers
now working, there is a shortage of nursery places, and in addition the
quality of care, especially in the crèches for young babies, is causing
anxiety. The length of paid maternity leave has now been matched or
surpassed in a number of countries (in Sweden it is seven months; in
Hungary, three years). The new family allowance system introduced

in 1974 allows only 12 roubles per month for children under 8 years in families with a per capita income of less than 50 roubles; Bernice Madison (1978, p. 321) notes that many families are sure to remain in financial difficulty. In fact, the strain of combining the care of small children with full-time work is undoubtedly one of the factors causing Soviet women to limit their families to one or at the most two children.

This situation has led some observers to conclude that the Soviet Union is not really sincere in its pro-natalist stance. David Heer has argued that the government is unwilling to lose female workers or to spend more on the increased housing, education and other needs of a larger population – hence its acceptance of abortion and contraception. In fact, 'the Soviet Union is not really committed to a higher rate of fertility' (Heer, 1965, p. 83). A closer look at the situation, however, will show that the government does have sound motives for increasing the birth rate, both economic and ideological, and that the apparent contradictions and hesitations in its policies reflect real dilemmas.

Economically, the USSR is faced with the growing problem of an inadequate labour supply. Industrial productivity is low, and attempts to persuade the workforce to try harder have been singularly unsuccessful. Large-scale immigration is not politically feasible (though there is an increasing number of East European guest-workers), so for the economy to expand in the future more workers must be 'produced'. In addition, the birth rate is significantly lower in the western industrialised areas than in the south, especially Central Asia, and this is likely to cause problems of regional imbalance and internal migration. The difficulty for the government is not whether to spend money on increasing the labour force, but how to achieve the desired effect. A simple increase in financial incentives to have children could worsen the regional problem; the possibility of the republics following their own family policies has been suggested, but carries with it the danger of being called discriminatory (Voronitsyn, 1978). An increase in maternity leave or the reduction of working hours for mothers of young children – both of which were promised at the 25th Party Congress in 1976 – have the disadvantage of reducing the efficiency of female labour and are not welcomed by enterprise managers (Lapidus, 1978, p. 316). There is also disagreement as to whether or not curtailing the nursery building programme would be economically effective.

There is a similar conflict in the ideological sphere between a pro-natalist policy and the problems of implementing it. Pro-natalism has always been part of Soviet policy, on the grounds that a growing population is proof of the superiority of socialism. This belief does have its roots in the early socialist movement, but it has come to be interpreted rather dogmatically in the Soviet Union. Initially it reflected not only a healthy opposition to neo-Malthusian ideas that blamed the 'teeming masses' of workers for their own poverty, but also an unfortunate weakness on the woman question, since it assumed that in favourable social conditions all women would want to choose motherhood. The early Soviet government took a number of pro-natalist measures (for example, maternity leave, nurseries) but at the same time proved responsive enough to the needs of women to legalise abortion – albeit as a regrettable temporary measure – and to initiate research into contraception. In a few years, the realisation began to grow that there might always be a need for abortion, or preferably contraception, to meet an individual woman's wish not to have a child at a particular time. A Soviet woman official, Lebedeva, speaking in favour of contraception said that 'motherhood should be conscious and not depend on blind games of chance', while in 1927 the 1st Ukrainian Conference of Gynaecologists passed a resolution urging more research into contraception as a priority (Higgins, 1977, p. 19).

Such views were by no means universally accepted; in fact the 1920s saw a heated debate on questions of marriage, the family and sexuality. With the coming to power of Stalin the proponents of more traditional and authoritarian views won out. Abortion on social grounds was banned in 1936 and contraception was quietly ignored; a rising birth rate was crudely equated with rising production figures. In part, this was due to the pressure of economic and military needs for more manpower, but a more fundamental cause of the change was the desire to tighten state control of all areas of life, including the personal. These measures were accompanied by a new emphasis on the family as 'the basic unit of society'; as such it provided a source of stability and also a mechanism of social control. Within its setting, motherhood became glorified:

> We alone have all the conditions under which a working woman can fulfil her duties as citizen and as a mother responsible for the birth and early education of her children . . . A woman without children merits our pity, for she does not know the full joy of life . . . We must safeguard our family and raise and rear healthy Soviet heroes! ('Krepkaya . . .,' 1936)

Since Stalin's time, pro-natalist policies have continued but have been modified by various political pressures. In the international sphere, the government has moved away from its firm opposition to any kind of population control in the Third World and now agrees with the Western powers that it may be necessary for economic development and stability (Brackett, 1968).

Within the Soviet Union, abortion and contraception were again permitted in 1956, during the more relaxed years of the Thaw, as a result of popular pressure. Motherhood is still portrayed as the true woman's destiny – after all, 'For a healthy woman not to give birth is unnatural!' and may even result in damage to her health, let alone her happiness (Orlova and Bykova, 1978). But there is a new emphasis on having children as the individual's means of personal fulfilment, rather than as a way of serving the state. Both husbands and wives are urged to put more energy into the art of child-rearing, to spend more time with one another, take family holidays and think more of their homes. A couple should not be content with only one child but have two, three or more.

The approach is reminiscent of the way family 'togetherness' was encouraged in postwar America, as a way of restabilising society. But the difficulty for the Soviet government is that women are needed both as mothers and as workers in production. This is why underlying the current debate about how to increase the birth rate there is, as Gail Lapidus (1978, pp. 324–33) has pointed out in her recent summary of this debate, a conflict of views about the future role of women in Soviet society. Three main tendencies can be distinguished. The 'moderates' believe that the existing dual role is more or less satisfactory, and that only minor adjustments need be made to help women cope (for example, improvements in the service sector and in women's working conditions). The 'conservatives' favour a greater emphasis on women's maternal role (for example, extended maternity leave and more part-time work for women), and with it a return to traditional notions of masculine and feminine aptitudes. The 'radicals' wish to confirm women in their role as production workers, but at the same time ease their domestic burden by encouraging role-sharing between the sexes.

The common framework shared by all these views is their commitment to the family. Likewise, the topics picked up for discussion in the press – what can be done about the divorce rate; how older people can meet suitable marriage partners; why so many young men remain unmarried – all see the problem as one of strengthening family life. The few concrete proposals that have so far been made – the establishment of marriage guidance centres; setting up a dating service; easier access to housing for young couples; opening baby-care shops and teaching men to change nappies – are on the same lines (Valentei, 1977).

They do not offer a solution, however, because they fail to deal with the problems raised by the existence of the family as such. It is the time-consuming and isolated round of housework needed to service the individual household; the continual presence of small children outside working hours; the responsibility for organising the smooth running of the home, that exhaust women's energies. Encouraging men to help with the housework only shifts the burden a little, and at the same time strengthens the family's ideological hold. If moves were made to put domestic life on a more collective basis, so that people remained in control of their home lives but shared the burdens with others whilst using state facilities as their needs required, then it is possible that women would feel able to have more children. Such an approach is unlikely to emerge as it would undermine the family's role as a conservative and stabilising force, one that reinforces the atomisation, the passivity and the growing consumerism of Soviet life.

To sum up, the Soviet government genuinely wishes to encourage motherhood, but is uncertain how to improve on the fairly limited incentives which it at present provides. The changes proposed by the 'moderate' tendency are unlikely to go far enough to make much difference; the policies of the 'conservatives' conflict with economic needs and with the traditional socialist commitment to women's emancipation via work in production; while the more 'radical' suggestions of role-sharing fail to confront the oppressive nature of the family. Motherhood may be glorified with words and medals, but it has yet to receive really substantial practical support.

THE FUNCTIONING OF THE ABORTION LAW

The existing Soviet law on abortion dates from 1955. The decree passed at that time was a simple statement repealing the previous restrictive law, but its preamble contained the important new principle that this was being done 'in order to give women the possibility of deciding by themselves the question of motherhood'. The right of a woman to make this decision 'in the interests of her own health' has since been written into the Public Health Act of 1969 (Hyde, 1974, p. 245), but evidently has not been considered fundamental enough to be included in the new constitution.

Though 'the right to choose' has been formally established, there are some legal restrictions on abortion. It is not normally permissible, except on medical grounds, after twelve weeks of pregnancy, or within six months of a previous abortion or birth, though in special cases (for example, a very young girl) it may be allowed. These limits are fixed on the grounds of the dangers to women's health, as the question of foetal rights, which is so controversial in the West, does not enter into Soviet considerations. The law fixes the start of independent life, or the moment at which abortion becomes murder, at the time the baby's head emerges during childbirth. Abortion is associated with criminality only when it is performed outside a clinic, by non-medical personnel, or for a profit (Juviler, 1978, p. 256).

The large number of abortions performed, however – Western estimates put it as high as 8 million a year (Lapidus, 1978, p. 299) – is considered to be a major problem. The main argument used against abortion is the risk to health, and there is a continual campaign in the popular press to persuade women of the dangers. It is described as 'a serious biological trauma for a woman's organism', and 'a delayed time-bomb' that, by leading to infertility in later life, can explode a woman's marriage and happiness. It is suggested that the possible complications following the operation are numerous (besides the favourite, infertility, there is inflammation, menstrual disorders, frigidity, obesity, and psychological illness) and also fairly common (affecting about 20 per cent of women). Even the rather remote chance of death is dwelt on (Zak, 1973; 'Tsepochka . . .', 1975; 'Chto . . .', 1975; Bodyazhina, 1977).

Soviet evidence regarding the actual rate of complications is patchy, but the overall impression is that it is around 12 per cent, and slightly higher for a first pregnancy. There is definitely some concern about complications in childbirth becoming more frequent because of women's previous abortions (Sadvokasova, 1969, pp. 121–3; Sokolova, 1975). Although it appears that the risks are being exaggerated to women, at the same time there is little to show that efforts are being made to eliminate them.

In the West, the spread of the vacuum-suction method which can be used on an out-patient basis has significantly reduced complications to well below 12 per cent. Though this method is known in the Soviet Union it appears that the routine procedure is still dilation and curettage (D and C), which requires hospitalisation for two or three days. A general anaesthetic should normally be given, but there are persistent rumours about this being withheld from women having repeated abortions as a 'punishment', and a Soviet sociologist has even commented on women's fear of painful or experimental methods being used on them in hospital abortions (Avdeeva, 1965, p. 75). This suggestion that the methods used may be rather rough and ready is borne out by the recently published account of the experience one British doctor witnessed in Kiev, when a fellow member of his tourist group had a spontaneous miscarriage and he accompanied her to hospital. The analgesia given for her operation (a D and C) was poorly administered, and throughout the proceedings 'the doctor chattered to her assistant and occasionally told the patient to be quiet. The woman nearly fainted with pain' (Levin, 1978).

In addition, it appears that abortions are not properly planned for. Soviet writers have complained of the shortage of doctors and beds; one recent article talked of abortion patients being either made to wait or sent home too soon after the operation because of the competition for gynaecological beds (Balashova and Muchiev, 1974). Problems like these can be found in all areas of medicine, but the difference with abortion is that a modern, out-patient service would be both cheaper and easier to organise. The failure to do so must raise some doubts as to whether enough is being done to make abortion a really safe option for women.

The situation regarding the provision of contraception is also far from ideal, though slowly improving. All the major methods in use in the West (with the exception of sterilisation) are now practised in the Soviet Union. The intra-uterine device (IUD) was officially approved in 1968, and although no similar statement has been issued regarding the pill it is being used by some urban women, particularly those with privileged access. (Evidence of its use can be found in research reports in medical journals and in statements in the popular press, for example Kiryushchenkov, 1977). There have, however, been problems with both the quality and supply of contraceptives (for example, awkward IUDs, shortages of the pill, unreliable condoms) and a significant absence of any propaganda campaign to promote their use. Many people still regard contraceptives as ineffective, unpleasant, pleasure-reducing or even harmful (Polchanova, 1972), and surveys show that only half the couples who do not wish to conceive bother to use them (Krasnenkov, 1973).

People's lack of enthusiasm for contraception and subsequent reliance on abortion is partly a result of circumstances (the much easier access to abortion until very recently), and partly due to the influence of peasant culture. (Himes [1970] a researcher into the history of contraception, has noted that abortion is preferred in less developed societies because it is dealing with a known fact rather than a hypothetical possibility.) The same lack of enthusiasm on the part of the government can be partly, but not wholly, explained by its pro-natalism. Since women do turn to abortion, the effective provision of contraception on a mass scale would probably improve the health statistics whilst leaving the birth rate much the same. Another, probably more important, motive is the government's reluctance to promote the separation of sex from reproduction. This is also reflected in official attitudes to sexuality, which punish homosexuality, discourage masturbation, and promote rigid stereotypes of appropriate male and female behaviour. Soviet backwardness on sex education is well known, and one critical Soviet observer has even called it 'a conspiracy of silence' which forces young people to learn about sex 'on the streets' (Madison, 1978, p. 313). The reason behind this attitude is the fear on the part of conservative officials that a self-determined sexuality, free from concern with reproduction, would threaten the stability of the family. Their suspicion of contraception may well be mistaken – and, in fact, Western experience shows that it gives only a potential freedom as much still depends on social attitudes – but it has deep roots in Soviet tradition. When these repressive attitudes come up against the reality of women's desire to control their own fertility, a tension is produced which leads to a number of difficulties being placed in the way of a woman seeking to exercise her right to abortion.

First, there is the campaign (described above) about the dangers to her health, and the lack of an efficient abortion service that would overcome any doubts. This will be backed up by pressure from the doctors to have the baby, especially if it is her first pregnancy. Although the woman does not have to go through the humiliating experience of arguing her case before a special commission, as in some other East European countries (for example, Hungary, Czechoslovakia), she may be asked to see the socio-legal bureau. These bodies try to deal with problems such as a father unwilling to acknowledge paternity or a lack of suitable child-care, but apparently they have had little success in preventing abortions (Madison, 1978, p. 317). At no time is the woman offered the kind of counselling that exists in the West and which, at its best, aims at helping the woman to appreciate her own wishes and feelings before coming to a decision.

Another common difficulty is refusal to provide the abortion because of the time limits: either the pregnancy has lasted more than twelve weeks, or less than six months has elapsed since a previous abortion or birth. As one East German doctor has noted, delay in the first case is not always the woman's fault but may result from the 'red-tape formalities' that exist in certain countries (Mehland, 1966, p. 86).

There is also the question of privacy. Women are entitled to ten days' unpaid sick leave, but it appears that many do not take it because they do not want their colleagues at work to find out. The magazine *Rabotnitsa* (Working Woman) recently published a number of letters from women complaining that the sick note issued has 'abortion' clearly written on it; some had even left their jobs rather than hand it to their trade union official (Sidorova, 1977; 'Vozvrashchayas' . . .', 1977). The ministry replied by promising to substitute a code of figures, but it is hard to see how this will not also become easily identifiable ('Spravka . . .', 1977). A point in the Soviet Union's favour is that money is not a barrier to abortion. The nominal charge is only 5 roubles, and even this is waived for women whose income is below 60 roubles a month, or whose abortion is for medical reasons (Juviler, 1978, p. 256).

The difficulties mentioned are also the reasons women most commonly give for having illegal abortions. These still take place on quite a wide scale, though obviously the true rate is unknown. Various Soviet estimates have conservatively put it at around 15 per cent of all abortions (Sadvokasova, 1969, p. 118; Avdeeva, 1965, p. 74).

Rather than trying to find solutions to these problems, the Soviet response is 'to improve health education', which in practice means publishing scare stories in the popular press. One article in *Zdorov'e* (Health) included an account of how the doctors at a women's clinic heard a knock at the door, and on answering it found an unconscious woman bleeding heavily from a perforation of the womb. The failed abortionist had brought her in a taxi and run away. She died (Zak, 1973). The prosecutions of people found guilty of performing criminal abortions are also occasionally reported, such as the case of a woman in Baku who was imprisoned for six years after the death of a woman she had aborted in the local bath-house (Shamorakov, 1978).

Although botched abortions undoubtedly do occur, especially in rural areas, the reality for most women is somewhat different. Many illegal abortions in the big cities are performed by qualified doctors using the most modern equipment, i.e. vacuum suction. A private arrangement involving extra payment may be made with a hospital, or the abortion may be performed in a private flat with little discomfort. According to one Western observer, the going rate in the late 1960s was 40 roubles, which is well within most women's means (Kaser, 1976, p. 66).

The existence of illegal abortion in the Soviet Union is an important political factor. It is admitted that its prevalence in the 1940s was the main reason for the introduction of the 1955 law, and that its continued presence is the main reason this law has not since been restricted. When a Soviet doctor was asked why, if abortion is such a risky operation it is not banned, the answer given was simple: 'It is the lesser of two evils' (Zak, 1973). The ability of Soviet women to exert this indirect pressure is the result of their unique historical experience – the period of free abortion from 1920–36 accustomed them to controlling their own fertility, and they continued to do so throughout the twenty years of restriction by organising illegal abortion on a large scale. Now it is clear that, whatever the official policy, women will try to choose for themselves. Several other East European countries have tried to overcome their population problems by introducing restrictions on abortion (Romania in 1968; Hungary and Czechoslovakia in 1973; Bulgaria in 1974), though these measures have not been popular ('Birth . . .', 1978). In Hungary a petition was even launched in protest ('Abortion . . .', 1978) and the government had to justify its move by making contraception universally available. In Romania the number of illegal abortions has soared. As the Soviet government is unlikely to risk unpopularity for a doubtful outcome, women's right to abortion there is more secure.

WHAT DO WOMEN WANT?

One Soviet doctor has complained in *Zdorov'e* that the reasons women often give for wanting abortions – we're too young; we're waiting for a separate flat; I want to defend my dissertation first – are trivial, and asks what use is a flat or a job without motherhood? (Zak, 1973). From the actual behaviour of Soviet women, it seems that they want to have both. The majority of women have at least one child, which shows a desire to experience motherhood, but very few have more than two, which shows a reluctance to devote their whole lives to it. Whether women's reluctance to have children stems from their desire for personal development, in the form of studies, a career, or simply a job outside the home, or whether from the pressures of material circumstances, has recently been the subject of some debate.

A number of surveys have been carried out in the attempt to find an answer, some asking women their motives for having an abortion, and some investigating the reasons why women fail to have the number of children they say they would like 'ideally'. Unfortunately the conclusions drawn are not very reliable, and often are influenced by the viewpoint favoured by the researcher in the debate around the birth rate.

One of the earliest and most influential surveys was carried out by E. A. Sadvokasova in 1958–9 and involved 26,000 women, representative of all regions of the Russian Federation; the details were published as part of a book in 1969. The women, who were having legal abortions, were asked to choose between ten possible motives; the results as presented by Sadvokasova are shown in Table 3.1.

In interpreting these findings, Sadvokasova divided the motives into objective, subjective and unclear categories, and where a woman had indicated both an objective and a subjective motive the latter was discounted. The most popular choice, 'mother doesn't want to continue the pregnancy', was considered subjective and its significance minimised. This enabled Sadvokasova to argue that the majority of abortions were for material or 'surmountable' reasons, which future progress towards communism – in the shape of reforms such as extended maternity leave – would eliminate (Sadvokasova, 1969, pp. 152, 163, 181). The motive 'mother doesn't want to continue the pregnancy' could, however, be interpreted quite differently – as a positive rejection of rationalisations for the abortion, a desire for self-determination. The fact that as social conditions have improved the abortion rate has risen rather than fallen must throw some doubt on Sadvokasova's interpretation. It remains, however, an influential model for other Soviet researchers. Her argument is repeated by Yu. P. Lisitsyn (1973, pp. 173–4) in his summary of more recent surveys on the reasons for abortion. He asserts that the main motives are poor living conditions, financial difficulties, child-care problems (i.e. both parents busy with work or studies) and poor marital relations – all reasons which progress will overcome. At the same time, he notes a

Table 3.1

Motives	% of women choosing	(a)	(b)
(1) No one to look after child and no possibility of nursery place	11·0	obj.	def.sur.
(2) Insufficient living space	9·1	unc.	def.sur.
(3) Financial difficulties	10·5	unc.	def.sur.
(4) A baby, or many children, in family already	9·6	obj.	unsur.
(5) Absence of a husband	6·5	obj.	sur.
(6) Illness of one parent	5·3	obj.	sur.
(7) Family troubles	5·2	unc.	sur.
(8) Mother doesn't want to continue pregnancy	35·6	sub.	unc.
(9) Father doesn't want the baby	3·0	sub.	unc.
(10) Multiple or other reasons	3·8	unc.	unc.

Notes:
(a)　obj. – objective reason
　　　unc. – unclear reason
　　　sub. – subjective reason
(b)　def.sur. – definitely a surmountable difficulty
　　　unsur. – an unsurmountable difficulty
　　　sur. – a surmountable difficulty
　　　unc. – unclear

Source: Compiled from Sadvokasova, 1969, pp. 137–66.

difficulty – also referred to by Lapidus (1978, p. 303) – namely, that the women choosing these material motives are not those in the most difficult circumstances.

Other researchers, using a similar questionnaire, have found that the proportion of women choosing a motive on the lines of 'unwilling to have the baby' rather than a material motive has reached 50 per cent (Polyakov and Kovaleva, 1976). This proportion tended to be higher among well-educated urban women, which led one writer (Polchanova, 1972) to conclude that the basic reasons for abortion are now psychological, and indicate that a more responsible attitude towards motherhood is developing. The author of a survey (Krasnenkov, 1973) among rural women also noted that although many chose material reasons, most who did so also considered themselves materially well off, and concluded that the predominant feeling among the women was that they already had enough children. (On rural women, see also Markov, 1973.) The unstated logic behind these arguments is that material incentives to have children will not have a great effect.

The many surveys on women's failure to have their ideal number of children tend to stress the material rather than the personal factors (Lapidus, 1978, p. 303). When the question has been put differently, however, and women have been asked if they would prefer to stay at home with the children if their husbands earned the same as their present combined income, the vast majority have said no. In one survey only 5 per cent of women wanted to be full-time housewives (Orlova and Bykova, 1978).

One point that does emerge with clarity is that it is the woman rather than her husband who decides, especially about abortion. In one survey a third of the women thought their husband's opinion irrelevant, while in another nearly a quarter had their abortion without his knowledge (Polyakov and Kovaleva, 1976; Polchanova, 1972). Less clear from the contradictory findings of these surveys is the extent to which women feel constrained by their circumstances when making their choice about whether or not to have a child, or the extent to which they feel satisfied with the options open to them. It is probable that with rising living standards women have gained a greater freedom from material pressures, and this can only be welcomed. At the same time, women's expectations about the priorities within their lives have been changing, so that their degree of satisfaction is much harder to assess.

What Soviet women really want is a question only they can answer. In a situation where, in common with other social groups, they are unable to meet together freely to exchange experiences and develop views, the answer is likely to remain hidden for some time.

CONCLUSIONS

The emergence of abortion as an international political issue is not a process which will by-pass the Soviet Union. On the contrary, the government's need to increase the birth rate for economic reasons, together with its concern about the stability of the family, have already made women's control of their fertility an important question. The debate around it is sure to continue as the final decisions have yet to be taken.

Meanwhile present-day feminists must look critically at the Soviet Union's claim, almost unique in the world, that it has established a woman's right to choose. Such an examination shows that it does exist, but only in its narrowest sense, that is, a pregnant woman may insist on a legal abortion. Women are unable to control the conditions under which health service abortions are performed, as is shown by the continued practice of illegal abortion. At the same time, the fact that many prefer to have abortions on their own terms, by going outside the law, gives women an indirect political power, and this is the main reason why the present abortion law has not been restricted.

In its broader sense, the right to choose to have a child is also limited by the difficult conditions in which women have to raise their children. It could be argued that social resources are not infinite and limitations on choice are inevitable in any society; but then Soviet women are not involved in the serious decision-making that shapes the framework within which they must choose.

As a result, Soviet women are resigned to the conflicts and strains of their present role, and, when they do have time to think, tend to dismiss their problems as eternal and inevitable – you cannot change women's biology. No, but as women elsewhere in the world are coming to realise, biology need not be a source of oppression. By organising together to gain control of their own bodies, which means in the long term gaining a full and equal say in the running of society, women are finding that their ability to reproduce can be a source of strength and solidarity.

BIBLIOGRAPHY

'Abortion petition in Hungary', *Labour Focus on Eastern Europe: Special Issue [on] Women* (1978), pp. 4–5.

Avdeeva, I. M., 'Izuchenie prichin i uslovii, sposobstvuyushchikh sover-sheniyu prestupnykh abortov, i mery po ikh ustraneniyu', *Voprosy predup-rezhdeniya prestupnosti*, vol. 2, 1965, pp. 73–8.

Balashova, V. G. and Muchiev, G. S., 'K voprosu o ratsional'nom ispol'zovanii fonda akusherskikh i ginekologicheskikh koek', *Sovetskoe zdravookhranenie*, 1974, no. 5, pp. 48–52.

'Birth rate politics', *Labour Focus on Eastern Europe: Special Issue [on] Women* (1978), pp. 15–17.

Bodyazhina, V. I., 'Sokhranite beremennost'!', *Zdorov'e*, 1977, no. 12, pp. 13–14.

Brackett, J., 'The evolution of Marxist theories of population', *Demography*, vol. 5, no. 1 (1968), pp. 158–73.

'Chto zavisit ot vas?, *Zdorov'e*, 1975, no. 11, p. 25.

Heer, D., 'Abortion, contraception and population policy in the Soviet Union', *Soviet Studies*, vol. 17, no. 1 (1965), pp. 76–83.

Higgins, J., 'Some Characteristics of the Fight with Abortion in the USSR, 1917–1936', unpublished research report (Birmingham: University of Birmingham, Centre for Russian and East European Studies [1977]).

Himes, N., *A Medical History of Contraception* (New York: Schocken Books, 1970).

Hyde, G., *The Soviet Health Service* (London: Lawrence & Wishart, 1974).

International Campaign for Abortion Rights, *Manifesto for Day of Action* (London: ICAR, 1979).

Juviler, P., 'Women and sex in Soviet law', in *Women in Russia*, ed. D. Atkinson, A. Dallin and G. W. Lapidus (Hassocks, Sussex: Harvester Press, 1978), pp. 243–65.

Kaser, M., *Health Care in the Soviet Union and Eastern Europe* (London: Croom Helm, 1976).

Kiryushchenkov, A. P., 'Gormonal'nye kontratseptivy', *Zdorov'e*, 1977, no. 1, pp. 18–19.

Krasnenkov, V. L., 'Nekotorye sotsial'no-gigienicheskie aspekty aborta sredi zhenshchin Kalininskoi oblasti', *Sovetskoe zdravookhranenie*, 1973, no. 5, pp. 20–4.

'Krepkaya sovetskaya sem'ya', *Pravda*, 28 May 1936.

Lapidus, G. W., *Women in Soviet Society* (Berkeley, Cal.: University of California Press, 1978).

Levin, B., 'If you've ever thought of falling ill in Russia, read on . . .', *The Times*, 21 July 1978.

Lisitsyn, Yu. P., *Sotsial'naya gigiena i organizatsiya zdravookhraneniya* (Moscow, 1973).

Madison, B., 'Social services for women: problems and priorities', in *Women in Russia*, ed. D. Atkinson, A. Dallin and G. W. Lapidus (Hassocks, Sussex: Harvester Press, 1978), pp. 307–22.

Markov, A. I. 'Sotsial 'no-gigienicheskie aspekty aborta zhenshchin v Tambovskom raione Amurskoi oblasti', *Sovetskoe zdravookhranenie*, 1973, no. 7, pp. 43–6.

Mehland, K. H., 'Combatting illegal abortion in the socialist countries of Europe', *World Medical Journal*, vol. 13 (1966), pp. 84–7.

Orlova, D. and Bykova, I., 'Odin, dvoe, troe?' *Zdorov'e*, 1978, no. 9, pp. 2–4.

Polchanova, S. L., 'Nekotorye sotsialno-psikhologicheskie aspekty rozhdaemosti', *Sovetskoe zdravookhranenie*, 1972, no. 5, pp. 15–19.

Polyakov, I. V. and Kovaleva, A. P., 'K sotsial'no-gigienicheskoi kharakteristike abortov v Leningrade', *Sovetskoe zdravookhranenie*, 1976, no. 12, pp. 43–6.

Sadvokasova, E. A., *Sotsial'no-gigienicheskie aspekty regulirovaniya razmerov sem'i* (Moscow, 1969).

Shamorakov, I., 'Harsh lesson' (*Bakinskii rabochi*, 15 April 1978), *Current Digest of the Soviet Press*, vol. 30, no. 15 (1978), p. 24.

Sidorova, K., 'Spravka na tainu', *Rabotnitsa*, 1977, no. 1, p. 26.

Sokolova, N. S., 'Izuchenie plodovitosti zhenshchin, ikh akusherskogo i somaticheskogo anamneza', *Sovetskoe zdravookhranenie*, 1975, no. 9, pp. 39–44.

'Spravka na tainu', *Rabotnitsa*, 1977, no. 9, p. 32.

'Tsepochka prichin i sledstvii', *Zdorov'e*, 1975, no. 4, pp. 25–6.

Valentei, D., 'Sluzhba sem'i: pervye shagi', *Nedelya*, 1977, no. 52, p. 7.

Voronitsyn, S., 'Controversy about demographic policy', (RL 205/78), *Radio Liberty Research Bulletin*, no. 39 (2983), 29 September 1978.

'Vozvrashchayas' k napechatannomu: spravka na tainu', *Zdorov'e*, 1977, no. 4, p. 27.

Zak, I. P., 'Abort – eto kak bomba zamedlennogo deistviya', *Zdorov'e*, 1973, no. 5, pp. 14–15.

Part Two

Education and Child Care

4

Secondary Education for All in a Forward-Looking Society

ELISABETH KOUTAISSOFF

INTRODUCTION

The Soviet Union is a land of contrasts, not merely in geographical terms. It aspires to be in the forefront of scientific progress and on the verge of achieving a rationally managed society organised in accordance with the laws of social development. Yet almost half of its child population is still taught in rural schools which are often small and ill-equipped, with poorly qualified teachers. Thus Soviet planners are confronted simultaneously with very novel problems of the planning of science and its social impact, while at the same time they have to provide tolerable conditions for village teachers, many of whom still have to cultivate a private plot or keep a cow to meet the needs of their family (Filippov, 1976, p. 84).

According to Marxist theory, the economic basis determines the superstructure of human institutions and psychological attitudes. Yet, the material and technical basis which should automatically give rise to new production and social relations – hence to a new society and, eventually, a New Communist Man – is taking a long time to build. Therefore the Soviet leadership has had for decades to rely heavily on propaganda and exhortation to overcome manifestations of undesirable behaviour, and to educate children and adults to understand the laws that govern both natural and social phenomena. It has had to make them internalise new attitudes to promote further scientific and technical progress, and a willingness to participate in productive work for the community, thus advancing the material and cultural potential of a homogeneous, forward-looking, scientifically managed communist society.

At present Soviet society is not homogeneous but rent by substantial differentials in earnings and status as well as the nationalism of its ethnic minorities. That there is widespread corruption and bribery, abuse of power by those in office, parasitism, breaches of labour discipline, drunkenness and other forms of anti-social behaviour has been admitted by no less an authority than L. I. Brezhnev, General Secretary of the CPSU (Brezhnev, 1976*b*, p. 537; 1977*b*; 1978).

So, while the laborious building of the material–technical basis is slowly progressing, the difficulties of educating the New Man within a still unsatisfactory environment have been many and varied. At the moment three very practical problems seem to be in evidence: (1) how to implement a genuinely secondary education in remote rural areas; (2) how to determine a satisfactory balance between general knowledge and vocational training at both secondary and tertiary level; (3) last, but not least, how to discover, nurture and harness human creativity without which further progress is unthinkable.

SECONDARY EDUCATION IN RURAL AREAS

The right of Soviet citizens to secondary education put forward at the 23rd Congress of the CPSU in 1966 and scheduled by the 24th Congress in 1971 to be implemented by 1975 has now been written into the New Constitution. In 1977, about 5 million teenagers, or 95 per cent of the relevant age-group, were completing their secondary education while another 1,700,000 people already in employment were studying at evening classes (Korotov, 1978, pp. 3–4).

Yet the implementation of a truly secondary education in rural areas has met with serious difficulties, due to geographical and historical factors such as a harsh climate, great distances, patterns of settlement and lack of roads and transport, as well as to demographic trends. Collectivisation, war losses and migration to towns have drained villages in many Union republics of their most active and fertile age-groups resulting (except in Moldavia and the republics of Central Asia with their high birth rates) in a dramatic fall in child population. The majority of primary schools which cater for children aged 7 to 9 are attended by fewer than twenty-five pupils, sometimes by only five. These small schools provide a family atmosphere, which is all to the good, but little intellectual stimulus. To attend an 8-year or a 10-year (secondary) school, children from smaller villages have to travel to larger ones, i.e. to a collective or state farm central settlement, or else they must go and live in a boarding school (*internat*). This usually has to be paid for by parents, who also lose the help which a teenager often contributes by cultivating the family plot or minding younger siblings while the adults are at work in the fields.

Even in the larger rural schools, the number of pupils is falling off. Thus in the RSFSR, the average school contingent in 1965–6 comprised 520 pupils; it fell to 471 by 1970 and is likely to drop to 275 per school by 1980 (Filippov, 1976, p. 71). To make up their statutory teaching load of eighteen hours per week, teachers have to take on subjects which they are not qualified to teach. Their pupils are consequently at a disadvantage when competing in entrance exams for establishments of higher education (*VUZ*). Even if country freshers are accepted on the strength of their final school marks, which are now taken into consideration as part of *VUZ* entrance qualifications (poor schools tend to rate their pupils' performance higher than the better urban ones), they may find *VUZ* courses too advanced and drop out even before completing the first year.

Recent regulations give preferential treatment to rural youths who apply for educational and agricultural *VUZy* because it is hoped that this will make them stay within their region and accept more willingly jobs in their home villages. Needless to say, these provincial institutions are not among the best in the USSR. Thus a vicious circle sets in: poorly prepared students attend second-rate *VUZy* and return as poorly qualified teachers to instruct inadequately the on-coming generation.

Apart from these unsatisfactory young graduates, there is still a back-log of ageing teachers who had been trained at *pedagogicheskie uchilishcha* (training colleges) in the days when these institutions provided two-year courses for pupils coming from a 7-year, later an 8-year school. These colleges still exist, though their courses have now been extended to four years and they rank as secondary specialised schools. Most are concerned with the training of nursery school assistants or with that of teachers of art, music or physical training.

For some years, particularly since 1968, numerous institutes as well as shorter courses for 'the improvement of teachers' (*usovershen-stvovaniya uchitelei*) have been set up and efforts are made to allow teachers to attend refresher courses every five years. Often the gap between their actual knowledge and the growing demands of a modernising society is difficult to bridge. Thus, of the teachers who attended courses for raising their standards at the University of Novosibirsk in 1970 only 20 per cent were able to solve problems in mathematics and physics normally set in *VUZ* entrance examinations, while many others were ignorant of the fundamental principles of the science that they taught and lacked an understanding of the basic ideas underlying the new school curriculum (Turchenko, 1973, p. 94).

Concern for the rural school has grown together with the more comprehensive attempts to improve agricultural performance and counter rural depopulation. In July 1973, a decree was promulgated to improve educational facilities in the countryside ('O merakh . . .', 1973). It envisaged the construction of new schools to accommodate an additional 7.25 million pupils and to house 772,000 children in boarding accommodation, as well as to provide housing for teachers estimated at 6,420,000 square metres. Collective farms were to contribute their share with the help of credits from the State Bank. Various ministries responsible for construction, transport and water works were enjoined to supply the necessary materials and blueprints. Moreover, the Union Republics' Ministries of Transport were to sell to state and collective farms 3,000 school buses in 1974, increasing this number between 1976 and 1980 to 5,000 per annum. The Union Republics' Ministries of Education were to furnish adequate equipment for school laboratories and workshops, books for their libraries and some machines to train tractor drivers and mechanics. As from 1975, 25 per cent of all boarders were to receive free meals three times a day while others would get theirs at half the cost price.

The decree also envisaged the building of student hostels for those studying at pedagogical institutes and the location of appropriate vocational schools in the countryside. The Komsomol was called upon to organise from among its members teams of builders to take part in the construction of new rural schools and the enlargement of old ones.

Indeed, during the 1971–5 period, three-quarters of all new school-building work was carried out in rural areas and under the current Five-Year Plan (1976–80) about half of all additional school places envisaged will be in the countryside ('O dal'neishem . . .', 1977).

Various measures taken to improve the infrastructure in rural areas in general (for example, the projected construction of 25,000 kilometres of hard surface roads) will benefit schools and keep the growing fleet of school buses in working order. Inevitably, in a vast country, these measures are likely to be implemented sooner and more effectively in the European parts of the USSR than, for instance, in the Magadan province where bare literacy, whether in Chukchi or in Russian, was achieved officially only in 1967 (Verin, 1969, p. 90).

Undoubtedly a great effort is afoot to make secondary education truly and not only nominally so throughout the Soviet Union. However, what should constitute secondary education in the latter quarter of the twentieth century is still a matter of debate in the USSR, as elsewhere (UNESCO International Conference, 1973).

WHAT KIND OF EDUCATION AND WHAT FOR?

Vocational Training

Ever since the introduction of polytechnical education in the early post-revolutionary years, the emphasis on general knowledge and practical know-how respectively have fluctuated from the 'withering away of the school' and its becoming 'one of the workshops of the factory' in the 1920s, to the rigidly academic curriculum of the later

1930s and 1940s, when the teaching of simple manual crafts was relegated to the narrowly vocational, low-level labour reserve schools (*shkoly trudovykh rezervov*). Then, with Khrushchev's reform of 1958, there was a swing of the pendulum towards a school that would prepare for life and work. Teenagers were encouraged to enter employment upon completing eight years of schooling and to obtain any further education at evening classes. In secondary schools, productive work became a major subject taking up one-third of all school hours. From 1966, a more academic, though up-dated and fairly flexible curriculum allowing for optional subjects was gradually introduced. The time spent on practical work was reduced to two hours per week, plus a month of productive labour during the last summer school vacation between forms 9 and 10, performed in local factories, on collective farms, in summer 'rest-and-work' camps, lumbering in forests or joining agricultural pupils' brigades.

Recently, optional subjects have verged on vocational training, and teaching-production centres (*uchebno-proizvodstvennye kombinaty*) have increased in numbers. These centres came into existence in the early 1960s, in the days of Khrushchev, to help schools to organise productive work as prescribed by the 1958 Education Act. In 1974, they received further impetus ('Ob organizatsii . . .', 1975; Kornitskii, 1978). Usually they are equipped by local industries and attended by pupils of several schools in turn. For instance, in Leningrad one such centre is sponsored by eight enterprises, including a major electrical equipment plant, the North-Western River Shipping Enterprise, a public transport central garage, a supermarket and a clothing store. Here pupils can learn to be turners, fitters, drivers, electricians, salesmen, cashiers, typists or seamstresses (Geizhan and Vasil'eva, 1976, p. 57). In rural areas, particularly in the region of Stavropol' (North Caucasus), there are agricultural pupils' brigades in charge of considerable areas of arable land, machinery and livestock (Zharkov, 1972; 'Primernoe polozhenie . . .', 1973; Brezhnev, 1976*a*; Brezhnev, 1977*a*). Some major industrial and mining enterprises, such as the Noril'sk mining complex situated beyond the Arctic circle, run their own teaching-production centre to train drivers, car mechanics, bulldozer operators, draughtsmen and assistants for chemical laboratories ('Ko vseobshchemu . . .', 1974).

Even more comprehensive is the educational network sponsored by the oil refineries and petrochemical works of the Groznyi region. They act as patrons (*shefy*) to ten secondary schools, three vocational schools (*professional'no-tekhnicheskie uchilishcha*), a chemical-technological college and two evening-class centres, as well as having technical teaching departments (*kabinety*) at each of their enterprises. Every workshop undertakes to sponsor one school form to which it delegates a tutor (*nastavnik*) who provides the teachers of physics, mathematics or chemistry with real-life problems and helps the teacher of labour and his class to carry out small industrial orders in the school workshops that are usually equipped by the enterprise. Pupils from senior forms are allowed to work for short periods in the enterprise's laboratories or workshops during their last vacation's practical work period; parents, as well as pupils and teachers, are invited on conducted tours through the works; young workers are seconded to the school to act as Pioneer leaders. Often meetings of school and factory Komsomol are held jointly. The help given to the sponsored *vocational* schools is even greater. Instructors from the works are seconded to conduct in-service training for teachers of labour and two- to three-months' courses in production processes are organised at the works for pupils of senior forms to prepare them for employment (Senchenko, 1976).

Establishing links between schools and industries has always been the policy of the Soviet authorities, even during the periods when the teaching of academic subjects has had the upper hand. More recently the December 1977 decree ('O dal'neishem . . .', 1977) on education has revived the view that the school should prepare teenagers for a working life. So the time allocated to practical work has been increased to four weekly hours, and forming links with an industrial or agricultural enterprise has become mandatory on every school. Optional courses are to be used deliberately as an initiation to productive work of the type needed by the regional industries, and the scientific principles underlying industrial processes are to be made clear to pupils. For instance, in the case of the school plot allocated by a collective farm to a rural school, the teacher should stress the scientific aspect of agricultural work; the plot should not be used merely to grow vegetables for pupils' consumption or sale, but for experimentation such as cross-breeding and selecting plants, learning the right use of fertilisers or for building hot-houses or frames to grow plants under glass. Emphasis on the scientific aspect of agriculture is particularly important in view of the very low esteem that it commands among school-leavers whose great desire is to migrate to the towns and who have a general contempt for manual work.

The undeniable social stratification of Soviet society has fostered among the young the desire to join the intelligentsia rather than seek employment in manufacturing industries, while reluctance to go into service industries or into farmwork is even greater. This was confirmed by numerous sociological studies on the career aspirations of the young conducted in the 1960s throughout the USSR. They showed some variations between boys and girls, the former choosing science-oriented occupations such as physicist, pilot, radio engineer, while girls were more inclined to take up medicine or teaching, but there were few who wished to become cleaners, cooks, salesmen or office clerks and even fewer who wanted to be stableboys or dairymaids (Koutaissoff, 1976, pp. 16–17, 36).

This is a truly disquieting trend since of the 7 million new recruits who are to join the labour force during the current Five-Year Plan (1976–80) – partly to replace older, retiring workers and partly to meet the requirements of an expanding economy – 5 million are needed for manual-type occupations.

Apart from its detrimental effect on the economy, contempt for work is contrary to communist ideology since, according to Engels (1940, ch. 9) it was work that transformed the ape into man and distinguishes him from other animals. Work for the community is the cornerstone of communist morality. Besides, in a society freed from exploitation, work should become an essential human need. This does not seem to be the case with Soviet citizens among whom absenteeism and job dissatisfaction are common and labour turnover high, especially in the case of young and consequently more mobile workers. This is damaging to the economy and demoralising for the individuals. Increasingly, measures are being taken to instil respect for manual work. The mass media glamorise it, for example by showing on television feats of young workers on major construction sites such as the Baikal-Amur railway line (the 3,000 miles of track crossing the swamps and mountains of Eastern Siberia), or else they relate biographies of dynasties of workers proud to toil at the same plant from father to son, or the ceremonial handing over of his first pay packet to a young worker.

Another approach to enhance the standing of semi-skilled manual occupations is the gradual up-grading since 1969 of vocational schools (*professional'no-tekhnicheskie uchilishcha*) to the status of secondary schools. These vocational schools originated as very low-standard labour reserve schools (*shkoly trudovykh rezervov*) in 1940. At that time they enrolled boys and girls aged 14 who had completed the obligatory minimum four-year schooling in rural areas or seven years in towns and workers' settlements. Initially enrolment was by compulsory draft as a percentage of the local population. The length of course varied from six months to two years, after which pupils were directed to work for four years in the jobs and locations assigned to them. Later, with the introduction of the universal eight-year school in 1958–9 and the lengthening of the course to two years and occasionally even to three, their standing improved and enrolment was on a voluntary basis. They also changed their name from labour reserve schools to vocational schools. Training remained narrowly specialised, preparing for 1,100 to 1,200 different occupations with two-thirds of school hours spent on practical work taught by a *master*, a workman skilled in the relevant work process. Now that the length of course in vocational schools converted to the status of 'secondary vocational schools' has been extended to four years, general academic subjects are given more time, lessons in social science and the economics of labour and production have been introduced. More significantly still, secondary vocational schools will no longer be geared to one of their former 1,100 to 1,200 specialities but will provide broad polytechnical courses grouped into five types: (1) chemistry and metallurgy; (2) radio and electrotechnology; (3) metal working; (4) mechanics and assembly; and (5) biology and agriculture (Foteeva, 1973, p. 139). On completing their stay at a secondary vocational school, pupils will be entitled to sit for *VUZ* examinations alongside other entrants; moreover, they will be entitled to certain priorities when applying to technical *VUZy* within their speciality. By 1976 the number of secondary vocational schools had risen to 3,071 out of a total of 5,777 ('O dal'neishem . . .', 1972; 'O merakh . . .', 1975; *Narodnoe khozyaistvo . . .*, 1977, p. 478).

The conversion of vocational schools into institutions of secondary education has been delayed by shortages of building and equipment and of appropriately trained teachers of labour. Formerly these were workers skilled in the performance of certain operations but with little understanding of the scientific laws on which these processes are based. Now they are being replaced by graduates of the new (and still few) engineering-pedagogical faculties and of some secondary specialised schools where pupils are instructed in teaching methods alongside appropriate technical subjects (Bondarenko, 1974; 'Ob uvelichenii . . .', 1977, p. 6; Glushko, 1977). There is also a shortage of graduates in other subjects because young graduates are now largely directed to rural schools in an effort to raise the formerly low standards of the latter.

Vocational Guidance

Since the late 1960s, great store has been set on vocational guidance. By matching aptitudes to jobs it is hoped to reconcile the interests of the economy with those of the individual. Vocational guidance implies an insight into the physical and mental make-up of the individual, on the one hand, and, on the other, a detailed knowledge of the work processes in various occupations and the demands they make on the human organism. Vocational guidance also involves information on existing employment opportunities. It is here that an element of propaganda in favour of needed skills inevitably comes in. Such *prof-propaganda* is often carried out by factories, mines, construction sites, and so on, seeking to attract young recruits by inviting them to open days; allowing them to come for short-term trial practice, which is often paid for; and promoting various forms of sponsorship, as already mentioned.

Important work in the study of man's physiological abilities is going on in many scientific research institutes of the Academy of Pedagogical Sciences of the USSR, in educational research institutes of Union Republics, the Institute of Labour Hygiene and Occupational Diseases of the Academy of Medical Sciences, the Central Scientific-Research Institute for the Protection of Labour of the Trade Union Council, the All-Union Scientific Institute of Technical Aesthetics, and several others engaged on improving the 'man-machine' interface.

In the USSR, the study of 'aptitudes and abilities' (*sposobnosti*) is mainly concerned with physiological and biomechanical factors such as sensory and motor reactions to external stimuli, for example the speed and precision of these reactions, the thresholds of discrimination to light, pitch, vibration, as well as measurements of short-term visual and verbal memory, of attention and fatigue, of the sense of time and spatial orientation. These measurements are combined into a 'psychodiagnosis' of the individual. However, it is assumed that aptitude and abilities are not static but have potential for development, so an assessment of such possibilities leads on to the more risky art of 'psychoprognosis'. Intelligence tests are still frowned upon because they measure intelligence indirectly through performance and the latter is strongly conditioned by social factors. Rorschach ink blots are seldom used.

Various refinements in establishing job profiles lead to the broader science of 'professiology' (*professiologiya*). Like the study of job profiles, it starts with a detailed break-down of the demands that various work processes make on the mind and body of a person. Yet it also takes into account work organisation, the social prestige of the occupation, the standards of general knowledge and acquired skills needed to perform a given operation and the opportunities to introduce innovations. This leads on to ergonomics and is sometimes described as the 'man-machine-environment-collective' system (Platonov, 1971; 1973; 1974; 1978).

The need and ability to estimate more elusive character traits and their neurological basis in both sensory organs and the brain cortex are of the greatest importance in appointments to responsible jobs, where the individual may have to cope with emergencies and stress situations, and when the amount and speed of on-rushing information taxes the human brain to its utmost. This makes further research into brain physiology very urgent. On the other hand, it is held by many that – within certain physiological limits – no special abilities are really needed for ordinary, run-of-the-mill manual occupations. Motivation, social conditioning and willingness to work are far more important. In other words, what should be promoted is a positive attitude to work and a more realistic appraisal among the young of their own limitations and those of their present-day society. So we are back to square one, i.e. *prof-propaganda* (Gurevich, 1970, chs 4–5).

The hope that, in time, work processes will become more meaning-ful and creative is a long-standing and much cherished one in the Soviet Union. The rising generation may be over-educated for present-day jobs, but later all will need their theoretical knowledge, and even more of it, so as to adapt to technological change and recurrent retraining. The trouble lies in the time lag. Unfortunately the experience of industrialised nations is undermining the belief that, in future, work will always be interesting and creative, for automation sometimes displaces highly skilled personnel, the machine takes over complex operations leaving the operator menial machine-minding and servicing functions. Creativity is more likely to find outlets in further scientific research, in art, sport and participatory social management.

CREATIVITY

No progress is possible without new inventions, insights into natural phenomena or novel ways of perceiving and making things. Whether creativity, like intelligence, is an innate faculty or the product of social factors may be a matter for debate. Soviet psychologists, unlike their Western counterparts, give greater weight to the latter. For them, human faculties can be stunted by an unfavourable environment or stimulated and developed by appropriate educational methods. Hence an increasing insistence on developing the reasoning powers of children and reducing the amount of memorised data. This is known as 'developmental instruction' (*razvivayushchee obuchenie*). At prim-ary level, the teacher will try to get the class to work out a concept, for instance in guiding them to a definition of 'What is a fruit?'. She displays visual material (actual apples, plums, etc.) and asks questions until the first answers 'Something nice to eat' or 'Grows on trees' leads on to the 'discovery' that all have pips or stones, i.e. seeds. Later pupils will be guided towards finding out solutions to scientific problems or answers to literary questions by consulting reference books more or less independently, carrying out simple experiments or analysing the theoretical principles underlying their productive work practice. This is known as 'problem instruction' (*problemnoe obuchenie*). Eventually at *VUZ* level some students will join a research team engaged on a real-life problem. The difficulty is to find a balance between the effective but time-consuming developmental method of discovery, and the amount of necessary knowledge accumulated by mankind over centuries which will still have to be conveyed, under-stood and assimilated without having to be 'rediscovered' by every child.

Despite their emphasis on development, Soviet psychologists do not deny completely the existence of special talents. Specialised schools have been established for those particularly gifted for mathematics, physics, languages, ballet, music, art or sport. Among the most famous schools for prospective mathematicians and physicists are those sponsored by the universities of Novosibirsk, Moscow, Kiev and Leningrad, though there are many others. Their value is disputed (Dunstan, 1978, pp. 73–5, 116–22). Thus, Academician P. I. Kapitsa came out against creaming off the brighter pupils because it is detrimental to ordinary schools to be deprived of their 'leaven' (Kapitsa, 1971, p. 23); moreover, the selected pupils may have been precocious rather than truly talented and suffer later from failing to live up to expectations. In the case of language schools, given the relative isolation of the Soviet Union, their pupils might not find appropriate employment (Filippov, 1976, pp. 59–61).

At a lower level, but on a larger scale, creativity is encouraged by promoting a variety of clubs and societies run within the school or outside by Pioneer or Komsomol organisations: there are circles of young naturalists, radio fans, bird watchers, model-makers, and many others. Initially, the inclusion of optional subjects in the curriculum after 1966 was designed to raise standards of achievement in the pupil's chosen subject, to encourage minor abilities and perhaps discover outstanding ones. In reality, even before the December 1977 decree made it mandatory, optional courses had often been used as vocational training for local industries.

Scientific interests and technical abilities are the most favoured, but plenty of encouragement is given to sport and theatrical events. Sport and games (apart from PE) have not been school subjects, but the concern of Pioneer and Komsomol organisations and, in the case of adults, that of trade unions. They are, however, increasingly introduced in *VUZy* ('Ob utverzhdenii . . .', 1978). One-fifth of the population is said to be taking part in some form of physical culture and 7 million people have achieved some kind of recognised award. With the introduction of the five-day week and the country's growing prosperity, which enables the Soviet government to allocate more resources to build stadiums, sports grounds and swimming pools, and to manufacture or even buy abroad the necessary equipment, sport is bound to gain further popularity, particularly with the Olympic Games scheduled to take place in Moscow, Tallin, Kiev, Minsk and Leningrad in 1980.

Apart from the attraction of physical prowess, sporting events also satisfy aesthetic needs, both in the display of fine human bodies and in the colourful trappings of large-scale festivals with their processions, national costumes and decorated grounds.

Similarly, official help is increasing extended to artistic and theatrical events. The April 1978 decree 'On measures further to develop amateur artistic creativity' states that 25 million people now take part in song-and-dance ensembles, bands, amateur theatricals and other artistic activities. The decree enjoins professional artists, actors, musicians and writers to help with amateur productions, write suitable songs and plays and, generally speaking, provide artistic guidance. Various ministries are to expand the production of materials for props, sets and costumes and of musical instruments, paints and brushes. An All-Union festival of amateur artistic activities was held in 1975–7 and a second one is scheduled for 1980–2. It is specified, however, that these events must not be purposeless manifestations of spontaneous popular exuberance but, under Party guidance, contribute to the political, moral and labour education of the masses, thus helping to overcome the survivals of the past in the minds of the people ('O merakh . . .', 1978). Like education and sport, art should contribute to the building of a rationally organised and managed society. In an increasingly complex society, organisation and management themselves become arts that have to be learnt and practised from an early age.

To this is related the wish to revive a certain amount of pupil self-government in schools ('O dal'neishem . . .', 1977). This was widely encouraged in the 1920s and given much prominence in the writings of the educationalist A. S. Makarenko. It fell into disuse with the return of a more rigid educational system in the later 1930s and 1940s. A semblance of self-government persisted only in Pioneer and Komsomol organisations, though their meetings were mainly concerned with Party-inspired campaigns to collect scrap metal or medicinal plants, or else to carry out anti-religious propaganda or mobilise their parents and other adults to vote in elections. The Russian word *samoupravlenie* is sometimes translated as self-government, but in a school context it comes closer to self-management. Thus in junior forms, self-management consists in sharing out chores among pupils; for example, who is to clean the blackboard before the next lesson or feed the pet rabbit or take the daily roll-call once the art of reading has been mastered. Inevitably, in the initial stages self-management is organised by the teacher whose job it is to weld his class into a comradely collective with a strong ésprit de corps. Later on, one or two pupils act in turn as form prefects (*dezhurnye*), particularly those who have enrolled into the Pioneer organisation. Members of senior forms establish a rota of 'on duty' prefects for the whole school. Their duties include supervising the younger children during breaks, keeping an eye on how the form *dezhurnye* serve meals, and organising the cleaning of classrooms and corridors at the end of the school day (particularly necessary if the building is used by a second shift). Competitions in the efficiency of carrying out duties are held between classes and judged by the school Komsomol committee. Self-management is of special importance during excursions to places of natural or historical interest, such as those linked in some way with the October Revolution. During such outings, everyone should know who is responsible for what, and therefore they are usually preceded by a pupils' meeting at which arrangements are discussed and finalised.

Each class sends a deputy to the school council, as well as to various circles interested in sport, music, astronomy or other hobbies. During meetings pupils learn to elect a chairman and other officers, take down minutes, vote on resolutions and later make sure that these are being carried out in accordance with the decisions of the majority, thus learning to observe the rules of democratic centralism. Older pupils who join the Komsomol attend meetings with those younger teachers (below 26 years of age) who are members of the Komsomol. The latter come under the influence of the Party, possibly represented by older teachers. Thus the Party–Komsomol linkage ensures a bond between generations united by their faith in a common ideology (Korotov, 1976).

As children proceed through school they learn to take on responsibilities, to submit to the spirit of the collective and obey rules that they have discussed and adopted themselves under the discreet guidance of older pupils whose standing is enhanced by their membership of the Komsomol. The latter also brings them into contact with the wider world, since Komsomol primary cells from different schools, as well as from local factories, may have joint meetings organised by the district Komsomol committee. This is itself subordinate to the regional Komsomol Committee and the latter comes under the Republican or the All-Union Komsomol Committee on the model of the structure of the Party itself.

Children who later become students at institutes of higher education will engage as part of their training in some form of socially useful practical activity, such as voluntary work on building sites during the summer vacation (known as the third semester), or delivering lectures on current affairs and Party policy at factory meetings – all activities designed to promote and test the organisational abilities of the prospective graduates and the forcefulness of their communist convictions ('Primernoe polozhenie . . .', 1974).

It has been observed that on paper Soviet citizens enjoy far more rights than they seem to exercise. Indeed, the Party itself is calling for democratisation and initiative from below. Decades of terror, however, have stunted initiative among citizens, and people who are entitled to take a decision apparently always await directives from above. It would seem that the Party leadership would be glad to devolve some decision-making to the masses provided it could trust them to have truly internalised the spirit of communism. According to one author, 'mature communism demands an ever broadening involvement of the masses in conscious, historically determined creativity, in the management of society, in the manifestation of initiative for which it is necessary to raise the professional training and political knowledge of the toilers, their communist conviction and democratic habits and traditions' ('Marksistsko-leninskaya . . .', 1978, p. 11).

SOCIAL ORGANISATION

Social planning, social engineering and a rational organisation of mankind have always been implicit in communist ideology. Indeed, the purpose of the Revolution was to bring it about. But, at first, there were more immediate tasks: the need for the Bolshevik Party to survive in a largely hostile environment, and hold on to power at all cost; and the need to defeat its internal enemies. First, there were the White armies, then an unco-operative 'petty-bourgeois-minded' peasantry, then thousands of alleged wreckers sabotaging industrial-isation and, during the long dark days of Stalinism, hundreds of thousands (and possibly millions) of ill-defined 'enemies of the people' who perished in the infamous 'Gulags'. It was also necessary to ward off external enemies, the powerful capitalist world encircling the first socialist state, its hostility culminating in the devastating on-slaught of the invading German armies. At last, after the tremendous material destruction wrought by them had been made good, the building of the material-technical basis began in earnest.

Social, as distinct from economic, planning began in the late 1960s with the first attempts at drafting long-term forecasts for periods of fifteen years upwards, which were required by very large-scale con-struction projects, and with the recognition of the impact that the scientific and technical revolution was having and would increasingly have on society. Attention had to be turned to the human factor, particularly if free labour was to be attracted to the forbidding wastes of Siberia.

During the same years, a movement for 'communist labour' appeared among some teams of workers at a few enterprises; these teams included in their group plans commitments not merely to increase production and ensure careful maintenance of machinery, but also they undertook to see that all their members learnt a second skill and attended Party schools or evening classes to complete either their secondary education or to obtain some technical qualification. Other groups undertook to improve and enlarge their hostels, to abstain from drunkenness and absenteeism, to publish the factory wall-newspaper and, generally speaking, to observe the rules of communist morality. The support of their enterprise was not always sufficient to achieve their laudable aims. For instance, since educational matters come under local authorities, if the latter failed to provide the necessary evening classes, the workers' endeavours to improve their education could be frustrated. Conversely, the town authorities might need the help of the enterprise with equipment. To complicate matters, larger enterprises situated within the city bound-aries might be subordinate not to the city Soviet but to an All-Union ministry in Moscow. The need for co-ordinating efforts became evident (Aldasheva, 1976).

Contending social needs could be satisfied only within budgetary constraints. The building of new towns posed problems of the types of housing to be built, that is larger communal flats with shared amenities, assumed to promote a spirit of collectivism, or smaller ones allowing for the privacy of family life. Often the choice lay between better shopping centres to reduce time-wasting queuing, or additional hospital accommodation, or the inclusion of sport centres or cinemas, the destruction of green belts for building purposes or their preserva-tion. Such decisions confront town and country planning authorities in any country, but are more acute in the USSR because of the rate and scale of urbanisation, connected with migration from the countryside and the number of industrial plants being built, and are complicated by a chronically inadequate supply of everything from bricks and mortar to telephone equipment and pipes for central heating on a district basis.

Although social planning is increasingly pervasive and determined, it is not a specially Soviet phenomenon; rather it seems to be inevitable in large industrial societies. Despite the prevalence of a market economy, the closure of unprofitable plants which deprives people from earning a livelihood now forces a Western government to step in with subsidies or devise alternative work; 'job experience schemes' are created for unemployed school-leavers; various tax rebates are devised to attract industries into depressed areas; statistics and sur-veys proliferate to estimate the future costs of welfare services; and a new ill-defined concept of the quality of life is becoming the concern of governments and environmentalists in industrialised nations.

Planned social development is still a novelty and some decisions have unforeseen results: thus high-rise dwellings apparently affect the birth rate adversely; the separation of residential from industrial zones may lead to transport difficulties for the night shift and thus to high labour turnover. The multiplicity of problems can be solved only by a 'complex' approach, by tackling many targets in an integrated way within larger territorial units, and it seems that the lines of communication lie through the Party organisations. For it is the job of the Party district committee (*raikom*) and, at the next echelon, that of the Party provincial committee (*obkom*) to co-ordinate the plans of individual enterprises and institutions with those of the city and those of the city with those of the region as a whole. Recurring statements on the growing importance of Party leadership for the development of the country may stem not from the desire of a non-elected, self-perpetuating oligarchy to retain power, but may reflect a genuinely integrative function of the Party's hierarchical structure. Be that as it may, social development is now a major concern in the USSR. Thus, the annual plan for the development of the national economy presented to the Central Committee of the CPSU by N. K. Baibakov, Chairman of Gosplan in December 1977, included for the first time the word 'social' in its title (Baibakov, 1977).

Economic planning was concerned with material production, whereas social planning aims at promoting the 'Soviet way of life'. This is no longer regarded as a distant utopia but as a slowly attainable goal, a further development of 'mature socialism'. It is also becoming evident that the shaping of the new society cannot be left to the spontaneous action of objective economic forces and that the 'subjective factor' has to play a greater role. In other words, social development must be guided by the élite of the nation – the Communist Party – by men appropriately selected and trained, capable of taking decisions, of enlisting support among the masses, undeterred by unforeseen difficulties and, above all, unflinching in their communist faith. Furthermore, those whom they will lead and whose whole-hearted support is essential cannot be passive robots but must be 'fully-developed' personalities, conscious of the great aims to be achieved, willing to strive for them, trained to think creatively and to act collectively in an organised way.

CONCLUSIONS

The Soviet educational system is designed to form knowledgeable, rationally minded, competent and dynamic human beings who have accepted without reservation and will conform to a nineteenth-century ideology. Whether this implies an internal contradiction and how it can be resolved, time alone can tell. Possibly the ideology may become more flexible or more vague. Already long-resisted theories in modern physics (such as relativity or the Heisenberg indeterminancy principle), as well as cybernetics and genetics have had to be accommodated into Engels's scientific heritage. The scientific and technical revolution is altering human existence more fundamentally than any political revolution ever did. But it is argued that this too is man-made and, in so far as many of its elements are amenable to human control, future developments can be both foreseen and directed towards desired goals. Hence the prominence given to 'the science of science' (*naukovedenie*), that is studies of the likely trends in scientific discoveries and possible ways of manipulating them, such as the allocation of resources to certain fields of science in preference to others, the training of technologists for selected industries, or the financing of research and development in specific types of complex apparatus and equipment (Lubrano, 1976; Gvishiani, 1978).

The study of the likely impact of future innovations on human societies is now the subject of the new science of 'social prognostics' (*sotsial'noe prognozirovanie*). Soviet social prognostics are more goal-oriented than the 'alternative scenarios' of Western futurologists who restrict themselves to scientifically objective predictions intentionally free of normative values.

Hitherto, social prognostication in the USSR has developed piecemeal in various research institutes concerned with the long-term planning of the economy, of urban construction, education, health services, ethnography, demographic trends and cultural activities. Several have set up departments of social prognostication within their own fields. A specialised Institute of Social Prognostics within the system of the Academy of Sciences of the USSR to co-ordinate the study of various aspects of future social change is now in the offing (Bestuzhev-Lada, 1969, 1970, 1975, 1977).

It is to be hoped that a rationally minded, technically powerful and forward-looking generation will be able to outgrow such transitory forms of human organisation as capitalism and communism and devise better ones to live in peace on the planet Earth.

BIBLIOGRAPHY

Aldasheva, Sh. B., 'Opyt raboty gorodskogo Soveta deputatov trudyash-chikhsya po planirovaniyu sotsial'nogo razvitiya predpriyatii i goroda', in *Planirovanie sotsial'nogo razvitiya*, ed. D. A. Kerimov (Moscow, 1976), pp. 84–99.

Averiev, Yu., 'Nuzhna produmannaya sistema podgotovki rabochei smeny', *Sotsialisticheskii trud*, 1974, no. 12, pp. 76–84.

Baibakov, N. K., 'O gosudarstvennom plane ekonomicheskogo i sotsial'nogo razvitiya SSSR na 1978 god', *Pravda*, 15 December 1977.

Bestuzhev-Lada, I. V., 'Social prognostics research in the Soviet Union', in *Mankind 2000*, ed. R. Jungk and J. Galtung (London: Allen & Unwin, 1969), pp. 299–306.

Bestuzhev-Lada, I. V., *Okno v budushchee* (Moscow, 1970).

Bestuzhev-Lada, I.V., 'Prognozirovanie kak kompleksnaya problema', *Vestnik Akademii nauk SSSR*, 1975, no. 7, pp. 43–52.

Bestuzhev-Lada, I. V., 'Prognozirovanie obraza zhizni', in *Problemy sotsialis-ticheskogo obraza zhizni*, ed. M. N. Rutkevich (Moscow, 1977), pp. 219–28.

Bondarenko, N. I., 'O sisteme podgotovki uchitelei trudovogo obucheniya', *Sovetskaya pedagogika*, 1974, no. 1, pp. 76–82.

Brezhnev, L. I., 'Uchastnikam Vsesoyuznogo sleta chlenov uchenicheskikh proizvodstvennykh brigad', in his *Leninskim kursom*, Vol. 5 (Moscow, 1976*a*), pp. 121–2.

Brezhnev, L. I., 'Otchet TsK KPSS i ocherednye zadachi partii v oblasti vnutrennei i vneshnei politiki; doklad XXV s''ezdu KPSS', in his *Leninskim kursom*, Vol. 5 (Moscow, 1976*b*), pp. 450–550.

Brezhnev, L. I., 'Raduet yunaya smena', *Pravda*, 5 August 1977*a*.

Brezhnev, L. I., 'O proekte konstitutsii (osnovnogo zakona) SSSR i itogakh ego vsenarodnogo obsuzhdeniya; doklad na sed'moi sessii Verkhovnogo soveta SSSR devyatogo sozyva', *Pravda*, 5 October 1977*b*.

Brezhnev, L. I., 'Vysokaya nagrada na znameni Baku', *Pravda*, 23 September 1978.

Dunstan, N. J., *Paths to Excellence and the Soviet School* (Windsor, Berks.: NFER, 1978).

Engels, F., *Dialectics of Nature* (London: Lawrence & Wishart, 1940).

Faure, E. (*et al.*), *Learning to Be: the World of Education Today and Tomorrow* (Paris: UNESCO, 1972).

Filippov, F. P., *Vseobshchee srednee obrazovanie v SSSR: sotsiologicheskie problemy* (Moscow, 1976).

Foteeva, A. I., 'Vospitanie molodoi rabochei smeny', *Sovetskaya pedagogika*, 1973, no. 3, pp. 137–41.

Geizhan, N. F. and Vasil'eva G. V., 'Iz opyta organizatsii professional'noi orientatsii shkol'nikov', *Sovetskaya pedagogika*, 1976, no. 2, pp. 55–63.

Glushko, M. P., 'O podgotovke inzhenerov-pedagogov', *Vestnik vysshei shkoly*, 1977, no. 12, pp. 61–3.

Gurevich, K. M., *Professional'naya prigodnost' i osnovnye svoistva nervnoi sistemy* (Moscow, 1970).

Gvishiani, D. M., 'Metodicheskie problemy modelirovaniya global'nogo razvitiya', *Voprosy filosofii*, 1978, no. 2, pp. 14–28.

Kapitsa, P. A., 'Nekotorye printsipy tvorcheskogo vospitaniya i obrazovaniya sovremennoi molodezhi', *Voprosy filosofii*, 1971, no. 7, pp. 16–24.

'Ko vseobshchemu srednemu obrazovaniyu', *Sovetskaya pedagogika*, 1974, no. 12, pp. 3–9.

Kornitskii, G. V., 'Organizatsiya trudovogo obucheniya, vospitaniya i proforientatsii shkol'nikov', *Sovetskaya pedagogika*, 1978, no. 2, pp. 11–19.

Korotov, V. M., *Samoupravlenie shkol'nikov*, 2nd edn (Moscow, 1976).

Korotov, V. M., 'Novyi etap v razvitii obshcheobrazovatel'noi shkoly', *Sovetskaya pedagogika*, 1978, no. 3, pp. 3–9.

Koutaissoff, E., 'Young people's choice of careers and manpower planning in the Soviet Union', in *Education and the Mass Media in the Soviet Union and Eastern Europe*, ed. B. Harasymiv (New York: Praeger, 1976), pp. 15–38.

Lubrano, L., *Soviet Sociology of Science* (Columbus, Ohio: AAASS, 1976).

'Marksistsko-leninskaya filosofiya i progress chelovechestva', *Voprosy filosofii*, 1978, no. 1, pp. 3–15.

Narodnoe khozyaistvo SSSR za 60 let: yubileinyi statisticheskii ezhegodnik (Moscow, 1977).

'O dal'neishem sovershenstvovanii obucheniya, vospitaniya uchashchikhsya obshcheobrazovatel'nykh shkol i podgotovke ikh k trudu', *Pravda*, 29 December 1977.

'O dal'neishem sovershenstvovanii sistemy professional'no-tekhnicheskogo obrazovaniya', *Pravda*, 29 June 1972.

'O merakh po dal'neishemu razvitiyu samodeyatel'nogo khudozhestvennogo tvorchestva', *Pravda*, 2 April 1978.

'O merakh po dal'neishemu uluchsheniyu uslovii raboty sel'skoi obshcheobrazovatel'noi shkoly', *Pravda*, 6 July 1973.

'O merakh po raspredeleniyu seti srednikh sel'skikh PTU i po uluchsheniyu ikh raboty', *Pravda*, 21 February 1975.

'Ob organizatsii mezhshkol'nykh uchebno-proizvodstvennykh kombinatov trudovogo obucheniya i professional'noi orientatsii trudyashchikhsya', *Spravochnik partiinogo rabotnika* (Moscow, 1975), pp. 369–71.

'Ob utverzhdenii instruktsii po organizatsii i soderzhaniyu raboty kafedry fizicheskogo vospitaniya vysshikh uchebnykh zavedenii', *Byulleten' Ministerstva vysshego i srednego spetsial'nogo obrazovaniya*, 1978, no. 9, pp. 7–16.

'Ob uvelichenii i povyshenii kachestva podgotovki inzhenerno-pedagogicheskikh kadrov v vuzakh SSSR dlya sistemy professional'no-tekhnicheskogo obrazovaniya', *Byulleten' Ministerstva vysshego i srednego spetsial'nogo obrazovaniya*, 1977, no. 12, pp. 6–7.

Platonov, K., 'Professiografiya i ee znachenie i metodika raboty', *Sotsialisticheskii trud*, 1971, no. 4, pp. 74–9.

Platonov, K., 'O sushchnosti i zadachakh professiografii', *Sotsialisticheskii trud*, 1973, no. 2, pp. 78–80.

Platonov, K., 'Protiv vul'garizatsii v primenenii testov pri psikhodiagnostike', *Sotsialisticheskii trud*, 1974, no. 12, pp. 95–8.

Platonov, K., 'Professiologiya i professiografiya v professional'noi orientatsii', in *Professional'naya orientatsiya molodezhi*, ed. L. A. Morsina (Moscow, 1978), pp. 130–52.

'Primernoe polozhenie ob obshchestvenno-politicheskoi praktike studentov vysshikh uchebnykh zavedenii', *Byulleten' Ministerstva vysshego i srednego spetsial'nogo obrazovaniya*, 1974, no. 9, pp. 22–4.

'Primernoe polozhenie ob uchenicheskoi proizvodstvennoi brigade v kolkhoze, sovkhoze', *Spravochnik rabotnika narodnogo obrazovaniya* (Moscow, 1973), pp. 318–26.

Rutkevich, M. N., 'Nekotorye problemy razvitiya sotsial'nogo planirovaniya', in *Planirovanie sotsial'nogo razvitiya*, ed. D. A. Kerimov (Moscow, 1976), pp. 23–30.

Senchenko, I. T., 'Rol' proizvodstvennogo kollektiva v trudovom obuchenii i vospitanii', *Sovetskaya pedagogika*, 1976, no. 8, pp. 71–6.

Turchenko, V. N., *Nauchno-tekhnicheskaya revolyutsiya i obrazovanie* (Moscow, 1973).

UNESCO International Conference on Education, 34th Session, 1973, *Main Trends in Education* (ED/BIE/Confined/34/4) (Geneva: UNESCO, 1973).

Verin, L. *Stanovlenie i razvitie narodnogo obrazovaniya na Kolyme i Chukotke* (Magadan, 1969).

Zharkov, S. M. (ed.), *Nekotorye voprosy proforientatsii i istorii pedagogiki* (Barnaul, 1972).

5

Socialisation in the Literature Lesson

FELICITY O'DELL

Literary criticism in any society can serve the sociologist as yet another indicator of the nature of that society. The doctrines of 'art for art's sake' and of socialist realism were spawned by very different environments. Literary criticism can also be used for more active social purposes as it forms one element of the socialisation process. The training in literary appreciation provided by schools, for example, both by indicating what should be looked out for in a story or poem and by evaluating fictional behaviour, cannot but colour pupils' perceptions in and out of school.

It is thus revealing of Soviet society in general, and Soviet socialisation in particular, to examine in some detail the attitudes towards literature which are taught to secondary school pupils in the USSR. Not only what is read but also how it is read is indicative. We ask, 'Is the emphasis on classical or contemporary works and why?'. But we also ask to what extent, and how, such controversial literary figures as Raskolnikov or Hamlet are interpreted.

The subject of this chapter is the Russian literature programme for use in Soviet schools in 1977/8 (*Programma* . . ., 1977). This exemplifies the importance attached to literary criticism by the Soviet Ministry of Education as it gives systematic, detailed guidance to the teacher. It lists the works to be studied from the fourth to the tenth form, determines the number of hours to spend on each book or author, outlines the aspects of the various topics which the teacher must emphasise and even lists which passages the pupils must learn by heart.

THE IDEAL LITERATURE TEACHER

The literature syllabus can prescribe what is to be studied in great detail, but there is no escaping the ultimate significance of the individual teacher. It is likely that most people remember far more about the personalities of the teachers that they had at school than about the nature of the textbooks used. Lenin's literary metaphor in speaking of teachers as 'an army of socialist enlightenment' is frequently quoted and the syllabus, not surprisingly, devotes some paragraphs to the qualities required by these soldiers of the aesthetic. First of all, the teachers must 'have had a broad ideological and political training and must be a good communist'. Second to this she needs 'a deep knowledge of literature and the theory relating to it'. (The teacher is referred to throughout as 'she' to avoid the clumsiness of 'he or she' and because 79 per cent of non-administrative Soviet teachers in 1975/6 were women.) Thirdly, come her pedagogic requirements; she must have 'knowledge of the fundamentals of educational theory and of the age characteristics of pupils' as well as 'creative initiative and constant concern about the perfecting of her teaching skills' (ibid., p. 8).

The order in which these characteristics are placed is telling. Both knowledge of the field and of teaching methods come second to a committed communist world-view. This can be accounted for, in part, by the early history of the political involvement of teachers after 1917. A Soviet essay on literature teaching in the first years of the Revolution summed up the situation as follows:

'What kind of teaching staff did we have then?' Lunacharskii used to reminisce in 1929. 'In Leningrad, then, apart from a few communist educationalists, there was no one at all. In Moscow, the teaching profession refused to teach and said "We announce that, until Soviet power disappears, we shall not teach the children." ' Things were a little better in the provinces. But, after a protracted campaign in Kostroma in 1919, Lunacharskii wrote that a section of the teachers and pupils at the *gymnasium* were still hostile to the new order.

Among those teachers who opposed or were actively hostile to Soviet power, a not insignificant role was played by the teachers of literature. A number of these put anti-Soviet pronouncements into print. (Rotkovich, 1965, p. 16)

The nature of their early history has helped to make the Soviet authorities anxious to have loyal teachers of literature. Having once known disloyalty among these teachers, they wish to avoid repeating the experience.

The very nature of the subject which they teach also makes such loyalty crucial. Unlike the school teacher of physics, the literature teacher is teaching not so much facts as an approach. The same point could be made for the teaching of history. Paul Neuburg, a Hungarian *émigré*, vividly discusses the conflict of Eastern European teachers, of whom many have tried 'positive' neutrality: exploiting the possibilities of the curriculum for putting over views of their own, even in the most difficult years. 'I remember my history teacher explaining about Fascism, must have been about 1952', a 29-year-old poet in Hungary told me. 'He described to us what it had been like to stand on a street corner and watch the Fascists march by, shouting slogans and holding their hands high. It was a long and very vivid description, as if he were talking about things that had happened not years ago but only the previous week, and slowly we began to realise that he was talking about not just Fascism, but our own marches too. He spoke very quietly, but he was almost spitting the words when he said, "I'll have you know, boys, I'm an individual. I hate crowds marching and shouting in unison. And you, too, every one of you, are individuals. Not a mob." I can still see him, in front of a hushed class, saying those words . . .' (Neuburg, 1972, pp. 107–8)

Even more than history, literature provides scope for the teacher to put across her particular opinions; as has already been said, books can be interpreted in different ways. Moreover, any story can provide a jumping-off point for digression along any lines chosen by the teacher. The literature lesson indeed provides unique scope for propaganda work at the discretion of the individual teacher. It could also be expected that the teacher's own study of belles-lettres would make her especially aware of style and thus able to put across her own views in an articulate, powerful way. At least one Soviet *émigré* now living in Britain considers that his eyes were first opened to contradictions in the Soviet system by his literature teacher at school (personal testimony). For all these intertwining reasons, the syllabus puts the literature teacher's political convictions first in its list of qualities required for the job.

METHODS OF TEACHING LITERATURE

The personality of the teacher, in the literature lesson especially, is seen as the cornerstone of effective teaching methods. Just as it is the teacher who has scope in her lessons for digression and debate unparalleled in any other classroom, so it is ultimately she who can either bring the stereotyped notes of the syllabus into life or who can present them so drily that the pupil's interest in literature is lost for ever. More significant than the harm done to the pupil's reading habits if the teacher's methods are inadequate is the damage to his social attitudes:

The basic problem, in character-education through a classroom subject, consists in the 'internalisation' of knowledge – i.e., the transformation of the information communicated into convictions and genuine principles of living for the individual. Here it is important that teaching in the social disciplines should be free from formalism and that textbooks should awaken the deep interest of the pupils and that the teachers themselves should be expert at their task. Bad teaching of history, literature or social science does not simply leave a gap in the pupils' knowledge, it causes direct harm to the political and social education of the rising generation. (Kissel', 1970, p. 60)

Teaching methods are to be dictated by the social rather than the aesthetic aims of literary education.

Consequently, the teacher is not left to deal with the texts listed by the syllabus just as she wishes. The official curricula lay down quite precisely how the works are to be studied, leaving the individual teacher freedom only within closely prescribed limits. She is permitted, for instance, to redistribute the time allotted to the consideration of particular themes if she feels this to be necessary and she may choose, say, which specific folk sayings her 11-year-olds discuss. But on more fundamental matters, the curriculum takes the decisions for her. It gives, therefore, guidance on the most effective methods of teaching the material in the programme.

Above all, it is stressed that everything must be done to make the lessons stimulating for the child and to inspire an emotional response in him. Where possible, thematic links should be created relating such courses as singing, history and art to the literature syllabus – for example, children should be encouraged to paint their favourite literary hero. Much use, it is stressed, can be made of other media as well: this is, of course, simplified in the Soviet Union because of the fact that all the media are aiming at putting over the same basic values. Thus, use of articles from children's magazines is suggested as well as pictures, musical works and tapes of literary readings – all of which can help to bring the lesson to life. The pupils are particularly to be encouraged to read at home. Appropriate reading lists are supplied in the syllabus. At least once a month, a lesson is to be devoted to discussing individual reading. The teacher is urged to enlist people outside the school to help in her task – librarians, keepers of literary museums and parents should all give the teacher support.

Thus the focus of the methods section of the literature syllabus is essentially to show how to arouse the child's interest and enthusiasm, rather than how to force most facts into him – although this is clearly largely because it is realised that the child will learn most if he is interested and emotionally involved with the subject.

At some variance perhaps, with the other ideas suggested on how to make lessons lively is the requirement to use constant and systematic repetition. This implies that the pupils' grasp of the facts and the correct approach is ultimately the aim of the course rather than a more rarified appreciation of literature which would hardly be encouraged by constant repetition. Repetition in another, possibly more positive, form is an element of the Soviet literature lesson in that it places great emphasis on learning by heart. Conversation with Russians frequently quickly reveals their ability to quote passages from their native poetry or prose by heart, an ability which is, regrettably many feel, not encouraged by contemporary British education.

The methodological notes with the syllabus are not the only guidelines easily accessible to the teacher. There is a journal, *Literatura v shkole* (Literature in School) published six times a year, and numerous books and articles written on individual authors or works, and on stylistic and pedagogical topics.

Despite all these official guidelines, the literature teacher need not lose the opportunity to make a lesson interesting in her own personal way. Rotkovich (1965, pp. 306–7) describes certain successful lessons carried out with an original and individual style – for example, a lesson on Nikitin's poem *'Utro'* (Morning) in which the poet describes a summer dawn. The teacher had all the pupils close their books and then led a discussion with them on their summer holidays in the country. Carefully he steered them into the delights of summer nights, of sunrise and early morning. After they had spent some time describing the latter, they opened their books and found Nikitin describing his summer morning in terms very similar to those they had used themselves. As a result of this imaginative introduction they read the poem aloud with great feeling and willingly learnt sections of it by heart.

To sum up, teaching methods certainly aim to awaken pupils' enthusiasm in as lively and as original ways as possible, but they should never lose sight of the underlying social purpose behind all Soviet education, not least that in literature.

GENERAL CHARACTERISTICS OF THE SYLLABUS

We now turn to examine the curriculum in which such methods are to be applied by this committed, conscientious teacher. We shall consider first the general characteristics of the syllabus before dealing with more specific aspects of literary criticism as practised in the Soviet school.

The course covers Russian literature from its beginnings to the present-day, from folk tales to Tvardovskii, and also includes some major foreign writers – Homer, Shakespeare, Hans Andersen, Molière, Goethe, Byron, Balzac and Cervantes. Its scope is thus very broad. A pupil is to leave school with a systematic general knowledge of literature rather than a deep understanding of a few particular works. Indeed, most Westerners who have met young Russians are impressed by their wide knowledge of both Russian and foreign literature.

A further significant feature of the curriculum is the attention paid to the literature of the Soviet period (see Table 5.1). From this, it can be seen that one-third of the time spent discussing literature is devoted to material written in the mere sixty years since the Revolution. Only in the eighth and ninth forms does a comprehensive survey of pre-revolutionary Russian oust Soviet writing from a significant position.

The content balance of the literature course has been a bone of contention ever since the new Soviet authorities began discussing what to include in their school syllabuses. Gor'kii felt strongly that the classics of Russian and world literature should play an important part in the school syllabus. Krupskaya, on the other hand, felt that these should be included only if they had an obvious political content; thus, she favoured the works of the revolutionary democrats and populists of the 1870s, for example *Chto delat?* (What Is To Be Done?) by Chernyshevskii and such politically loaded novels as *Uncle Tom's Cabin*. More ambiguous works should have a secondary use only and should be published with detailed notes explaining their social background and their Marxist interpretation. (For details of the development of the literature syllabus, see Rotkovich, 1965.)

Nowadays, the literary classics of tsarist Russia are in fact well represented in the syllabus. Nevertheless, Soviet literature has proportionally a more-than-generous share. This reflects perhaps a continuation of the authorities' early sensitivity in their awareness of the ambiguities which can come to the surface in a prolonged discussion of pre-revolutionary literature. On the other hand, it may in part be a simple pedagogical acceptance of the fact that pupils there, as in the West, respond more willingly in school to modern novels than to the classics.

Whether the work under discussion is Soviet or not, socialisation is a factor in its treatment. Although the character-education content of most Soviet books is obvious and deliberate – hence, perhaps, their predominance in the earlier, more impressionable classes – it is not difficult to find ways in which non-Soviet works fit the authorities' requirements for character education. For example, they may show the injustices of the tsarist regime or, by demonstrating an ardent Russian patriotism, they may illustrate a virtue which clearly transcends the revolutionary barrier.

Character education is a vital ingredient of the literature lesson, as is suggested by the programme's demands for a teacher with a broad political and ideological training. Character education is used here as a

Table 5.1 Distribution of time in the Soviet secondary school literature programme

	1	2				3	4
		Periods spent discussing work read in class					
Form no.	Total periods available	Russian classical literature	Soviet literature	Translated foreign works	Total	Periods spent discussing out-of-class reading	Periods spent in speech development
4	70	25	25	4	54	8	8
5	68	32	16	4	52	8	8
6	68	28	19	5	52	8	8
7	64	29	20	0	49	8	7
8	100	76	(see col. 3)[a]	6	82	8	10
9	136	97	(see col. 3)[a]	12	109	12	15
10	102	10 (revision)	81	3	94	0	8
Total	608	297	161	34	492	52	64

[a] The out-of-class reading suggested for these classes is predominantly Soviet.

translation of the Russian word *vospitanie* which means that aspect of education which trains political, moral and social attitudes and behaviour. Indeed, the teachers' notes go on to state that 'The most important goal of the study of literature at school is the formation of a communist worldview and the ideological, political, moral and aesthetic education of the pupils' (*Programma* . . ., 1977, p. 5). Quite explicitly, then, the aesthetic goal is secondary to the less obviously literary goals of the study of poetry or prose. Instruction in the arts, like the arts themselves, is not seen as being primarily concerned with the cultivation of sensitivity; its fundamental worth depends on its social role, on the influence it has on the child's moral and political development. Significantly, in the very first form at school the child is taught the slogan '*Kniga — vash drug i uchitel*' (A Book is Your Friend and Teacher). The educative aspect of reading is never to be forgotten.

It has been shown above that the literature curriculum followed in Soviet secondary schools has three basic characteristics. First, it covers a large number and wide variety of writers. Secondly, Soviet works occupy a possibly disproportionately prominent position. Thirdly, the ideological content of the books studied is clearly of key importance.

THE IDEOLOGICAL CONTENT OF THE SYLLABUS

What is the exact nature of the ideological content of the syllabus? What virtues are emphasised through the medium of works of literature? What vices are decried?

Broadly speaking, of course, the pupil is to be educated 'in the spirit of communist morality' (ibid., p. 5) but certain elements of this spirit receive more frequent mention in the notes for teachers.

Above all, the syllabus emphasises that pupils must have a deep feeling of Soviet patriotism. The notes on individual works refer to this time and time again, starting from the very first item on the programme, the folk-tale *Ivan — krest'yanskii syn* (Ivan, the Peasant's Son), the patriotic significance of which is firmly maintained. Both classical and Soviet writers are shown to display great patriotism in their works. In looking only at works studied by 11-year-old pupils (fourth form) we see that Lermontov is shown as depicting in his poem *Borodino* the 'heroic victory of the Russian people' (ibid., p. 12) in their defence of the Motherland against Napoleon. Paustovskii, on the other hand, is said to show his love for his native land through his lyrical descriptions of the countryside. Furthermore, several stories about the Second World War ('The Great Patriotic War of the Soviet Union') are used to illustrate patriotism. Examples of these are

Kataev's *Syn polka* (Son of the Regiment) and Gaidar's *Timur i ego komanda* (Timur and His Team).

In later forms, also, various types of works are similarly used to encourage this feeling of patriotism. Stories of war exploits are particularly helpful; Russia's history of heroic defence against invaders has provided much useful matter for literature. The *byliny* (epic folk ballads) show the victories of the early Russian warriors. Russian heroism in the Napoleonic wars is reflected in *War and Peace*, and the triumphs of the other Patriotic War are amply represented in the curriculum by such works as Polevoi's *Povest' o nastoyashchem cheloveke* (Story of a Real Man) (a novel depicting the 'patriotism and selflessness of the partisans' and the 'solidarity of the Soviet people in the cruel years of the war' [ibid., p. 18]) and *Vasilii Terkin*, an epic poem by Tvardovskii which deals with the adventures of a down-to-earth, humorous private in the Soviet army.

Patriotism is not only exemplified in works on military themes. The poets Pushkin, Lermontov and Esenin are all seen to be primarily expressing their love for the motherland in their lyrical native poetry. Indeed, 'patriotism' and 'love for Russia' are the most regularly recurring words in the notes on the various works to be studied; of the thirteen Russian authors and themes to be discussed in the fifth form, nine are described by the syllabus notes in terms of their patriotic content.

But of course a deep sense of patriotism, though of first importance, is not the only quality felt to be necessary as part of imbuing a young person with the spirit of communist morality. The Moral Code of the Builder of Communism also requires the aspiring communist to have a feeling of proletarian internationalism and this does receive a certain amount of attention in the literature course. (The Moral Code was formulated by the Communist Party of the Soviet Union in 1961; for text see *Programma* . . ., 1961, pp. 119–22). It is encouraged in part by inspiring sympathy for other workers through stories of the oppressed masses in pre-revolutionary Russia, as in Nekrasov's *Na Volge* (On the Volga), telling of the harsh lives of the Volga boatmen, or Korolenko's *Deti podzemelya* (Children of the Underground). But this is a diachronic feeling of proletarian bonds rather than an international one (i.e. the bonds emphasised are those between Russian workers of all eras rather than between workers of all countries today).

Another facet of the interpretation of proletarian internationalism is its treatment as simply feelings of friendship among the different peoples of the USSR. An article in the journal *Literatura v shkole* (Literature in School) by A. V. Gorskaya (1978) considered the problem of internationalist education as being merely a matter of encouraging non-Russian and Russian pupils in Soviet schools to love each others' languages and literatures. Nowhere is there any suggestion of a broader understanding of the word 'internationalist'. The non-Russian nationalities are well represented in the literature curriculum, but only in the lessons reviewing Soviet literature in the tenth form and in the out-of-school reading lists for the eighth and ninth forms. Shevchenko, the Ukrainian romantic poet, is the only writer of a non-Russian Soviet nationality to whom entire lessons are to be devoted. (He is given two in the sixth form.)

As regards Western literature, the teacher is expected at the end of the tenth form to give a brief survey of contemporary foreign literature. Through this, she must demonstrate 'the struggle of progressive writers against the ideology of imperialism and the influence of reactionary, bourgeois literature' (ibid., p. 51). She is allowed a freedom here (in the choice of which particular works she uses as examples) that is not paralleled anywhere else in the syllabus. This unusual laxity suggests the true weight of proletarian internationalism as a Soviet virtue. These vague foreign works seem likely to be the part of the syllabus most neglected by the teacher who has an overwhelming list of stipulated titles to cover. The relative attention afforded in the curriculum to the potentially contradictory values of patriotism and proletarian internationalism leave one in no doubt as to which, in the event of a clash of loyalties, is to take precedence.

There is in the curriculum never any suggestion that there might be a clash of loyalties – because patriotism is invoked also in the very works which are intended to foster a sense of proletarian internationalism. This is done easily in stories of pre-revolutionary Russia, for Russians, past and present, are shown as being linked by a common intense bond of love for the motherland. To sum up, a fairly marked lip-service is paid to the Marxist virtue of proletarian internationalism, but it is clearly both qualitatively and quantitatively subordinated to the somewhat less well-known Marxist virtue of patriotism.

A communist attitude to labour is a further fundamental characteristic noted by the Moral Code of the Builder of Communism and this is unequivocally stressed in the syllabus. Tvardovskii's poem *Lenin i pechnik* (Lenin and the Stove-Maker) is a useful work in connection with this theme for it describes 'Lenin's respect for labouring man' (ibid., p. 14). Other poems by Tvardovskii are used to illustrate the brotherhood in labour of all Soviet people. Similarly, Mayakovskii's *Rasskaz o kuznetskstroe* (Tale about the Building of Kuznetsk) describes 'the heroism of daily labour' (ibid., p. 26). Therefore it is largely Soviet literature which is used to teach a love for work, though the plot need not necessarily be about the Soviet period: A. N. Tolstoi's *Petr pervyi* (Peter the First), for example, is seen as depicting with fervour 'the creative labour of the Russian people forming a new culture' (ibid., p. 47).

On the other hand, the nineteenth-century works selected which deal with the question of work are frequently condemnations of the cruelties of serf labour – for example, Turgenev's *Mumu* and Griboedov's *Gore ot uma* (Woe from Wit). The point that the disastrous lives of Evgenii Onegin and Pechorin could well be blamed on the lack of useful work their society provided for them to which they could have devoted themselves is, surprisingly, not brought out. Soviet children are frequently reminded through the literature lessons that work is noble, to be respected and enjoyed as long as it is not the exploited work of the pre-revolutionary regime.

Attitudes towards the motherland, internationalism and work are, in this way, felt to be proper areas of concern for the literature class. On the other hand, there is one Soviet virtue which is notably absent despite its presence in the Moral Code of the Builder of Communism.

The notes for teachers at the beginning of the curriculum point out that the works listed in it 'provide rich material for the pupils' anti-religious education, showing how belief in God morally weakens a person, depriving him of freedom of belief in his own strength, making him weak and defenceless' (ibid., p. 6). Yet hardly ever do the notes on individual works refer to this point again. Speaking of Lermontov's epic poem, *Mtsyri*, they mention as one of its major ideological themes its protest against religious morality; the only other direct singling-out of religion as a theme to be discussed is in relation to Odysseus and the ancient Greek gods. It is surprising that such obvious springboards for atheist instruction as, say, corruptness within the Church in Radishchev or the conversion of the heroine in Gor'kii's *Mat'* (Mother) from Christian to revolutionary zeal are not highlighted – even if it is less unexpected that attention is not drawn to the religious threads in Dostoevskii's *Crime and Punishment* or Tolstoi's *Resurrection*. And so the teacher is, in fact, allowed considerable initiative as to how she incorporates atheist education into the literature syllabus – although it is stressed that she must do so in some way.

It is difficult to surmise reasons for this relative neglect of atheist education. By and large, since the truce between Church and State during the war, the Russian Orthodox Church, at least, has been tolerated in Russia. As long as it is not found to be campaigning to convert children and as long as it continues to render Caesar his dues and keeps out of unofficial politics itself, the Orthodox Church is seldom the subject of direct persecution. The Soviet authorities probably believe that eventually, as poverty decreases and education spreads, religion will indeed wither away of its own accord. They doubtless note the signs of doing so that it shows in the West, despite the lack of alternative institutions and rituals to fulfil the functions of religion such as have been deliberately established in the Soviet Union.

THE APPROACH TO LITERARY CRITICISM

Let us now look in more detail at other aspects of the presentation of the literature curriculum. Apart from the moral elements of a book, what characteristics does the teacher single out in discussing a work with her class? What role does character study play? Is much attention paid to language and style? Are literary critics discussed at all?

First, let us consider the role of character study in Soviet schools. 'Compare the characters of Brutus and Cassius' is a familiar English school textbook question. Is the approach similar in the Soviet Union?

Character presentation is looked on as a major method of training in the civic virtues and, as such, is much stressed in the official approach to Soviet literature represented by the syllabus. The noble side of an appropriate character in a book is developed and an effort is made to persuade children to adopt him as a model for their own behaviour.

This method is used extensively with the Soviet literature included in the syllabus. The introductory notes set out as an important aim of the course 'to awaken in pupils the desire to emulate the noble deeds of the positive heroes of pre-October times and, more especially, of Soviet literature and thus to promote the formation of creative, skilful and independent people' (ibid., p. 6). The concept of the inspiring role of the 'positive hero' is central to literature for Soviet adults. This must follow the prescriptions of the artistic theory of socialist realism, one of which is a demand for heroes who embody all that is good in Soviet terms. It is believed that the influence of the positive hero can be even more prolonged and formative on the developing personality of the child than on the adult.

In each of the Soviet works read in the fifth form (at an age – 11 to 12 – when children are particularly susceptible to hero-worship), there are definite positive heroes who are held by the educational authorities to be worthy of imitation. For example, Kataev's *Beleet parus odinokii* (Lone White Sail) tells of children helping their elders during the upheavals of 1905. It traces the formation of the characters by the revolutionary events. L. A. Kassil's *Rasskaz ob otsutstvuyushchem* (Story of an Absent One) and B. N. Polevoi's *Story of a Real Man* both present military heroes of the Second World War.

The most positive of the positive heroes is Lenin. His role as a model for behaviour is paramount. In reading books for primary school children he is a prominent figure and he continues as such even after pupils have progressed from classes in 'reading'. to those in 'literature'. He receives particular attention in the fourth form which studies Tvardovskii's *Lenin and the Stove-Maker*, Inber's *Na smert' Lenina* (On the Death of Lenin), and Marshak's *Lenin*. The fifth form read about Lenin in Isakovskii's *Duma o Lenine* (Thought about Lenin) and in Bednyi's *Snezhinki* (Snowflakes). Neither is he neglected by the older forms. These all read either one or two works about him or else discuss his comments on various nineteenth-century writers.

Who are the other positive heroes with whom Soviet secondary school pupils are encouraged to identify? Two of these are Nastya and Mitrasha in Prishvin's *Kladovaya solntsa* (The Sun's Larder). The lessons which they teach are that man should be 'a good and wise master over nature' and that there must be friendship and mutual help among people. The heroes of Kassil's *Story about an Absent One* are the fallen soldiers of the last war who are seen to demonstrate above all 'courage and humanity'. Their selfless patriotism is also, as we have seen, the most highly valued Soviet quality.

The title of Polevoi's *Story of a Real Man* in itself indicates that the hero of this novel is considered a worthy model for behaviour. It is the story of a war pilot, crippled in a forced landing, who manages to overcome a series of huge obstacles and resume his active duty in the air force. Marc Slonim says of him 'A cripple with artificial limbs, he displays iron will, endurance, contempt for suffering and high moral virtues' (Slonim, 1967, p. 285).

Such then are the types of heroes with whom Soviet school-children are presented in literature lessons and on whom it is considered desirable that they should model themselves. The chief unifying feature of these characters and others like them is their love of the collective with its ultimate expression in patriotism, actively demonstrated by their readiness to sacrifice themselves for their country.

Thus far, it has been shown how the approach to literature in Soviet schools centres round the aspects of the pupils' characters which can be moulded through the works studied. There is another facet of the Soviet approach which is reflected very strikingly in the syllabus. This is the preoccupation of Soviet literary criticism with the historical context of the work under discussion – the historical interpretation being the current Soviet Marxist one. Thus, when in the eighth and ninth forms the students are given a systematic course on pre-revolutionary literature, eleven hours in all are devoted to providing a general historical background to the works under discussion. For example, at the beginning of the ninth form the students are said to be studying 'the literature of the second period of the Russian liberation movement' and they are to be given four lessons on 'the socio-political struggle in Russia in the 1860s and 1870s and its reflection in literature, theatre, art and music' (*Programma* . . ., 1977, p. 35). The Soviet works studied in the tenth form are likewise clearly placed in their historical context.

As a result the curriculum sets each writer or literary movement against a revolutionary historical background. Byron is noted chiefly for his connections with the 'national liberation in Italy and Greece' (ibid., p. 32). Gor'kii is described as 'the new type of writer given birth to by the revolutionary epoch' (ibid., p. 42) and one of the most highlighted aspects of Pushkin is 'his role in the liberation movement of the Russian people' (ibid., p. 31). Foreign, Russian classical and Soviet authors are wherever possible placed in a framework of the motion of society – especially revolutionary change. Similarly, the content of a work is almost always related to its historical, or social and political background. In this way, Griboedov's play, *Woe from Wit*, is summed up as showing 'the protest of the leading people of the nineteenth century against the reactionary political and spiritual values of a land-owning society' (ibid., p. 30). Similarly the teacher is reminded to draw attention to the 'historical events depicted' when discussing Tolstoi's *Kavkazskii plennik* (Caucasian Captive) (ibid., p. 13).

Thus the Soviet child is frequently reminded of the fact that, to a Marxist, literature is part of a superstructure determined by an economic base. This is, of course, a justifiable approach to the study of literature but its constant re-emphasis perhaps suggests that the authorities also find it a useful intellectual mechanism for legitimating the present.

Soviet literary criticism in schools therefore, first and foremost, emphasises a work's educational significance and its historical background. What place is left for aesthetic appreciation?

A sense of the aesthetic, say the teacher's notes, is a quality to be developed in Soviet youth. Children must be given an appreciation of what is beautiful. The reason for giving them this is not so much the wish to open them up to the intense personal joy which an awareness of the beautiful can provide, but rather the will to inspire in them the desire to fight for what is beautiful in life. Again, the utilitarian and social rather than individual and personal aspects of art are stressed. An extension of teaching children an appreciation of art is that they will learn to love, in particular, their native Russian literature. And so once more the virtue of patriotism is invoked.

The question, 'What is beauty?', too, is given a social answer in the Soviet Union. The nature of the beautiful is explained below by the psychologist, K. K. Platonov, in a discussion with a laboratory worker who claims that, as a man of science, he knows nothing about art or beauty:

'The sense of the beautiful came into being in human history as a product of social development and, in each person, this manifests itself in the process of personal aesthetic education, which is inseparable from general development.'
'But tastes differ', my opponent persisted.
'I think you also have a wrong idea of this saying . . . Chernyshev-skii convincingly demonstrated that the criteria of beauty really differ with the different classes but are uniform enough within that

class. According to their criteria, all peasants consider beautiful a fresh complexion, high colour covering the whole cheek, and sturdy build – i.e. the result of continuous physical work under good natural conditions. Their taste differs from that of the people who have developed the ideal of the woman of fashion with small, delicate hands, unhealthy pallor, weakness and languor which are the result of a rich, but physically inactive life . . .'

'But what is the beautiful? How can one learn to see it?' my interlocutor began to give in.

'Then listen to me', I said. 'The beautiful is life. That being is beautiful in which we see life as we think it should be. That thing is beautiful which manifests life or reminds us about life. These are Chernyshevskii's words.' (Platonov, 1965, p. 213)

Thus beauty, as it is interpreted to the Soviet child, is no abstract ideal of truth set in a sphere of existence isolated from the practicalities of science; it is totally dependent on social conditions and finds its very nature in them.

In the notes on individual works, the purely aesthetic aspects of a particular novel or poem are comparatively rarely mentioned. In the remarks about *Hamlet*, for example, no mention at all is made of the poetry or the beauty of the language, although this can perhaps be explained by the fact that Soviet children are reading it in translation and the poetic language loses something in translation, despite the excellence of the Russian version. But yet even the comments on Esenin make no allusion to the very characteristic artistic features of his style – to, say, the richness of his vocabulary or the vividness of his imagery. The notes deal solely with content:

> His poetisation of his native heath. His love for the Motherland. His tragic awareness of his own alienation from the *avant-garde* of the revolutionary masses. His aspirations to put an end to this alienation. The complete sincerity and deep lyricism of Esenin's poems. Folk-song traditions in Esenin's works. (*Programma* . . ., 1977, p. 45)

The comments show a similar tendency, even when treating Push-kin and Mayakovskii, both of whom in their different ways are very significant from the point of view of language, since both introduced remarkable innovations in style and versification. These are referred to in the notes but only in the vaguest of terms. About Mayakovskii, for example, all that is said is 'The continuer of the best traditions of the nineteenth century. The innovations of Mayakovskii.' (ibid., p. 46). Detail, on the other hand, is given about the themes and content of his various works. And so, although an appreciation of the aesthetic and of style is given a place in the teacher's notes, it is certainly in a subordinate position in relation to the content or the social significance of the work in question.

Russian teachers' literature recognises this teaching of style and literary methods as 'the weakest link in the literary instruction of secondary school pupils'. It is regretted that the overwhelming majority of school-leavers cannot distinguish an iamb and has not fully mastered 'such basic concepts of literature as national spirit (*narodnost'*) and party spirit (*partiinost'*), socialist realism, and so on' (Rotkovich, 1965, p. 309). One of the ways in which the school literature syllabus has changed since the early 1970s is that notes have now been added throughout headed 'theory of literature'. These are usually vague. For instance, on the nineteenth-century writer Fonvizin, the theory note says 'Understanding of the literary school, classicism' (ibid., p. 28). After Sholokhov the notes say 'Development of the pupils' understanding of the party spirit of literature. Party spirit and national spirit in Soviet literature' (ibid., p. 48).

Which theorists are acknowledged as the originators of the approach to literature presented in the school curriculum?

Apart from Lenin, critics are mentioned only rarely in the syllabus. Attention is drawn to Lenin's views on Radishchev, Herzen, Belinskii, Turgenev, Nekrasov, Tolstoi, Saltykov-Shchedrin, Chernyshevskii, Chekhov and Gor'kii. His on the whole unfavourable opinion of Mayakovskii is not referred to. The lessons given over to the general historical background of literature also draw heavily on Lenin's writings. For example, in the ninth form, two hours are to be devoted to 'the world significance of Russian literature' (ibid., p. 40) and the notes for these two lessons open with the words 'Lenin on the universal significance of Russian literature'. In the few introductory lessons before pupils follow a systematic course on Soviet literature in the tenth form, pupils are to be told of Lenin's writings on the party spirit of literature and of his belief in the need for the mastery of the classical heritage. They are to be directed to two specific articles by Lenin on literary criticism. Indeed, the introductory teaching notes at the beginning of the curriculum claim that 'the teacher's main task is to make the pupils deeply aware of the basic ideas and stances of the works of Lenin and of the documents of the Party on questions of literature and art' (ibid., p. 7). The teacher is even here recommended a book on how to work with Lenin's writings in literature lessons for the eighth to tenth forms. This is the only case in which such guidance is given to specific teacher's notes elsewhere.

Apart from Lenin, the only other individual critics whose writings are discussed at all are the classical ones of the nineteenth century – Belinskii, Dobrolyubov and Pisarev – all of whom are notable for their radical approach, which stresses the social rather than the aesthetic significance of a work and is thus in line with the main strand in Marxist–Leninist criticism.

Mention must also be made here, however, of the Party itself as a literary critic. In the quotation above attention was drawn to the basic stances both of Lenin and of the Party. Like Lenin, the Party is much more prominent in the 1977/8 syllabus than it was in the otherwise very similar syllabus for 1971/2. The Party is said in the notes to 'stand for variety and richness in form and style worked out on the basis of socialist realism. It highly values the talent of an artist, the communist tendency of his work, his irreconcilability to all that prevents our movement forward' (ibid., p. 8). In the notes on specific works throughout the tenth-form Soviet literature course, the teacher is told to refer to the Party as a literary authority. In particular, pupils are to learn about the statements of the 24th and 25th Party Congresses on the tasks of Soviet literature.

A significant result of the approach to literary criticism described above is that no room is left for conflicting schools of thought about the meaning and significance of a work. Nowhere in the syllabus is there any suggestion of different interpretations of, say, Hamlet's behaviour, the character of Pechorin, or the conflicts in Mayakovskii. The one approach is set out very simply in a way that may be helpful in conveying a clear and coherent account to school-children; for the upper forms, at least, though, the degree of dogmatism in the programme does seem excessive. In this, however, it reflects the state of Soviet literary criticism as a whole in displaying a remarkable uniformity and monolithism of approach.

We have seen above the way in which the Soviet child is taught to read literature, if – and this is important – he is taught by someone who undeviatingly follows the official guidelines. He is encouraged to look on novels and poems as social instructors providing him with positive heroes, models of patriotism and the other Soviet virtues, whom he can emulate. He will set each work read in its historical context as presented to him, and try to glean from it illumination about society rather than individual psychology. For him, the litera-ture class is less likely to be deadened by discussions of anapæsts and litotes than it is – or until recently was – for many an English pupil. Content can thus legitimately interest him far more than method and he is taught to accept that there is only one true interpretation of that content – the Marxist–Leninist one. The approach described above is intended to lead to reading habits which, teachers are told, need to be taught in Soviet schools; they must significantly affect the reading of the child (both in and out of school) and of the adult.

Durkheim assigned to the teaching of literature 'only a secondary and accessory role in moral education' (Durkheim, 1973, p. 267). It has been demonstrated that the Soviet authorities would not agree with him in this. Durkheim saw the teaching of literature and the other arts as simply instruction in aesthetics and the appreciation of the beautiful, with a moral value only in so far as it lifted pupils above themselves and their own everyday concerns. Soviet educationists attribute a much broader function to the teaching of literature in schools. Not only is the content of the works studied in school usually seen to be morally instructive, but also the approach to the interpretation of the works has a deliberately educative nature.

This approach to literary teaching in Soviet schools is characteristic of Soviet society as a whole in its patriotic collectivist and thoroughly goal-directed emphases. It also typifies Soviet society in the way that the literature lesson is so explicitly and systematically used as an agent of socialisation.

BIBLIOGRAPHY

Durkheim, E., *Moral Education* (London: Collier-Macmillan, 1973).
Gorskaya, A. V., 'Vospityvat' internatsionalistov', *Literatura v shkole*, 1978, no. 1, pp. 25–8.
Kissel', A. A., 'K analizu problemy sotsial'nogo vospitaniya' in *Voprosy filosofii i sotsiologii*, Vol. 2 (Leningrad, 1970), pp. 57–61.
Neuburg, P., *The Hero's Children; the Post-War Generation in Eastern Europe* (London: Constable, 1972).
Platonov, K., *Psychology as You May Like It* ((Moscow: Progress, 1965).
Programma Kommunisticheskoi partii Sovetskogo Soyuza, prinyata XXII s"ezdom KPSS (Moscow, 1961).
Programma vos'miletnei i srednei shkoly na 1977/8 uchebnyi god; russkaya literatura (Moscow, 1977).
Rotkovich, Ya. A., *Ocherki po istorii prepodavaniya literatury v sovetskoi shkole* (Moscow, 1965).
Slonim, M., *Soviet Russian Literature* (Oxford: OUP, 1967).

6

Soviet Boarding Education: its Rise and Progress*

JOHN DUNSTAN

INTRODUCTION

A campaign to establish a countrywide system of boarding schools, heralded as the schools of the future, was launched in the USSR in 1956, but by the early 1960s was already foundering; by the middle of the decade the development of the schools had been halted, on the grounds of cost to the state and, so it was rumoured, unpopularity with the public. This is the customary miniature of the boarding school episode. Basically a faithful representation, it nevertheless scales down a reality that was much more complex.

The topic has received some attention from earlier writers. The fullest work hitherto is the doctoral thesis of Schapker (1972); this gives a comprehensive though rather 'official' picture of the daily life of the school. There are two especially useful articles by Kaser (1968, 1969). Other studies in English are those of Ambler (1961), Bakalo (1964), Roberts (1966), and Weeks (1962, 1965). Several Western works on Soviet education and social institutions deal in passing with residential schools; of these the most informative is probably Madison (1968). A general study of boarding education which includes the Soviet case is Fraser (1968). There are hundreds of Soviet articles and pamphlets on the subject, and a small number of more extensive works ranging from scholarly studies to autobiographical or semi-autobiographical accounts.

Recently a substantial piece of research on residential education in

* This is a slightly altered and abbreviated version of a paper presented to the 4th International Conference of the Institut für Pädagogik, Ruhr-Universität Bochum and the Deutsche Gesellschaft für Osteuropakunde at Vlotho in October 1977, and first published as 'Die sowjetische Internatserziehung-Entstehung, Zielsetzungen, Probleme und Ergebnisse' in O. Anweiler (ed.), *Erziehungs- und Sozialisationsprobleme in der Sowjetunion, der DDR und Polen* (Hannover: Hermann Schroedel Verlag, 1978). It appears with the kind agreement of Messrs Schroedel. An earlier draft was read to the last meeting of the CREES Soviet Education Group to be chaired by Geoffrey Barker.

England was reported (Lambert, Bullock and Millham, 1975), and to that end a useful conceptual framework was devised (Millham, Bullock and Cherrett, 1975). Although the latter explains little in itself, it does clear the ground for explanation, and both studies provide insights which may contribute to an understanding of the historical development of the boarding school system in the USSR. Millham and his associates dub their scheme 'a working compromise between sociological irreconcilables', incorporating structural-functional features as well as a consideration of the individual's perceptions of his social situation and his expectations of it. Ideally, one would identify and analyse not only different types of the institution's goals (described by Millham, after Parsons, as *instrumental* or concerned with the transmission of skills and acquisition of qualifications, *expressive* or concerned with desired states of being, and *organisational* or concerned with the maintenance of the organisation itself) and its functions, but also the individual's perceptions of and reactions to these goals and functions and the effect of such perceptions on the latter's changing relative preponderance over time.

This second desideratum, however, is primarily the object of future action. The present contribution attempts to build on earlier work by tracing the Soviet origins of the boarding school and its development over the twenty years 1956–75, establishing the goals set, the problems and conflicts thereby encountered, and their outcomes, which reflected noteworthy but certainly not complete change from the original concept. Boarding schools with specific allocative functions, being a different genre, are excluded from our considerations; those for children of high ability have been examined elsewhere (Dunstan, 1978).

ORIGINS

The pre-Soviet history of residential education in Russia, dating back to the beginning of the eighteenth century, is outlined in Kaser (1969). The Revolution came, and with it the increasingly urgent need to map out and begin to implement a plan for the schooling of the future. Ideological principle and socio-economic reality combined to heighten interest in boarding education. The stormy debates of 1918 in the Commissariat of Education (Narkompros) revealed deep differences as to the context of education: while both the Petrograd and the Moscow groups favoured progressive methods and polytechnism, the more extreme Moscow line was that children should belong less to the family than to the school, which should take the form of an all-the-year-round working community. They would acquire their labour skills in the process of running this collectively organised, self-supporting commune (Anweiler, 1964, pp. 112–16; Fitzpatrick, 1970, pp. 29–30). Vera Pozner declared: 'The new school-commune forms the germ-cell of the future communist society' (*Protokoly . . .*, 1919, p. 32). This exaggeration of the undoubted importance of productive labour, to the extent of the school being so fused with life that it would lose not only its function of mediating subject knowledge but its very identity, was rejected by the Petrograd group. Their more moderate view prevailed and is represented in the Decree on the Unified Labour School of 30 September 1918. Secondary sources on the 1918 debates in the RSFSR give the impression that at an early stage the specific role of boarding was scarcely a predominant issue – only N. A. Polyanskii's proposals for a 'school-village' come to mind (Anweiler, 1964, pp. 171–2) – but the notion of the 'full school day' in the Moscow programme anticipates that of the extended day introduced later.

Discussion continued, however, experimentation thrived, and 'life itself dictated' the creation and preservation of residential institutions, many of which came to be regarded as models for the communist upbringing of the future. The tsarist *vospitatel'nye doma* had been taken over to be run as children's homes or colonies by the Commissariat of Social Security, being transferred to Narkompros in 1919; and, as additional weapons in the battle against child neglect and vagrancy, school-communes and children's villages (*detskie gorodki*) were set up. They varied widely, but had a common official goal, the rearing of a new type of person, and shared the organisational principle of collective self-help (Fitzpatrick, 1970, p. 227; Prokoshev, 1964). Their immediate function, however, was that of a comprehensive child-welfare agency. Although the Soviet encyclopedia of education gives two quite separate definitions of the term *shkoly-kommuny*, the first referring to experimental institutions and the second to social-care organisations (*Pedagogicheskaya entsiklopediya*, 1968, col. 726), such a distinction was not initially intended. Rather, the welfare institutions were regarded as seedbeds for new socialist upbringing. They varied in calibre and in the ability to cope with adverse circumstances; but those same circumstances often helped to create a sort of embattled solidarity cloaking a dysfunctionalism which more peaceful times would expose.

In the Ukraine, however, a different pattern was emerging. In July 1919 it was decreed that its Narkompros should draw up fundamental statutes for the social upbringing of all children from birth to maturity (Kobzar', 1967, p. 17). With the extended school day as a traditional measure, the goal of full residential education for all children became, for the first time in Soviet educational history, the official line in the 'Declaration on the Social Upbringing of Children' of 1 July 1920. (Extended-day schools were also set up in Petrograd in 1920 and were commended by Lunacharskii and Krupskaya [Opitz, 1965, pp. 227, 229].) The Ukrainians proposed to make the 'children's home' the basic unit of the public upbringing of children to the age of 14 or 15, as the highest – and in the future the only – form of this. The Declaration saw virtue in lessening the influence of the individualistic family and also referred candidly to the 'incipient' withering away of the school (Anweiler, 1964, pp. 151–2, 173–5). This latter notion was sharply criticised by Lunacharskii at the 1st Party Conference on Public Education at the turn of 1920–1 (Kobzar', 1967, p. 18); the tensions in the situation were evident from the compromising tone of the Conference's resolution that although the children's home was the most appropriate form for socialist education, in Russia boarding education for all was not yet feasible.

The Ukrainians nevertheless went ahead, and for a time children's homes, the great majority catering for pre-school as well as school-age children, expanded along with 'day children's homes' (extended-day schools), homes for adolescents aged 14 to 17, and, as the most advanced form of public upbringing, children's villages, which included up to twenty-five homes and a production enterprise. The famine year 1921 accelerated the development of children's homes. But they were costly – the annual expenditure per pupil being 160 gold roubles compared to 15 in an ordinary school (Kobzar', 1967, p. 19) – and at the start of 1923 much of the funding of educational institutions was transferred to local budgets. Meanwhile, large numbers of homeless and starving children kept their welfare function to the fore. The 1923 education census reported that during 1922 the school had gained ascendancy and 'the role of the children's homes as the ideal form of social upbringing is gradually being sullied and ultimately amounts to more or less organised child care (*prizrenie*)'. 'Day children's homes' were in actual decline (*Narodnoe obrazovanie Ukrainy* . . ., 1924, pp. ix, xli, xliii, xlvii). This erosion of the children's home ideal was also noted in the RSFSR at about the same time by M. V. Krupenina, one of its staunchest supporters (Anweiler, 1964, p. 229).

Numerically, children's residential welfare institutions and their inmates were at their zenith in the Ukraine on 1 January 1923, with provision for some 94,000. By December 1927 nearly one in four had closed and their complement had almost halved (*Narodnya osvita* . . ., 1928, p. xix). An alternative total for 1923, cited by Anweiler (1964, p. 198n), is 114,000. Even with this higher figure, the ratio of children in welfare institutions to those in schools would have been only one in twelve or thirteen; by the end of 1927 the ratio was one in sixty-four. An exact picture of the relative capacity of schools and residential establishments as providers of education is not possible, however, partly because the 1923 education census reflects the disorganisation of the day and also because a minority of children attended outside schools full- or part-time.

The notion of the complete institutional upbringing of children was again extensively discussed at the end of the decade in connection with the planning of the new 'socialist cities', and in 1930 even showed some signs of becoming reality with its forceful advocacy by that fiery prophet of the death of the school V. N. Shul'gin and with temporary Party backing. Shul'gin and the majority of the left were not, however, in favour of segregating children from adults, because sharing in adult working life was to be the primary context of learning; parents should have limited access to their children in a communal setting (Shul'gin, 1930, pp. 11, 16–19). But such views were inopportune. The reassertion of the school's role by the Central Committee decree of 25 August 1931 meant in fact that the Ukrainian episode as an instance of implemented policy was the first and last forerunner of the universal boarding school project of the Khrushchev era. As such it ought to have received more attention thirty years on, as in spite of very different social conditions it would have taught a number of lessons that had to be learnt all over again.

Lofty societal goals were set and precipitately pursued, apparently without realistic appraisal of the physical resources necessary to achieve them. These included not only funds and materials but also, probably, qualified personnel – the problems of fluctuating cadres and 'casual persons' (*sluchainye lyudi*) cited elsewhere (Anweiler, 1964, pp. 229–30) with respect to 1927–8 are likely to have applied earlier once the homes and communes were developed beyond a few model institutions – and even the charismatic Makarenko sometimes had problems with his staff (for example, Makarenko, 1973, pp. 247–51, 261–5). A recent Ukrainian commentator adduces a further cause of failure: temporary difficulties, having brought about a certain economic weakening of the family, were mistakenly exalted by prominent educators into 'socialist legality', leading allegedly to the family's complete destruction and the liquidation of family upbringing (Leshchenko, 1969, p. 13). Residential education was to give family child-rearing the final push into oblivion.

It is also arguable that the obvious necessity for the homes and communes as welfare institutions generated by socio-economic conditions, coupled with the physical limitations on their development which those same circumstances induced, tended to conceal parental opposition to them which would find expression in less dislocated times. But nevertheless hostility was experienced even then by the model communes. We need not limit ourselves to the Ukrainian experience. The Narkompros School Commune was founded by P. N. Lepeshinskii in his native village of Litvinovichi in Belorussia in autumn 1918; he assembled a group of pupils only in the teeth of fierce resistance by the local people. When a revolt broke out in Gomel' province the following year an attempt was made to destroy the commune; and circumstances necessitated its permanent evacuation to Moscow with twenty-two pupils, the rest being kept back by their parents (Molotkov, 1966, pp. 142–4). In 1920 Krupskaya commented, during her journey on the *Krasnaya zvezda*, that the population of Rybnaya Sloboda 'hates the word "school-commune" ' (cited in Fitzpatrick, 1970, p. 55). Once opposition had been overcome, however, and the parents had adapted to the new situation, a fresh problem might arise which only a few extremists welcomed: abdication of all parental responsibility. The pitiful appeal of the children of the Banner of Labour Commune, Kurganinsk district, in their wall newspaper won a sympathetic hearing from Shul'gin himself:

> We so want to tell you what our life's like today,
> How we're doing in our Sakhalin far away . . .
> Oh, in you, mums and dads, we don't strike any chords:
> You yourselves sleep on pillows, and we sleep on boards.

This is my translation from Raskin (1930, p. 121); Sakhalin was, of course, a traditional place of banishment. Complete isolation of children from parents, except those deemed unfit to exercise parental rights, has never been part of official Soviet policy; but varying degrees of contact have been tried out, and parents' sometimes contradictory attitudes to these and to the residential idea will require further attention.

The residential idea need not detain us long over the next twenty-five years; I omit arrangements for young people in vocational training. In the mid-1920s the first boarding schools had arisen for children of the nationalities, for example in the Far North, and annexes at rural schools had begun to be expanded; a statute on school hostels was approved in September 1941 and another in June 1948. These may be the institutions that Beatrice King (1942) described as weekly boarding schools; 'though where possible', she added, 'homes are found in the neighbourhood, as home life is considered preferable to institutional life'. In accordance with a RSFSR Council of Ministers decree of November 1955, extended-day groups for forms 1 to 4 were opened in the schools of Moscow and Leningrad (this development was put on an all-RSFSR basis a year later), and the draft directives for the 20th Party Congress published on 15 January 1956 called for expansion of the school hostel network. These are reminders that Khrushchev's boarding school reform, though announced suddenly, was not an isolated phenomenon, nor should it have been very astonishing in view of recent discussion in educational and government circles. But it was.

GOALS

During the summer and autumn of 1955 there had been a public debate on the improvement of young people's standards of conduct, culminating in the RSFSR Ministry of Education decree published on 19 October in *Uchitel'skaya gazeta*, the teachers' newspaper, 'On Strengthening Conscious Discipline in the School'. The burden of the decree was that upbringing in general must receive much closer attention by education agencies, and a lack of parental efficacy is clearly implied. The launching of the boarding school project by Khrushchev in the Central Committee's report to the 20th Congress on 14 February 1956 must be seen against this background. The schools were to be the main centre of interest in a general campaign to improve all forms of state upbringing, the most thoroughgoing way to achieve the ends served by extended-day education and residential annexes, and yet more; and the chiliastic utterance seems to have been very much Khrushchev's own. Boarding schools were not mentioned, for example, in the pre-congress editorial of the February issue of *Sovetskaya pedagogika* on the new stage of development of the Soviet school; not until the April issue was anything said, and then not in detail until June. The Academy of Pedagogical Sciences (APN) appears to have been taken by surprise. Minister of Education Kairov's tribute to 'Comrade Khrushchev's proposal' in the congress discussion looks suspiciously like a late insertion ('XX s"ezd . . .', 1956). Even *Uchitel'skaya gazeta* ran no articles on the subject until 14 April.

Khrushchev's initial remarks on boarding schools, and their immediate setting, demand closer scrutiny. They were made in the context of creating the spiritual wherewithal for completing the transition from the lower stage of communism to the higher. Khrushchev then referred to the child-rearing difficulties of widows and working parents. Alluding to forms of residential upbringing favoured by privileged classes in the past, he said that the socialist state must organise this much better, to form the builders of a new society. Well-designed and equipped boarding schools with good staff should be established in pleasant localities. Children should be admitted on the request of parents, who could visit them during holidays or after hours. Fees should be related to family size and income, varying from zero to full cost. No expense of effort or funds on the schools' behalf should be spared (Khrushchev, 1956). From this three main points may be extracted: the schools are to be model institutions, raising model citizens (but not an élite – this early Western misinterpretation sprang from a failure to consider Khrushchev's remarks within their social context); they are also to perform a welfare function; and they envisage the voluntary cession of children by their parents, not absolutely, but certainly from their home environment. How carefully Khrushchev had thought through these ideas might well be asked.

Before moving to a consideration of the ensuing problems it is appropriate to examine how the stated goals of the boarding schools were elaborated during their earlier years. To fill out the Khrushchevian picture as a starting point, reference may be made to the Statute on Boarding Schools (*V pomoshch'* . . ., 1958, pp. 17–28; a very free translation is to be found in Redl, 1964, pp. 167–76) approved by the RSFSR Council of Ministers on 13 April 1957 after over a year of drafting and redrafting, reflecting controversy among educationists and administrators. Its opening section on aims is very close to the preamble of the Central Committee of the Party and Council of Ministers decree 'On the Organisation of Boarding Schools' of 15 September 1956, which called them 'a new type of educational institution . . . to solve at a higher level the problems of training educated, thoroughly developed builders of communism' (*Spravochnik* . . ., 1957, pp. 289–92). The most favourable conditions were to be created for all-round general and polytechnical education, the inculcation of high moral qualities, physical and aesthetic development, and training for various branches of the economy. Lenin's demand to combine teaching with productive labour must be constantly implemented. These phrases indicate clearly that the schools were also to have an important role in the polytechnisation of secondary education which was already the subject of wide experimentation and was soon to become law. But the welfare function, singled out in the very limited discussion at the 20th Congress (Voroshilov, 1956; 'XX s"ezd . . .', 1956) is not presented as a *goal* – perhaps this would be illogical as many of the factors necessitating it ought to disappear with social progress – although priority for need cases is made explicit later in the document. As to Khrushchev's high expectations of the family's capacity for self-abnegation, the statute modifies these by allowing home visits and the admission of day pupils to the schools.

The holistic official view of Soviet education doubtless contributed to the frequent definition of the goals of residential schooling in global terms. The aims of, first, contributing substantially to the achievement of eight- or ten-year education as more systematic and efficient provision, especially for underprivileged groups (rural and nomadic children, Moslem girls), and secondly, becoming an educational vanguard ('the prototype of the school of the future', Kairov's successor as minister called them [Afanasenko, 1961*b*, p. 14]) combined instrumental and expressive elements. Thus the functions to be served by the schools in pursuance of these goals were allocative (producing model citizens, training for *specific* occupations); integrative (transmitting skills, values and norms of behaviour); and administrative (welfare). But the first allocative function was not immanent; inevitable at first, it was to disappear as the vanguard became the mass.

A third general aim is interesting because of its far-reaching implications as well as changing attitudes to it. It was first broached, apparently, by an educationist: 'The main purpose of the boarding school is to begin the transition to the public upbringing of *all* children in state institutions . . .' (Lyalin, 1956; my italics). However, he rejected the isolation of children from the family. N. A. Petrov, who at this time may be regarded as the spokesman of the Academy of Pedagogic Sciences on boarding schools, saw them as 'becoming a mass institution catering for all children', but only in the long term (Petrov, 1956, p. 7). When Kairov recovered his breath he began to speak of them in somewhat millenarian language: when complete they would include a nursery and a nursery school, too (Kairov, 1956). The following day *Pravda* itself stated that the boarding school must in the long run become the school for all children ('Shkoly-internaty', 1956). But after this, teething troubles muted such talk until the eve of the 1959–65 plan period, when Khrushchev urged: 'The sooner we provide nurseries, nursery schools and boarding schools for all children, the sooner and more successfully the task of the communist upbringing of the rising generation will be achieved' (Khrushchev, 1958). At the 21st Party Congress he stated that such a possibility was planned, and not less than 2·5 million children would be in these schools by 1965 (Khrushchev, 1959). What the people thought about it will be considered below; meanwhile it may be noted that the general line on the development of residential education expressed to members of the Comparative Education Society a few months earlier had not tallied with this, the relief of need being the sole (and limited) criterion; the only significant exception, taking a wider view, had been the Uzbek Deputy Minister of Education (Bereday, Brickman and Read, 1960, p. 208).

Fourthly, boarding schools were to enhance the social and economic position of women. Khrushchev also pointed this out at the 21st Congress. (Previously the social and economic advantages of boarding had customarily been presented in terms of benefit to parents of both sexes.) This may be seen either in expressive terms as a contribution to the quest for an end-state, the *de facto* achievement of women's emancipation, with improved opportunities for participation in production and public life; in expressive-instrumental terms as providing women with the chance to develop their interests, skills, knowledge, qualifications and economic independence as ends in themselves; or as the instrumental goal of releasing women for jobs or training for jobs in order to supplement the workforce, or alleviating the pressures on those already employed and thus perhaps improving their performance. Lack of child-care facilities has been cited as the major reason why jobs are not sought by women of working age who are unemployed (26 per cent in 1959 – figure derived from Dodge, 1966, p. 37). The 1959–65 Seven-Year Plan aimed at an additional 5 to 6 million women workers; the interests of women and the state appeared in this to be one.

Expressive goals are evident in the enhancement of the child-rearing aspects of the school's work (*vospitanie*). The character education mentioned in the statute was to be promoted by continuity of tutorial oversight through the school, and 'unified demands' would be facilitated through the elimination of parent–teacher conflict and, as far as possible, that of unfavourable environmental influences. Extreme cases where boarding schools had an obvious compensatory or indeed surrogate role were those of child neglect or cruelty, but more specialised tasks of value inculcation came to be assigned to them in countering strong cultural, religious or nationalistic influences (Mirbabaev, 1956; Namsons, 1966, pp. 66, 71–2). Except in really atypical circumstances, however, the family was not to be excluded, but, as in other sectors of Soviet education, necessitated systematic intervention by the teacher. Thus, drawing up a detailed plan of work with her class's families, a tutor notes that she must have a chat with Sima Sidorova's grandmother, who gave the girl a crucifix (Alpatov, 1958, p. 66). The school–family relationship was often presented in terms of a goal of 'helping' parents with upbringing: if a boarding pupil only saw his parents relaxed and receptive to him, the family was strengthened (Gmurman, quoted in Bereday, 1960, p. 210). The brevity of the encounters, presumably, would obviate spoiling.

Residential education within the collective of peers would also compensate for demographic factors likely to mar upbringing; in the early 1960s, approximately half of families with children had only one child, who ran a heightened risk of growing up over-indulged and self-centred (Redl, 1964, p. 75; Kharchev, 1964, p. 272). Other demographic factors caused a different kind of need for assistance with upbringing. The law of 1944, exempting unmarried fathers from alimony payment with the aims of boosting the birth rate, had led to a tenfold increase in the number of single mothers receiving child allowances between 1945 and 1957 when they peaked at some 2·8 million (deduced from Sonin, 1967). By 1956, substantial numbers of these children must have been in primary school, and some were beginning to enter the secondary stage. This presages an increasing demand for boarding education by such cases of need which would not decline until 1965. Except for the children of war disabled, other need categories presumably remained fairly constant. Poor conditions for child-rearing due to cramped housing were another problem which residential education was intended to alleviate. (This is rarely mentioned in the press, but see Fraser, 1963, p. 82, and Bronfen-brenner, 1968, p. 111.) Even after its heyday, the vanishing *babushka* (grandmother) and the consequently increasing incidence of latchkey children were to sustain a demand for more public upbringing in one form or another.

The predominantly instrumental goals of residential schooling were twofold and closely related. First, as the statute made clear, the new schools should become beacons of polytechnical education. The combination of labour with learning and the linking of the school more closely with life were to be achieved with maximum efficiency by means of sustained and systematic exposure to desired influences including local production activity, a superior technical base, the finest cadres, and good teacher–pupil ratios. The number of pupils was laid down as thirty per class (contrasting with day schools, where according to legislation of 1959 the maxima were forty for forms 1 to 8 and thirty-five thereafter); classes with at least twenty pupils could be split for foreign language and labour. The inter-relationship with expressive goals in the mutual reinforcement of performance and attitude is indeed patent, but here we wish to stress the immense expectations placed in the schools regarding the development of cognitive and conative abilities and the improvement of careers guidance, with consequent enhancement of young people's life chances and reduction of inequality of opportunity. Good examples of this were the comments expressed at the All-Union Conference on Boarding Schools of April 1957 by V. N. Stoletov, then Deputy Minister of Higher Education, and Academician Nesmeyanov, President of the USSR Academy of Sciences, who wished the conference success in the discovery and training of Mendeleevs (Kazmin', 1958, pp. 127, 129–31). Secondly, such model institutions were to serve as research centres for experiment and innovation in polytechnical education ('The new stage . . .', 1959, p. 7).

Organisational goals, developed by an institution to facilitate its own self-maintenance, might have been expected to arise in a situation where the prospects for order, regimen and control in the everyday life of the inmates were so often described as particularly favourable. A typical account, listing the advantages of boarding schools over ordinary ones, cites not only good teaching conditions and material conditions but also round-the-clock supervision by experienced pedagogues and the possibility of organising a correct routine (*rezhim*) of study, labour and leisure (Gud and Senkevich, 1963, p. 4). Part of the Soviet tradition of the purposeful approach, such features are unexceptionable, unless perhaps one is a believer in progressive education; but great vigilance would be necessary lest the means to the end of more effective education became the end in themselves and conflicted with other goals. Finally, although this was never explicit, it is possible to regard the original boarding school project as an idiosyncratic self-strengthening device of the state, in that, by virtue of their very existence and performance of their function of producing a higher type of Soviet person, these establishments reflected, if in narrow confines, the state's task of consolidating and perpetuating itself. These, it is suggested, were the goals of 1956, official or potential. But what was the reality?

PROBLEMS

The boarding schools were born in chaos. As soon as the press discussion opened there were complaints of the absence of guidelines and supplementary funding (Korenev, 1956; 'Byt' na urovne . . .', 1956), which was blamed on the Ministry of Education; other voices warned against excessive haste (Mer, 1956; Gamagelyan and Pluzyan, 1956); while the Central Committee held a special conference, attended by Khrushchev, which resulted in an *Uchitel'skaya gazeta* editorial criticising ministers of education, local education authorities and executive committees of local Soviets for their faint-heartedness and exhorting them to action and economy ('Soveschanie . . .', 1956; 'Delo . . .', 1956). Staff were hurriedly selected and seminars and summer courses organised in some places. The first intake of pupils in the autumn of 1956 comprised 56,000 but the shortage of time to prepare meant that a number of buildings were ill-adapted and lacked satisfactory residential, teaching and/or recreational facilities (Naumov, 1957). Most boarding schools were converted from ordinary schools and others from teacher-training schools or children's homes. Although good tutors might sometimes be transferred from children's homes, the teachers were mainly young and inexperienced and the children predominantly disadvantaged youngsters from many different schools (e.g. *Pervye shagi*, 1958, pp. 6–7; Demidenko *et al.*, 1960, p. 9). There then followed the problem of developing well-integrated collectives of teaching and tutorial staff and pupils.

Against all this, it was often said, the directors, initially at least, were outstanding for their leadership qualities; they selected staff who made up in enthusiasm for anything they lacked in expertise, and together they quickly developed know-how along with the solidarity of fighting the good fight. Many of the schools were highly successful; evidence of this can be adduced from contemporary accounts. (Nearly ten years on, it was to be authoritatively stated that the very first schools were still the best [Shirvindt, 1966]). However, it is necessary to take the long, retrospective view, and with hindsight it is clear that some of the troubles facing the first schools were in fact endemic, springing from their very nature, and although they would not kill them they would certainly stunt their growth. It will be convenient to examine these problems in accordance with goal categories, i.e. in relation to the schools' expressive goals (and their child-rearing and welfare functions); instrumental goals (their teaching and training functions); and their combined goals (vanguard of the universal institution with its wider benefits). It will be necessary to discern their relationship with organisational goals.

Something of the nature and extent of the tasks of these pioneering institutions can be pictured from an analysis of their pupil composition. This is available in terms of social need for three republics (see Table 6.1). The conflated data do not match perfectly but are nevertheless serviceable. It appears that between 80 and 100 per cent of the schools' intake comprised cases of need. If large numbers of these were from unsatisfactory home backgrounds, problems of behaviour and attainment might be expected; the boarding school would have to compensate for the inadequacies of the family and at the same time work out some kind of relationship with it.

There were certainly many reports of difficult children. In the early days they were usually coupled by the heirs of Makarenko with success stories. In 1956 there had in fact been public discussion as to whether the new schools should indeed admit such children, but the ministry ruled that there should be no selection. Later Roy Medvedev, who was concerned about exaggeration, quoted boarding school directors as saying that from 30 to 50 per cent of entrants were fully normal, and the great majority of the neglected children quickly returned to the norm (Medvedev, 1962, p. 71). Yet half, perhaps many more, arrived ill-prepared. With expansion, it was hoped that the problem would be diluted; with an increasingly affluent society it was believed that it would diminish. But the first two years of the Seven-Year Plan showed a rate of growth in pupil numbers (400,000 on 1 January 1960, 540,000 on 1 September) not nearly fast enough to bring them up to the desired 2·5 million by 1965, and in 1961, the year of the 22nd Party Congress and Khrushchev's euphoric Party Programme, when the schools were once again officially eulogised, the question of selection was authoritatively cited (by Afanasenko and Kairov) as their main problem, and the preponderance of backward (academically poor and undisciplined) pupils designated as incorrect; the range of children should reflect that in the mass schools (Redl, 1964, p. 206). A sort of negative selectivity prevailed, interfering with certain of the new schools' tasks.

Such statements may appear to conflict with the findings of the only known empirical research on Soviet boarding as contrasted with day education which endeavours to gauge the effectiveness of its upbringing. Having demonstrated his hypothesis that Russian 12-year-olds in boarding schools were less likely than their American coevals in day schools to experience peer pressure as conflicting with adult values,

Table 6.1 Composition of Boarding Schools by Categories of Need, 1956/7

	RSFSR ?1956[a]	%	Ukraine 1 January 1957	%	Latvia (? 1 January) 1957	%
Orphans	1,860	9.3	1,323	13.1	133	13.5
Children with only one parent	n.s.[d]		2,712	26.8	n.s.[d]	
Children of unmarried mothers	7,112	35.6	2,408	23.8	375	38.0
Children of war and/or industrial disabled	1,882	9.4	1,277	12.6	n.s.[d]	
Children from large families and in poor circumstances	4,817	24.1	1,476	14.6	200	20.3
Children from [other] families unable to cope with their upbringing	232	1.2	927	9.2	159	16.1
Total need cases	15,903	79.5[b]	10,123	100.0	867	87.8[b]
Others (deduced)[c]	4,097	20.5		—	120	12.2
Grand total	20,000[a]	100.0	10,123	100.0	987	100.0

Notes:

a The RSFSR figures (grand total approximate) were quoted in respect of 105 schools at a conference in January 1957. Either they are a sample, or they date from 1 September 1956. On 1 October 1956 there were 165 schools with 37,071 children (Narodnoe khozyaistvo . . ., 1959, p. 510).

b Sub-totals do not add up to total because of rounding.

c May include certain categories of need not otherwise stated.

d n.s. = not stated.

Sources: RSFSR – Naumov, 1957, p. 6; Ukraine – Kazmin', 1958, p. 28; Latvia – Namsons, 1962, p. 153. Percentages added.

and were thus able to identify more strongly with adult standards of behaviour (Bronfenbrenner, 1967, pp. 199–207 and 1974, pp. 77–8), Urie Bronfenbrenner proceeded to carry out the same experiment in a similar number of Russian day schools. The boarders evinced stronger resistance to anti-social behaviour and less discrepancy in reaction to pressure from peers *vis-à-vis* adults (Bronfenbrenner, 1974, p. 78). The experimenter himself indicated the small size of his sample, and his work may be criticised on other methodological grounds: the evidence is based on unfulfilled self-predictions and not actual behaviour. Furthermore, few data are supplied on the second stage of the experiment; and one would like to know which particular boarding schools Bronfenbrenner visited. Elsewhere, there is much evidence of a range of quality, and one cannot be sure that the schools in question, while undoubtedly efficient and perhaps extremely efficient socialising agencies, were in fact a representative sample.

The relationship of residential schools to the family is a somewhat ambiguous one. Much may be written and said about the school being meant to help the family; but despite compensatory talk about the school welcoming the family's support, the relationship is unequal and implies that the family is failing in one of its primary roles, for need is basically a negative reason. Mutual assistance, even in an officially monistic society, may yet be impeded by disparate values, so much so that the school as public value-bearer may be tempted to reduce the contacts it is supposed to sustain. Residential institutions have a built-in tendency to become custodial and induce dependency for both expressive and organisational ends (Lambert, Bullock and Millham, 1975, p. 213; Millham, Bullock and Cherrett, 1975, p. 209). This brings the possible consequences of alienation of children from the family and abnegation of their responsibility by parents. The boarding school cannot provide the love without strings which parents usually do; and to consign their children to residential education tends to cause deprivation to parents too. The fact that the case may be one of need does not lessen this problem, though there may be compensations. It appears to be only in the most extreme instances that severance from the family is justifiable; and for such children, as with orphans, the boarding school has unquestionably a dual role. What they need is a surrogate home for seven nights a week, rather than five. The Soviet evidence on these points will next be considered.

It has already been indicated how the implications of Khrushchev's remarks in 1956 about the role of parents were modified in the statute. It is not surprising, therefore, that radically differing views about this were expressed at the All-Union Conference on Boarding Schools of April 1957. Afanasenko, supported by A. I. Markushevich, a vice-president of the Academy of Pedagogical Sciences, repudiated the claim that these schools would lead to alienation between children and parents, insisted that they were not in opposition to the family, and urged school–home links (Kazmin', 1958, pp. 23–4, 135). Yet the Azerbaidzhani Minister of Education stated bluntly, 'The boarding school takes children away from their parents, replaces their parents, and brings them up in the name of the state' (Kazmin', 1958, p. 70). Talk of rearing *all* children in state institutions, however strenuously opportunities for parental contacts might at the same time be advocated, seems to have been widely construed as an attack on the family. Denials continued, the voluntary principle was repeatedly asserted, and practical and positive ways of parent–school interaction were demonstrated and discussed. True, there is little hard evidence of parental concern, for it was scarcely something to publicise. But travellers' reports, such as the one by a 1959 eyewitness, according to whom nearly everyone regarded the new schools with mingled disbelief and disquiet (Werth, 1969, p. 56), are given credibility by the frequent rebuttals and occasional radical comments. An eminent psychologist wrote in 1960: 'In contrast to the general school, where upbringing is effected not only by the school but also by the family, the boarding school must encompass the whole life of the child with its pedagogical influence' (Bozhovich, 1960, p. 8). In the same year, the veteran economist S. G. Strumilin's prophecy of the reduction of family life within two decades to the dimensions of a couple in love, with child-rearing in special sectors of communes and occasional parental visits only (a resurrection of one model of the socialist city), caused much discussion and authoritative refutation; this is conveniently reviewed in Bronfenbrenner (1974, pp. 82–4). Thus at the 22nd Congress of the CPSU, while residential education was exalted in the Party Programme (*Programme* . . ., 1961, p. 89) and its further development was said by Khrushchev to be of great importance, he also found it necessary to assert the associated role of the family, which would grow stronger under communism (Khrushchev, 1961). This, despite Afanasenko's talk of 'unanimous acceptance' of the schools by the people (Afanasenko, 1961*b*, pp. 13–14), suggests a degree of tension in the situation.

The usual pattern in Soviet residential education was, and is, weekly boarding, the children going home on Saturday after lunch and returning early on Monday morning, so that parent–child contact was frequently renewed. Although this was a basic principle of the system, there were sporadic complaints that such regular visits undid the school's good work, for certain children, having been exposed to very different values and behavioural norms, came back unmanageable for a time (Shirvindt, 1960, p. 16). The schools might react by turning in upon themselves and rejecting the outside world, even though this flagrantly breached the principle of linking with life. They were exhorted to adopt an aggressive attitude towards negative phenomena (Shirvindt, 1960, p. 16) and to seek active relationships with local production collectives, youth organisations and other schools. In an artificially cocooned environment, children would not develop the ability to resist the bad, excessive tutelage would sap self-reliance, and lavish material provision would cause an undesirable consumerism to be inculcated. Physical work of various kinds, not only within the school's precincts, was the best antidote for this, and sometimes involvement of the pupil in the school's budgeting was advocated (Noskov, 1964, pp. 21–2); for the instillation of the right attitudes, parent education was extremely important.

As Shul'gin and his associates had noticed, the underplaying of the family's role in upbringing might bring about a parasitical outlook and behaviour in the parents themselves, were they to cast all the cares of child-rearing upon the state. Interestingly, this is also presented, in quite different ways, as a consequence of the funding arrangements for maintenance: certain parents, those exempt from payment, might develop a spongeing attitude (Rostovshchikov, 1959), while fee-paying ones might demand their money's worth (heavily hinted in Sytin, 1967, p. 228) or refuse to pay their full share (Field and Anderson, 1968, p. 408). In the face of such behaviour, or indeed in any event, the children might react by becoming alienated from their families, though as a rule tutors were required to intervene and promote good parent–child relationships (see *Shkola-internat . . .*, 1958, pp. 204–16, for one of the fullest accounts).

How frequently this parental attitude was manifested is impossible to judge. It is probable, however, that a sense of deprivation was a far more likely consequence of separation. In the case of the children, there was some discussion of the possible negative results of lack of close individual contact with adults, particularly regarding the mother–child relationship (Bozhovich, 1960, p. 10), and much debate about the best kind of children's collective; many schools brought together older and younger ones as substitute siblings. Notwithstanding the prospect of weekend reunions, fear of deprivation lay behind the parental disquiet. A seasoned visitor found that the only women who spoke well of the plan were mothers of large families in poor conditions (Hindus, 1962, p. 291). A British delegation reported in 1967: 'On several occasions it became clear to us that the notion of sending one's children away from home to boarding school without some compelling reason was to Russians an incomprehensible notion' (Universities . . ., 1967, p. 28; see also Madison, 1968, p. 74n). There were social pressures against it; one account cites a Party meeting at which the integrity of a woman candidate for membership was questioned because her daughter was at a boarding school. ' "What sort of public-minded person is she, if she even refuses to bring up her own child?" ' it was asked. She got in, but only on a majority vote (Garitskaya, 1971). Reports also suggest that residential education was not popular with the intelligentsia and the more affluent (Weeks, 1962, p. 211; Madison, 1968, p. 160); and the present writer, going round a congenial boarding school in 1961, heard a Russian say with amused surprise, 'Better-off parents have got two or three rooms and a maid – why should they send their children here?' The general attitude has been candidly stated in a more recent Soviet pamphlet intended for foreign consumption: we are told that 'parents do not send their children there except as a last resort' (Soloveichik, 1976, p. 13).

Orphans, and children in a similar situation, presented particular problems of deprivation, suffering emotional upsets because of school–parent contacts and feeling the empty hours at weekends. Sometimes the staff were able to pay them special attention, but they could not receive the care and sympathy which they might have had in children's homes. This led to calls to set up separate residential schools for such children (Shirvindt, 1960, pp. 17–18; Shirvindt, Mironova and Moroz, 1963), and apparently such 'closed' schools did exist in some areas.

When one turns to the problems encountered in the pursuit of the boarding schools' instrumental goals, by which are meant, essentially, teaching and training for work, one again finds that they were handicapped from birth. The shortage of equipment, facilities and accommodation was, in general, not overcome; appropriations were not fully used, building lagged, targets were not met; authorities at various levels were upbraided repeatedly for indifference or dilatoriness (for example, Kazmin', 1958; 'V Ministerstve . . .', 1962). These material inadequacies hampered teaching in conditions already difficult enough because of the diversity of gaps in pupils' knowledge on entry. Although the schools had been heralded as pace-setters, few of them could show higher success rates than ordinary schools. One writer actually recommended admitting 'a few able pupils' (Zosimovskii, 1962, p. 83), but this, apparently, was easier said than done. Attempts to make up deficiencies by loading on the work were counter-productive; quantity was no recipe for quality. There was much debate about an optimum daily routine, but complaints in 1961 about the universal lack of time were still being echoed ten years later (compare Shirvindt, 1961, with Garitskaya, 1971).

Lack of facilities was not a problem peculiar to residential schools, but it had particular significance in that it encumbered the realisation of their role as model institutions. Labour training suffered for similar reasons and with similar consequences. A further tendency common to schools, whether boarding or day, was for polytechnical education to become narrowly vocational. Although this might mean a limitation of its role, it could also lead to such an exaggeration of it that the general-education aspects of the school's life were jeopardised. Markushevich referred with obvious disapproval to school heads planning their own self-supporting factories, or developing great agricultural concerns, like the school near Barnaul with its 1,600 hectares and 250 head of cattle (Kazmin', 1958, pp. 132–3). Possible dangers were that children might get squeezed out of the production process (Barsov, 1960; Shirvindt, 1960, pp. 19–20), or that their academic and recreational activities might be curtailed. Their presence all day long made them more vulnerable than day pupils to the latter hazard. The permanent tension between the general and the vocational became more explicit as the 1960s drew on. But it was inherent in the future-oriented residential tradition for the labour component of education to become dominant; the question was, if the Moscow Left of 1918, the Ukrainian Narkompros and the Shul'gin line of 1930 may be cited, how far it should go.

The attainment of both expressive and instrumental goals was frustrated by the staffing problems. 'Experienced, skilled teachers and tutors' had been promised (Petrov, 1956, p. 5), and although, as already mentioned, the actuality was much more diverse than this, the earliest schools seem in the main to have been staffed by people of reasonable calibre. The chief complaint at the 1957 conference was not, yet, that staff were incompetent but that the standard establishment was inadequate; there were many calls for full-time posts of teachers of PE and of music and singing. A deputy chairman of Gosplan, objecting to this, struck a discordant note by asserting that all graduates from pedagogical institutes should be trained to teach music, drawing and PE (Kazmin', 1958). This indicates a further problem that soon became paramount: the reform was embarked upon without due preparation of tutorial cadres (*vospitateli*). Two tutors were assigned to each of forms 1 to 7 and one to form 8 and above (in practice there were variations), but all were supposed to have higher education; consequently most of them had qualified as teachers but had had little training in upbringing, might not be interested in it, and in particular were not used to dealing with primary-age children. Pedagogical institutes, in general, appear to have taken the line that upbringing work could be learnt on the job (Kutsenko, 1958). When the schools expanded beyond the original handful, this lack of training proved to be a deterrent, as did the inferior salary. There was also disagreement among educationists as to whether tutors should be prepared in special departments or whether teacher-tutors should be trained. The Ministry of Education rejected the former alternative, and the training of teacher-tutors began, in a few academic fields only, at pedagogical institutes in Kiev and Khar'kov in 1956/7 and at the Lenin Institute in Moscow from 1959/60 (Kazmin', 1958, p. 32; 'O podgotovke . . .', 1962, p. 5). By

1962, there existed some twenty-four courses – a degree of provision described as 'timid groupings' (Suvorov, 1962, pp. 53, 55). Especially when underpinned by such training, the notion that every teacher must be a tutor was theoretically commendable; but in practice it seems to have led to overloading, dissatisfaction and fluctuation of staff. In 1962 an authoritative figure in boarding education was still referring to teachers and tutors as separate categories; this separation, in his view, led to the latter being overburdened (Shirvindt, 1962). The teamwork of tutors and teachers has remained a contentious issue.

By 1961, the unsatisfactory staffing position, particularly in respect of tutors but affecting teachers as well, was being discussed more vigorously, and the situation was no better five years later (for example, Afanasenko, 1961a; Suvorikov, 1964, p. 60; Izyumskii, 1966). The children were typically awkward and needed the most careful handling. But, partly for that reason, people avoided boarding schools unless they could find a job nowhere else, and local authorities were staffing them with anyone they could get. This meant that the better people regarded their work as temporary, which worsened the turnover rate, while those who remained tended to be of lesser calibre (sometimes they had been sacked from day schools). The higher education requirement seems, in practice, to have been abandoned, yet some posts remained empty. It was impossible to find enough able directors to cope with all these problems.

The difficulties under which the schools had to labour evidently led to some of them developing an unofficial organisational goal: to survive from day to day. Purposeful intervention was essential in the early days if a motley collection of untutored young individuals were to be welded into a 'healthy collective'; but sometimes this was carried too far and brought about excessive dependence in the pupils (Vysotina, 1958, pp. 53–4). This was officially deplored, but in some ways it made life easier. The routine and the rule book became king and excessive organisation prevailed, 'creating the appearance of well-being' (Kondratenkov, 1967, p. 41). Such a goal, however, conflicted with that of meeting a social need and impeded the schools' pastoral function. Thus a parent complains of the regimentation and emotional coldness in one of the schools ('Cold and cramped', 1957). It is difficult to quantify this problem and to see what kind of reaction harsh external control provoked in the pupil's informal world; when discussed it tends to be linked with a weak informal society – the children seeming not to be interested in one another – but occasionally they are portrayed as rebelling, as when sixteen of them at a terrible school sent a petition for help to a national newspaper (compare Komov, 1966, with Benderova, 1966).

In the literature, problems of discipline and control are sometimes linked to school size. Governed by economic considerations and the need to fulfil admissions plans, the RSFSR Ministry of Education favoured a standard complement of 800. Workers in the schools, however, felt that the optimum number of pupils was 300–350. With 500–600 or more, the daily routine was inevitably intensified and rushed, causing increased tension, necessitating strict external discipline, and losing individuals from view (except the naughty ones) ('Otkrovennyi . . .', 1960). A dissentient thought that alleged problems of size were being confused with those arising from poor architectural planning and with disorganisation due to poor educational work (Medvedev, 1962, p. 77). (He did not consider whether size might be a factor in the latter.) A balanced commentator stressed the administrative and pedagogical drawbacks of big schools, but conceded that they were cheaper for the state and afforded a superior technical base; a maximum of 480 seemed a reasonable compromise (Nikov, 1962, pp. 84–5). Financial considerations apparently prevailed.

Economic factors have now emerged; and although lack of space precludes detailed treatment, they must be mentioned briefly as important obstacles to the boarding schools' achievement of their goal of becoming model institutions, and as major causes of change in the official concept of them. A perceptive visitor noted apprehension as to their cost in manpower, resources and cash as early as 1956–7 (Gould, 1957, p. 287). In July 1956 Gosplan and the USSR Ministry of Finance were accused in a *Pravda* editorial of standing aloof ('Shkoly-internaty', 1956) – hardly a good augury – and they allegedly did nothing about capital investment for construction purposes for nearly two years (*Zasedaniya* . . ., 1959, p. 445). (One thing they did do, on 15 November 1956, was to lay down the procedure for the payment of fees – 'V pomoshch' . . ., 1958, pp. 32–4.) The capital cost of providing one pupil place was said to have been four times higher in 1960 in boarding schools than day (Noah, 1966, p. 108). Annual current expenditure per child by the state was then, and subsequently, rated about seven times higher (Noah, 1966, p. 108; Katz, 1973, p. 72), while other sources said ten (Buzlyakov, 1962; Kobzar', 1967, p. 24; Madison, 1968, p. 75); and this was at a time of slowdown in economic growth. In the summer of 1962, measures were passed to run the schools more economically. But would it be more rational to use the enormous sums involved for the improvement of the education of far more children, in day schools?

OUTCOMES

If a graph is drawn of the progress of Soviet boarding schools in terms of their pupil numbers from the school years 1956/7 to 1975/6, certain trends are indicated which reflect official attitudes to them, and also to some extent the outcomes of their problems. The graph rises steadily but not spectacularly from September 1956 to September 1958, after which it ascends sharply until 1962, with a much slighter rise until 1963, then it fluctuates, though moderately, until 1968, next descending fairly steadily until 1972, and tending, but for a temporary rise in 1973, to even out thereafter. Expanding gently, the first schools, despite undoubted problems, were reasonably successful. In the main they attracted enterprising teachers, they had novelty value and even a certain trail-blazing appeal, and were in heavy demand; for example, when Moscow Boarding School no. 19 opened, there were eight applications for each place (Vetrov, 1960, p. 5). Then came the sweep of Khrushchev's broom with the 1958 education reform and the Seven-Year Plan, and a furious programme of development began, with a target of 2·5 million boarders by 1965. It was a profound mistake, for the infrastructure was lacking. Quality ceded to quantity; the plan was the thing. Yet its financial implications had not been realistically pondered, and in any case the plunge into mass polytechnism itself created immense organisational strain. Local authorities were blamed for failing to recruit usually non-existent staff. The schools continued to be filled with pupils, but standards degenerated. Headteachers and their deputies were sacked for inability to cope with impossible conditions. The reality that had been forced upon the schools discredited the very notion of boarding education. Meanwhile, this headlong rush into the future was interpreted by some parents as a threat, intensified in 1961 by Khrushchev's talk of the schools as universal institutions and press references to the schools of tomorrow, and only partially allayed by tributes to the family in discussion of the Party Programme.

The year 1962/3 marked a change of thinking. Shortly before this the educationist A. M. Arsen'ev had forecast that by 1980 about 55 to 60 million pupils, some 80 per cent, should be in boarding and extended-day schools, with a slight majority in the latter (Arsen'ev, 1962, p. 9, cited in Anweiler, 1968, p. 108). This is interesting, because he appears to envisage a still prominent role for boarding schools in the context of the Programme's promises of social upbringing, but combines it with possibly the first statement on the strongly enhanced role of the extended day. What actually happened, however, was that development of residential education slowed down and stopped, while attention concentrated on extended-day facilities; these provided supervision of the child during most of his waking hours at far less expense, viz. 'one-sixth the per-student cost of the regular boarding school' (Field and Anderson, 1968, p. 408). This appears to refer to maintenance only; it matches Buzlyakov (1962), but Kobzar' (1967, p. 24) makes the cost one-fifth. Aggregated per-pupil costs (capital outlay plus maintenance) were said in 1958 to be about four times lower in extended-day schools than in boarding schools (Rostovtseva and Golikova, 1958); Kaser (1969, pp. 137, 139) gives three estimates for such costs and concludes that in 1962 the boarding schools were at least 4·3 times as expensive and possibly far more. Extended-day schools and groups thus obtained promotion from constituting in 1958 a transitional phenomenon on the way to residential education (Rostovtseva and Golikova, 1958) and from being still juxtaposed in the 1960 legislation developing them to boarding schools as 'institutions of a higher type', to achieving equal status in 1962, and to being actually superior by the mid-1960s, certainly from the economic point of view (Lerman, 1969, p. 53). They were also claimed to be in tune with such features of social development as improving conditions of everyday life and work and increasing time for family upbringing (Kostyashkin, 1967, pp. 48, 52).

With Khrushchev safely out of the way, the special status of the boarding school as a higher type of school of the future could be denied (Vasadze, 1965, p. 5). There was, however, some resistance to talk of cutback in the boarding school programme; but power lay with the paymasters, and the important education decree of November 1966 settled the matter by enacting that boarding pupil numbers were to be kept at their current level for the next five years. Interestingly, the *Pravda* paraphrase glossed over this point, and in fact enrolments started to fall sooner. It was conceded that the schools had a continuing role in meeting exceptional needs. But even their function of providing for pupils from thinly populated rural areas was to be appropriated more and more by the undoubtedly less costly agency of the residential annexe (Prokof'ev, 1968), especially after 1968, which seems to mark a further if less conspicuous shift of emphasis.

Figures of growth and decline for individual republics showed some variety. In 1963, when boarding accounted for an estimated 980,000 Soviet pupils, or 2·43 per cent of all in day general schools, it peaked also in the RSFSR with 2·2 per cent, thereafter fluctuating slightly until 1968, and probably in Lithuania with 2·9 per cent (3·4 per cent including day boarders), and in Armenia with 2·4 per cent (though in Armenia there were most boarding pupils the next year). In most of the other republics for which data series are available, 1965 was the high mark; Latvia showing the highest proportion with 3·8 per cent. Boarding and extended-day pupils together represented 6 per cent of all in Soviet day general schools in 1963 (RSFSR 5·2 per cent; Lithuania 10 per cent; Armenia 3·9 per cent), and 13·8 per cent of all Latvian pupils in 1965. In the USSR as a whole, the extended day had begun to outpace boarding in 1960, but in Georgia and Armenia this did not occur until 1966. By 1975, the total of Soviet boarders had sunk to 750,000, or 1·8 per cent of all day general pupils, with an estimated 8,050,000 boarding and extended-day pupils, or 19·1 per cent, betokening a steady increase over the period but the obvious abandonment of the goal announced by Arsen'ev. (These data were obtained directly or indirectly from numerous statistical handbooks, plan fulfilment reports, etc.)

That a less ambitious target might be expected could have been deduced from a statement by F. F. Korolev late in 1964 that it was not to be advocated that all schools should be converted into extended-day or boarding schools (Korolev, 1964, p. 1,105). This was in the context of a reconsideration of the role of the family in socialist upbringing. Interest in this grew as the 1960s proceeded; since the state was unwilling to shoulder the whole burden of child-rearing, for whatever reason, the family should be strengthened and taught to perform its part of the task as efficiently as possible. This new official confidence in the family meant that any vestigial public encouragement to send children to boarding schools, except in cases of need, was finally abandoned, and these schools, if discussed at all, were presented primarily as welfare institutions, usually with problems.

The origins of the children at two Leningrad schools had already been exposed to public view in a well-known work by A. G. Kharchev:

It is characteristic that a significant number of the pupils of present-day boarding schools consist of children from incomplete or 'unfortunate' families (not infrequently these two attributes coincide). At Boarding School no. 36, Leningrad, of 422 pupils, 325 have only a mother, 15 only a father, 16 are orphans, and only 66 have both parents, many of whom lead an abnormal way of life. At Boarding School no. 9, the parents of approximately 100 children out of 330 are on the books of a psychiatric clinic. (Kharchev, 1964, p. 273)

A study conducted in 1967–9 in Vladimir Region and Moscow uses overlapping categories which graphically portray the complexities of the schools: the children of unmarried mothers constituted 62 per cent, from big families 27 per cent, with parents in prison 5–7 per cent, with mentally ill parents 5 per cent, with alcoholic parents 24 per cent, and from completely happy families 8 per cent. Over 60 per cent of children in boarding schools were to varying degrees pedagogically neglected. Though this figure is similar to that of Medvedev for 1962 cited earlier, the author seemed to suggest the trend was accelerating (Tsypurskii, 1970, pp. 4–5). About the same time, the (?countrywide) proportion of boarding school pupils who were orphans or had only one parent was stated to be 57·7 per cent (Kobzar', 1967, p. 25). In

1968, the Soviet Minister of Education stated categorically that the remedial orientation must increase (Prokof'ev, 1968). The associated difficulties continue to be articulated occasionally by administrators and teachers. 'Boarding schools have been turned into schools for "difficult" children with the aim of raising their achievement and behaviour to the norm' (Garitskaya, 1971). 'In essence, we are being turned bit by bit into a kind of correctional institution' (Kosarev, 1973), for rejects from other schools. But perhaps the most trenchant comment came much earlier in the last issue of the journal *Shkola-internat* (The Boarding School) before it significantly rose from the ashes as *Vospitanie shkol'nikov* (Bringing up Schoolchildren): 'Even in the best of these schools the basic idea . . . has been in many respects perverted' (Akimova, 1965, p. 20).

A second concomitant of the official strengthening of the family, reflected in legislation of 1968 which included the reintroduction of paternity suits, was that cost-conscious economists and some educators began to express disapproval not only of young men licensed under the 1944 law to sow their wild oats but also of irresponsible unmarried mothers, whose methods of upbringing were likened to those of the cuckoo. This both increased the number of unfortunate children and was a further charge on the state (Izyumskii, 1966). Parental irresponsibility, as has been noted, was a built-in hazard of residential education, and by 1964/5 single mothers had come specially under fire (Madison, 1968, p. 172). They were exempt from boarding fees, and growing awareness of costs caused it to be pointed out that the 'surplus' of women were now past childbearing age, abortions were permitted and there was no longer any good reason for a woman to become a single mother (Sonin, 1967). This, incidentally, is further indirect evidence of the great strains on the boarding schools by the early 1960s. In 1967 one birth in nine was illegitimate (Belyavskii, 1967); if this situation could be improved, the development of the schools could be stabilised once the hump arising from the 1944 law had been surmounted. As to more recent trends, the direct evidence cited by Madison (1977, p. 319) is too sparse and contradictory to pronounce with certainty, but other demographic factors make an increase in illegitimacy credible.

When the draft 'Legislative Principles on Public Education' were discussed in 1973, it was suggested that, because some parents thought that the school should be entirely responsible for child-rearing, a point about primary parental responsibility should be added. The state, however, intended to bear the consequences of leadership, and a new article on pedagogical propaganda was inserted instead ('Osnovy . . .', 1973). As for institutional upbringing, the draft document listed residential annexes as one means of ensuring the school's accessibility to pupils, it attributed to extended-day schools and groups the purpose of facilitating their all-round development and helping the family, and it described boarding schools and children's homes as for those deprived of parental care and lacking the conditions for family upbringing. The final version, however, detached boarding schools from children's homes and linked them with the extended day. The aims of extended-day provision remained the same, but along with residential schools it acquired the further aim of expanding public upbringing. Boarding schools alone were said to be for children and adolescents without the conditions for family upbringing, and in a separate article children's homes were stated to be for those deprived of parental care. This suggests that, on reflection, the authorities decided yet again to reassert the role of the school *vis-à-vis* the family, made a token gesture towards rescuing the boarding school from the limbo into which it had fallen, and by giving it a more specific function freed it from the complexities of coping with orphans and non-orphans simultaneously. Since it was recently stated that children without parents live in such schools (Soloveichik, 1976, p. 13), little difference may have been made in practice; according to the regulations, they may admit these youngsters when accommodation in children's homes is not available ('O prieme . . .', 1975). In the Ukraine, however, some superior experimental boarding schools have been established specifically for children bereft of parental care, and other republics are said to be following suit (Agafonova, 1977, p. 29).

CONCLUSIONS

Considered over the years 1956–75, the boarding school saga nevertheless makes depressing reading. Heroic efforts were expended by a small band of people to realise a lofty plan foredoomed to ultimate failure. The schools' achievements were that they provided a second chance for at least some of their many thousands of underprivileged pupils – indeed, it should be stressed that they continue to offer enhanced opportunities to children in certain remote rural areas – and they gave thousands of women, particularly unmarried mothers, the possibility of improving their socio-economic position. Their tragedy was that they were established with contradictory and, in some respects, impossible goals, and usually without the means to pursue them.

Certain kinds of expressive goals (to provide more effective upbringing for children in need, thereby assisting certain parents) tend to conflict with certain instrumental goals (to become a beacon of formal education), and expressive-instrumental ones (to develop into a general-purpose educational vanguard as the prototype of a universal institution); and the organisational goal of self-maintenance, fostered by difficult circumstances, may seriously interfere with the attainment of expressive ones. The conflict is complicated by parents', especially mothers', own goals, their perceptions of their functions, which are strongly influenced by emotional ties and may impede the enhancement of their socio-economic position.

Earlier and more recent Soviet history shows, in somewhat different ways, that welfare and exemplar functions are incompatible in the same institutions on a wide scale without immense resources of material support and leadership, and even they are not necessarily enough. Official precepts carry no conviction unless backed by practice, but official practice still has to reckon with popular attitudes and behaviour. Short of coercion, a model stands no chance of mass adoption if it conflicts with basic human relationships, or at least unless it brings gains which clearly outweigh losses. To Soviet parents at large, the boarding schools could offer only disadvantages. The stars in their courses fought against them.

BIBLIOGRAPHY

Afanasenko, E., 'Shkoly bol'shogo budushchego', *Izvestiya*, 7 March 1961*a*.

Afanasenko, E., 'Let us greet the 22nd Party Congress with further progress in the school reorganisation', *Soviet Education*, vol. 4, no. 2 (1961*b*), pp. 3–17.

Agafonova, K., 'Bol'she udelyat' vnimaniya rabote shkol-internatov', *Narodnoe obrazovanie*, 1977, no. 8, pp. 28–9.

Akimova, A., 'Chtoby kazhdyi vyros chelovekom . . .', *Shkola-internat*, 1965, no. 6, pp. 15–21.

Alpatov, N. I. (ed.), *Vospitatel'naya rabota v shkolakh-internatakh Yuzhnogo Urala* (Chelyabinsk, 1958).

Ambler, E., 'The Soviet boarding school', *Slavic Review*, vol. 20, no. 2 (1961), pp. 237–52.

Anweiler, O., *Geschichte der Schule und Pädagogik in Russland vom Ende des Zarenreiches bis zum Beginn der Stalin-Ära* ([West] Berlin: Osteuropa-Institut in Kommission bei Quelle & Meyer, Heidelberg, 1964).

Anweiler, O., *Die Sowjetpädagogik in der Welt von heute* (Heidelberg: Quelle & Meyer, 1968).

Arsen'ev, A. M., 'Edinstvo tekushchikh zadach perestroiki sovetskoi shkoly i perspektiv sozdaniya kommunisticheskoi sistemy narodnogo obrazovaniya SSSR', *Doklady APN RSFSR*, 1962, no. 1, pp. 5–12.

Bakalo, I., 'Soviet boarding schools and extended day schools', *Studies on the Soviet Union*, vol. 4, no. 1 (1964), pp. 41–8.

Barsov, B., 'Pod sen'yu tsitat', *Izvestiya*, 27 July 1960.

Belyavskii, A., 'Ostorozhno – zakon!', *Literaturnaya gazeta*, 26 April 1967.

Benderova, V., 'Plokhaya devchonka', *Komsomol'skaya pravda*, 1 March 1966.

Bereday, G. Z. F., Brickman, W. W., and Read, G. H., *The Changing Soviet School* (Boston, Mass.: Houghton Mifflin, 1960).

Bozhovich, L. I. (ed.), *Psikhologicheskoe izuchenie detei v shkole-internate* (Moscow, 1960).

Bronfenbrenner, U., 'Response to pressure from peers versus adults among Soviet and American school children', *International Journal of Psychology*, vol. 2, no. 3 (1967), pp. 199–207.

Bronfenbrenner, U., 'The changing Soviet family', in *The Role and Status of Women in the Soviet Union*, ed. D. R. Brown (New York: Teachers College Press, 1968), pp. 98–123.

Bronfenbrenner, U., *Two Worlds of Childhood* (Harmondsworth: Penguin, 1974).

Buzlyakov, N., 'Chto nam dayut obshchestvennye fondy', *Izvestiya*, 2 June 1962.

'Byt' na urovne novykh zadach', *Uchitel'skaya gazeta*, 16 May 1956.

'Cold and cramped', *Times Educational Supplement*, 22 November 1957.

'Delo vsego naroda', *Uchitel'skaya gazeta*, 6 June 1956.

Demidenko, V. K., *et al.*, *V nashei shkole-internate* (Moscow, 1960).

Dodge, N. T., *Women in the Soviet Economy* (Baltimore, Md: John Hopkins Press, 1966).

Dunstan, J., *Paths to Excellence and the Soviet School* (Windsor, Berks: NFER, 1978).

XX [Dvadtsatyi] s''ezd Kommunisticheskoi partii Sovetskogo Soyuza. Rech' tovarishcha I. A. Kairova', *Uchitel'skaya gazeta*, 25 February 1956.

Field, M. G. and Anderson, D. E., 'The family and social problems', in *Prospects for Soviet Society*, ed. A. Kassof (London: Pall Mall Press, 1968), pp. 386–417.

Fitzpatrick, S., *The Commissariat of Enlightenment* (Cambridge: CUP, 1970).

Fraser, W. R., 'The traditional and the distinctive in Soviet education', in *Communist Education*, ed. E. J. King (London: Methuen, 1963), pp. 78–96.

Fraser, W. R., *Residential Education* (Oxford: Pergamon Press, 1968).

Gamagelyan, M. and Pluzyan, A., 'On boarding schools' (*Kommunist* (Erevan), 19 May 1956), *Current Digest of the Soviet Press*, vol. 8, no. 20 (1956), pp. 44–5.

Garitskaya, O., 'Dve nedeli v internate', *Pravda Ukrainy*, 14 January 1971.

Gould, Sir R., 'Russia revisited', *Phi Delta Kappan*, vol. 38, no. 7 (1957), pp. 285–7.

Gud, V. P. and Senkevich, G. G. (eds), *V shkolakh-internatakh BSSR* (Minsk, 1963).

Hindus, M., *House without a Roof* (London: Gollancz, 1962).

Izyumskii, B., 'Kak v rodnom dome', *Pravda*, 13 November 1966.

Kairov, I., 'Nekotorye voprosy sozdaniya shkol-internatov', *Uchitel'skaya gazeta*, 27 June 1956.

Kaser, M., 'Soviet boarding schools', *Soviet Studies*, vol. 20, no. 1 (1968), pp. 94–105.

Kaser, M., 'Salient features in the history of state boarding schools', *Annuaire de l'URSS 1968* (1969), pp. 131–9.

Katz, Z., *Patterns of Social Mobility in the USSR* (Cambridge, Mass: MIT, Center for International Studies, 1973).

Kazmin', N. D. (ed.), *Vsesoyuznoe soveshchanie po shkolam-internatam, 19–23 aprelya 1957g.* (Moscow, 1958).

138   *Home, School and Leisure in the Soviet Union*

Kharchev, A. G., *Brak i sem'ya v SSSR* (Moscow, 1964).

Khrushchev, N. S., 'Otchetnyi doklad Tsentral'nogo komiteta Kommunisticheskoi partii Sovetskogo Soyuza XX s''ezdu partii', *Pravda*, 15 February 1956.

Khrushchev, N. S., 'Kontrol'nye tsifry razvitiya narodnogo khozyaistva SSSR na 1959–1965 gody', *Pravda*, 14 November 1958.

Khrushchev, N. S., 'O kontrol'nykh tsifrakh razvitiya narodnogo khozyaistva SSSR na 1959–1965 gody', *Pravda*, 28 January 1959.

Khrushchev, N. S., 'O programme Kommunisticheskoi partii Sovetskogo Soyuza', *Pravda*, 19 October 1961.

King, B., 'Agricultural education in the USSR', *Times Educational Supplement*, 15 August 1942.

Kobzar', B. S., 'Pedagogicheskie problemy razvitiya shkol-internatov, shkol i grupp s prodlennym dnem (na opyte Ukrainskoi SSR)' (Tbilisi, 1967). Author's abstract of thesis.

Komov, V., 'Dostan'te papki iz shkafa', *Izvestiya*, 4 February 1966.

Kondratenkov, A., *Kollektiv otvechaet za kazhdogo* (Moscow, 1967).

Korenev, D., 'Pervye shagi', *Uchitel'skaya gazeta*, 25 April 1956.

Korolev, F. F., 'Neue Fragen für die pädagogische Wissenschaft', *Pädagogik*, vol. 19, no. 12 (1964), pp. 1,105–13.

Kosarev, A., 'Vchera, segodnya, zavtra', *Uchitel'skaya gazeta*, 5 May 1973.

Kostyashkin, E. G., 'Sem'ya i prodlennyi shkol'nyi den'', *Sovetskaya pedagogika*, 1967, no. 4, pp. 47–57.

Kutsenko, V., 'O nastoyashchem vospitatele', *Uchitel'skaya gazeta*, 5 December 1958.

Lambert, R., with Bullock, R. and Millham, S., *The Chance of a Lifetime?* (London: Weidenfeld & Nicolson, 1975).

Lerman, L. M., 'Education and the development of production in the Uzbek SSR', in *The Economics of Education in the USSR*, ed. H. J. Noah (New York: Praeger, 1969), pp. 45–62.

Leshchenko, N. N., 'Razvitie sistemy narodnogo obrazovaniya v Ukrainskoi SSR (1917–1934 gg.)' (Kiev, 1969). Author's abstract of thesis.

Lyalin, N., 'Shkola novogo tipa', *Uchitel'skaya gazeta*, 14 April 1956.

Madison, B. Q., *Social Welfare in the Soviet Union* (Stanford, Cal.: Stanford University Press, 1968).

Madison, B. [Q.], 'Social services for women: problems and priorities', in *Women in Russia*, ed. D. Atkinson, A. Dallin and G. W. Lapidus (Hassocks, Sussex: Harvester Press, 1978), pp. 308–32.

Makarenko, A. S., *The Road to Life*, Vol. 1 (Moscow: Progress, 1973).

Medvedev, R., 'O nekotorykh voprosakh razvitiya shkol-internatov', *Shkola-internat*, 1962, No. 1, pp. 70–8.

Mer, F., 'Opirayas' na opyt A. S. Makarenko', *Uchitel'skaya gazeta*, 18 April 1956.

Millham, S., Bullock, R. and Cherrett, P., 'A conceptual scheme for the comparative analysis of residential institutions', in *Varieties of Residential Experience*, ed. J. Tizard, I. Sinclair and R. V. G. Clarke (London: Routledge & Kegan Paul, 1975), pp. 203–24.

Mirbabaev, K., 'Stroim detskii gorodok', *Uchitel'skaya gazeta*, 14 April 1956.

Molotkov, G., 'Ozarennoe Il'ichem', *Neva*, 1966, no. 9, pp. 141–6.

Namsons, A., 'Die Sowjetisierung des Schul- und Bildungswesens in Lettland von 1940–1960', *Acta Baltica*, vol. 1 (1960/1 [1962]), pp. 148–67.

Namsons, A., 'Das Schulwesen und die ideologische Umerziehung der Jugend in Sowjetlettland', *Acta Baltica*, vol. 5 (1965 [1966]), pp. 36–76.

Narodnoe khozyaistvo RSFSR v 1959 godu (Moscow, 1959).

Narodnoe obrazovanie Ukrainy na 1 yanvarya 1923 g. Uchrezhdeniya sotsial'nogo vospitaniya (Kharkov, 1924).

Narodnya osvita na Ukraini na 15 grudnya 1927 r. (Kharkov, 1928).

Naumov, N. V., 'Pervye itogi raboty i ocherednye zadachi shkol-internatov', in *Pervye itogi. Materialy Vserossiiskogo soveshchaniya direktorov shkol-internatov* (Moscow, 1957), pp. 5–31.

The new stage in development of the schools and the tasks of pedagogic science, *Soviet Education*, vol. 1, no. 5 (1959), pp. 3–8.

Nikov, G., 'Eshche raz o shkolakh-internatakh gigantakh', *Shkola-internat*, 1962, no. 3, pp. 84–5.

Noah, H., *Financing Soviet Schools* (New York: Teachers College Press, 1966).

Noskov, Ya., 'Odin iz pokazatelei politicheskoi zrelosti', *Shkola-internat*, 1964, no. 6, pp. 21–3.

'O podgotovke uchitelei dlya shkol-internatov i shkol prodlennogo dyna', *Sbornik prikazov i instruktsii Ministerstva prosveshcheniya RSFSR*, 1962, no. 7, pp. 3–9.

'O prieme detei i podrostkov v shkoly-internaty i detskie doma', *Narodnoe obrazovanie*, 1975, no. 8, p. 103.

Opitz, R., 'Zur Geschichte des Tagesschulgedankens in der Sowjetunion', *Wissenschaftliche Zeitschrift der Karl-Marx-Universität Leipzig, Gesellschafts- und sprachwissenschaftliche Reihe*, vol. 14, no. 2 (1965), pp. 225–37.

'Osnovy zakonodatel'stva Soyuza SSR i soyuznykh respublik o narodnom obrazovanii', *Uchitel'skaya gazeta*, 5 April (draft), 7 July, and 21 July (final version), 1973.

'Otkrovennyi razgovor', *Pravda*, 19 February 1960.

Pedagogicheskaya entsiklopediya, Vol. 4 (Moscow, 1968).

Pervye shagi (Moscow, 1958).

Petrov, N. A., 'O novoi sisteme obshchestvennogo vospitaniya', *Sovetskaya pedagogika*, 1956, no. 6, pp. 3–12.

Programme of the Communist Party of the Soviet Union (Moscow: Foreign Languages Publishing House, 1961).

Prokof'ev, M. A., 'O sostoyanii i merakh dal'neishego uluchsheniya raboty srednei obshcheobrazovatel'noi shkoly', *Pravda*, 2 July 1968 and *Uchitel'skaya gazeta*, 3 July 1968.

Prokoshev, V., 'U istochnikov shkol-internatov', *Shkola-internat*, 1964, no. 2, pp. 69–72.

Protokoly I-go Vserossiiskogo s"ezda po prosveshcheniyu (Moscow, 1919), cited in Anweiler (1964), p. 114.

Raskin, L. E., 'Problemy vospitaniya detei v s.kh.kommune', in *Problemy nauchnoi pedagogiki. Sbornik V: Pedagogika perekhodnoi epokhi* (Moscow, 1930), pp. 92–167.

Redl, H. B. (ed.), *Soviet Educators on Soviet Education* (New York: Collier-Macmillan, 1964).

Roberts, H. C., 'Russian boarding schools', *Educational Forum*, vol. 30, no. 4 (1966), pp. 457–63.

Rostovshchikov, V., 'Siroty pri roditelyakh', *Izvestiya*, 9 June 1959.

Rostovtseva, O. and Golikova, N., 'Prodlennyi den'', *Uchitel'skaya gazeta*, 2 December 1958.

Schapker, P. E., 'A Study of the Role and Significance of the Soviet School-internat within the Framework of the post-Stalin Educational Scene', PhD thesis, Marquette University (Milwaukee, Wis., 1972).

Shirvindt, B. E., 'Nereshennye problemy shkol-internatov', *Sovetskaya pedagogika*, 1960, no. 12, pp. 16–21.

Shirvindt, B. [E.], 'Mozhno i nuzhno po-novomu', *Izvestiya*, 24 March 1961.

Shirvindt, B. E., 'Berech' vremya uchitelei i vospitatelei', *Shkola-internat*, 1962, no. 5, pp. 62–5.

Shirvindt, B. [E.], 'A budushchee u nikh est'', *Izvestiya*, 13 January 1966.

Shirvindt, B. [E.], Mironova, L. and Moroz, E., 'Na vsem gotovom', *Izvestiya*, 11 September 1963.

Shkola-internat. Voprosy organizatsii i opyt vospitatel'noi raboty (Moscow 1958).

'Shkoly-internaty', *Pravda*, 28 June 1956.

Shul'gin, V. N., 'K voprosu o sisteme narodnogo obrazovaniya', in *Problemy nauchnoi pedagogiki. Sbornik V: Pedagogika perekhodnoi epokhi* (Moscow, 1930), pp. 5–23.

Soloveichik, S., *Soviet Children at School* (Moscow: Novosti, 1976).

Sonin, M., 'Snova ob alimentakh? Da!', *Literaturnaya gazeta*, 25 January 1967.

'Soveshchanie v TsK KPSS po voprosam organizatsii shkol-internatov', *Uchitel'skaya gazeta*, 12 May 1956.

Spravochnik partiinogo rabotnika (Moscow, 1957).

Suvorikov, V., 'Drug i mudryi nastavnik', *Shkola-internat*, 1964, no. 2, pp. 59–64.

Suvorov, N. P., 'Highly educated teachers for schools', *Soviet Education*, vol. 4, no. 12 (1962), pp. 53–7.

Sytin, G. V., 'K voprosu o sovmestnoi rabote shkol-internatov s roditelyami i obshchestvennost'yu', *Uchenye zapiski. Moskovskii oblastnoi pedagogicheskii institut imeni N.K. Krupskoi*, Vol. 184 (1967), pp. 227–41.

Tsypurskii, V. G., 'Vospitanie pedagogicheski zapushchennykh detei v usloviyakh shkoly-internata' (Moscow, 1970). Author's abstract of thesis.

Universities of London, Reading and Oxford, 'Comparative Education Tour to the USSR, Easter 1967' (London, 1967). Duplicated typescript at University of London Institute of Education Library.

'V Ministerstve prosveshcheniya RSFSR. Ob uluchshenii raboty shkol-internatov', *Narodnoe obrazovanie*, 1962, no. 1, pp. 122–3.

V pomoshch' direktoru shkoly-internata (Moscow, 1958).

Vasadze, N. Sh., 'Osnovnye voprosy vospitatel'noi raboty v shkolakh-internatakh Gruzii' (Tbilisi, 1965). Author's abstract of thesis.

Vetrov, Ya. M., *Zapiski direktora shkoly-internata* (Moscow, 1960).

Voroshilov, K. E., speech at 20th Party Congress, *Pravda*, 21 February 1956.

Vysotina, L. A., 'Vospitatel'naya rabota s det'mi mladshego shkol'nogo vozrasta v shkole-internate', *Sovetskaya pedagogika*, 1958, no. 5, pp. 52–61.

Weeks, A. L., 'Brain surgery on Soviet society', *Phi Delta Kappan*, vol. 43, no. 5 (1962), pp. 206–11.

Weeks, A. L., 'The boarding school', *Survey*, no. 56 (1965), pp. 83–94.

Werth, A., *Russia: Hopes and Fears* (Harmondsworth: Penguin, 1969).

'XX s"ezd . . .', *see* Dvadtsatyi.

Zasedaniya Verkhovnogo Soveta SSSR pyatogo sozyva (vtoraya sessiya). Stenograficheskii otchet (Moscow, 1959).

Zosimovskii, A., 'O nekotorykh nereshennykh voprosakh', *Shkola-internat*, 1962, no. 5, pp. 83–4.

7

Soviet Child Care: its Organisation at Local Level

MADELINE DRAKE

INTRODUCTION

All modern European states take some measures to care for their most disadvantaged children – those in need of care and protection because of poverty, the loss or breakdown of their family, or exposure to moral danger. The exact form taken by the provision and administration of these services differs in different countries, but all include case-work by field workers and substitute family or residential care for those who cannot be cared for in their own families. In Britain, these services are provided by the local social services departments under the Social Services Act, 1970. In this chapter, I describe how they are provided in the Soviet Union. I shall deal with that area of child welfare which the British call 'child care' – support in the community or in children's homes for physically healthy children. The Russians use the terms *opeka* (care) and *okhrana detstva* (protection of children). In this chapter, I use the term 'child care' as the closest English functional equivalent of these two Russian terms. These functions are carried out by workers in the education department, who are called inspectors for the protection of children (*inspektory po okhrane detstva*). I discuss the organisation of child care, not policy itself, the description focusing on the regional (*oblast'*) and district (*raion*) levels. The district is the lowest complete government unit and the delivery point for child welfare and for other welfare services. Reference will be made to some of the major principles of Soviet public administration, particularly when these differ from our own.

There is little information available in either Western or Soviet literature about the organisation of child care at local (regional and district) level in the USSR. This study is based on the existing published sources, supplemented by data which I collected on a six-month field trip to the Soviet Union in 1972. This visit followed the issuing of the 1969 code of family law, the latest legislative revision in the field ('Kodeks . . .', 1969). I spent five months in Leningrad and one month in Moscow. In both cities I visited academic institutions and child welfare agencies, and was able to interview a number of officials working in the field of child care at republican, regional and district levels. Visits in 1974 and 1979 to study Soviet social security have confirmed my view that the organisation of child care has changed little since then, even though the rapid growth of Moscow and Leningrad has brought about an increase in the numbers of child care workers employed.

The legislative basis of the present Soviet child welfare system was laid in 1928 by a joint regulation issued by the Supreme Soviet and the Central Committee of the Communist Party ('Polozhenie . . .', 1928). Responsibility for child welfare at local level was laid on the president of the local executive committee in urban areas and of the village soviet in rural areas. In practice, however, this responsibility is carried out by specially appointed officers. In the case of child care for physically healthy children, the function is delegated to the education department. This joint regulation rationalised incremental changes which had been made in the 1918 code of family law ('Kodeks . . .', 1918), the major change being the transfer of responsibility for child care from the social welfare to the education system. Under articles 184 and 185 of the 1918 code, social security departments had been given child care duties. But child care increasingly became part of the functions of schools and other educational institutions. In 1920, child care responsibilities were transferred to the education department ('Ob iz"yatii . . .', 1920). Further clarification of the education department's role was made in an instructional circular from the Ministry of Education issued in 1950 ('Instruktivno-metodicheskie . . .', 1956).

This contrasts with the English system. Our own child care system has been part of a composite social services provision since the Social Services Act, 1970. Before this, it had been the responsibility of a separate child-care department under the Home Office. The English education department's welfare role is limited to educational welfare such as absenteeism, poor attainment and backward children. In contrast to the Soviet *raion*, English districts no longer have child care responsibilities (except for metropolitan districts).

It is difficult in the Soviet context to apply the British distinction between statutory and voluntary agencies. The Soviet education department relies on assistance from 'social' (*obshchestvennye*) organisations, which have responsibilities defined by statute in the same way as those of the education department. (Of the British voluntary child care associations only the National Society for the Prevention of

Cruelty to Children has legislatively defined powers.) The term *obshchestvennost'* may be variously translated. Churchward (1968, p. 269) used the English terms 'mass participation' or 'popular participation'. Berenice Q. Madison (1968) translated it as 'voluntary organisation'. Here we use the direct translation – 'social service' – retaining inverted commas for this term and for 'social', to remind the reader that these are peculiarly Soviet institutions which cannot be translated directly in our terms.

Soviet child care administration may be represented as two overlapping spheres of activity. On the one hand, there is the local soviet education department, on the other, the organisations – the Party, Komsomol and trade unions – responsible for organising 'social' workers. Their activities are linked by various bodies which harness the energies of the 'social' sector and integrate them with professional activity. I shall now go on to examine these various elements in the organisation of child care.

THE STATE STRUCTURE

The Ministerial and Soviet Hierarchies
Child care in the Soviet Union is a republican concern. It is part of the Ministry of Education's functions and there is a deputy minister in charge of questions of child care and children's rights (*opeka i okhrana prav detei*). Child care is represented at each of the four levels of republican government: the republican, the regional (territorial, autonomous republic and large city), the district and town and, at the lowest level, the village or urban settlement. This hierarchy is summarised in Figure 7.1. A general description of Soviet governmental hierarchy is given by Churchward (1968, ch. 12).

Like our own local government officers, those in the USSR are legally the servants of the local soviet and report to the executive committee or its subcommittees. Churchward (1968, p. 179) has stated that local soviets have more statutory powers than British local government bodies, but that in practice they are more subordinate to central government ministries. Soviet informants have described it to me as an expression of dual subordination, one of the basic principles of democratic centralism, maintaining centralised control as well as local autonomy. Formally both lines of authority – ministerial and local – pass through the executive committee to the departments. In practice, however, the informal links between units in the education hierarchy are very strong. The two chains of authority are shown in Figure 7.1, the ministerial chain with a dotted line and the soviet chain with a continuous line.

According to information given in interviews with personnel at all levels, the ministerial chain of command is maintained by various

Figure 7.1 The organisation of child care, showing dual subordination of the local child care agencies to the ministerial and soviet hierarchies

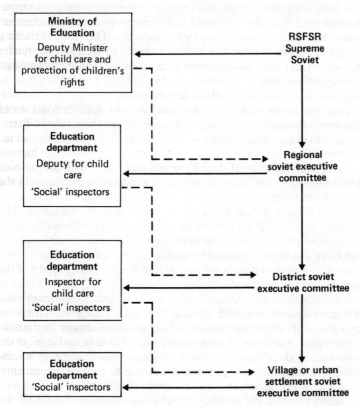

mechanisms. First, the ministry issues guidance through its publishing house, *Prosveshchenie* (Enlightenment). Secondly, local education departments refer their plans up through the hierarchy for ratification. Thirdly, a twice-yearly check (*otchet*) is carried out by officials at the higher levels of government over the work of officials at the lower levels. Case records are sent from the district departments to the regional. There they are collated and the regional officers present a report giving the statistical break-down of children in care, their problems and the actions taken. The check also provides the basic information for planning and budgeting. The deputy minister supplements this information by visiting or sending his or her staff to visit local offices. A fourth means of control is the regular reception periods (*priemy*) held by officials at all levels. Clients may have access to high-ranking officials to express their grievances or to complain against their particular welfare worker. Reception periods may even be held at the ministry itself. The officials whom I interviewed felt that being accessible to the client was an important means of keeping in touch with everyday problems and activities of their subordinates. It also provided a channel of redress for clients. The RSFSR Deputy Minister, during an interview with the author, answered a call about a case which had been passed directly on to her without going through the regional or district departments. She decided on the action to be taken without reference to these departments.

The ministerial chain of command is also maintained by the superiors' running regular training courses for their subordinates. Incentives in the form of bonuses, prizes and privileges are offered for good workers.

Alongside this powerful professional structure runs the state or soviet hierarchy. Officials at each level are accountable to the local soviet of elected representatives. The head of the department is normally a Party member and sits on the executive committee. The deputies responsible for each of the department's functions report to meetings of the executive committee and to full soviet meetings. The executive committee appoints standing commissions (*Posto yannye kommissii*) and committees to provide day-to-day management of the department's activities.

It is important to note that in the Soviet system each unit of state administration is matched by a Party unit. This exemplifies the principle of parallel organisation of Party and state organs. In the field of child care, the Party plays an active role both in organising 'social' personnel and in uniting within its ranks the leadership of the education departments. Thus many workers in paid or 'social' positions are Party members (just as many of the more active social workers in Britain are members of religious denominations, political parties or voluntary organisations). As in other aspects of Soviet life, the Party controls the key posts in child care through its 'nomenclature' (*nomenklatura*), or list of approved personnel for key posts. It has the right to nominate its members to a certain number of posts. In addition, it directs its members to posts outside its nomenclature as part of their training as Party members. The Party also runs regular training and propaganda courses covering political and professional issues.

The Region
This level includes a wide range of geographico-administrative entities, the government of a small republic, a region or large city such as Moscow or Leningrad. There is little Western information or analysis of regional Soviet government. The information presented here is derived from the author's field trip in 1972 and, in particular,

from extended visits to the Moscow and Leningrad departments. Moscow and Leningrad are, of course, not typical of the Soviet Union. They are the largest cities. There appears to be some rivalry between the two cities for the place of professional excellence. The Leningrad department is said to be the model department for child care. This may be partly because the number of district units with responsibility for child care is greater in Leningrad than in Moscow, even though Leningrad has the smaller population. In 1972 Leningrad (population 4 million) had nineteen districts employing children's inspectors. Moscow, on the other hand, (population approximately 7 million) had thirteen districts employing children's inspectors. Moscow is more densely populated than Leningrad and has a more transitory population.

The structure of the Leningrad department is shown in Figure 7.2. Child care functions are carried out by a deputy head for child care. Beneath the deputy there are four heads of sections responsible for child care, pre-school institutions, boarding schools and children's homes. Within the department there are also senior instructors (*instruktory*) responsible for specific activities. One of these instructors dealt with schools for defective children and special labour training

Figure 7.2   *An example of the organisation of child care services under the education department at intermediate level: Leningrad city education department*

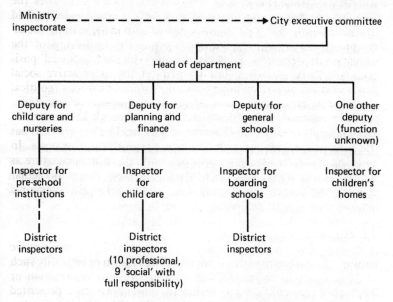

Source: Interview with departmental staff during field trip in 1972.

schools (*spetsial'nye proftekhnicheskie uchilishcha*). Another senior instructor was concerned with special schools for difficult children. She was also the deputy head of the Commission for Work with the Population at the Place of Residence and secretary of the city Commission for the Affairs of Minors. Such overlapping responsibilities and membership help maintain the links between the 'social' and strictly local government soviet spheres.

This intermediate level of government has three main child care responsibilities. First, it is responsible for planning and policy-making for its area. Secondly, the inspectors at this level oversee the functioning of the district departments under them. They check the work of the district inspectors, conduct in-service training and co-ordinate the district's needs and resources. This is no mean task. Not all districts have inspectors for child care. Many rely on 'social' inspectors alone or on a general schools inspector who takes on child care as an extra function. This patchy provision means that the regional inspector may have to take more part in the work of some districts than others. A further complication is the geographical dispersal of some districts. It can take days to reach outlying districts. This problem is discussed in an article by three inspectors in the Vologda region (Povarova, Godubov and Khvostov, 1969). The regional inspector is expected to travel round to all the districts at least twice a year when the reports to the ministry on the regional and district departments are made.

A third function of the intermediate level is to take decisions which are not within the legal competence of the district department. Residential placement, for example, requires the agreement of the regional inspector. Changes of the family status of a child – such as adoption, or the assumption of parental rights by the soviet – will be referred to the city or regional inspector before the district inspector takes the decision to the district executive committee.

The District

Like the British district, the Soviet *raion* is a multi-functional agency. It is the lowest level of government with the full range of local functions (the village and urban settlement soviets, like our parish councils, have more limited functions) and it is the point where the government most fully articulates with local people and the 'social' organisations. According to one of the few authoritative sources on the functions of the district:

The administrative district has specific rights in the sphere of socio-economic, socio-political and socio-cultural development. It is the district organs which play the important, and, in the last analysis, the leading role in the development of such social institutions as public education, health services and social insurance within its territory. The district organs through the direction of trade, food services, communal and day-to-day living services, building, have the ability to regulate the standard of living of the population. It can be stressed that the realisation of the social functions of society, linked with the satisfaction of material and spiritual needs of its members, is brought about to a significant degree through the agency of the organs at district level. The material expression of this is the district budget which constitutes part of the national income created and distributed on the governmental scale. (Pashkov, Dmitriev and Mezhevich, 1972, p. 33)

To fulfil these tasks the district organs make a social development plan. Pashkov, Dmitriev and Mezhevich (1972) described the general principles of the Leningrad City Plan; its primary function is to mediate between local and state interests. The social development plan has the following headings:

Transforming the social structure of the districts' population:
Bettering the residents' well-being, improving social insurance, communal, day-to-day services and living conditions.
Developing the health services and perfecting the physical culture of the population.
Improving the education system and upbringing of pre-school age and school age children.
Perfecting socio-political work in the area.
Communist upbringing of the workers and the general population.
Raising the workers' general educational and cultural level.
The district is also responsible for building new enterprises and for maximising industrial production. (Pashkov, Dmitriev and Mezhevich 1972, p. 35)

Child welfare appears in this district plan under the item for improving the education and upbringing of pre-school age and school-age children.

The district is the delivery point for child care provisions, and it has wide executive powers. The district executive committee carries out child care functions under the supervision of the intermediate level (Ershova, 1959, p. 24). The following account of the role and structure of the district education department is derived from information gained in 1972 through interviews with staff in the Vyborg and October districts of Leningrad.

The district education department has a general duty to ensure the welfare of any child in its area. It is empowered to place a child in substitute family care or guardianship. But the district must refer any decisions concerning property or changes in the legal status of a child, such as adoption, to the executive committee of the regional soviet. Decisions to place a child in a children's home or boarding school must be approved by the regional education department which controls placements in institutions. It advises the local court – either the People's Court or the District Court – on cases concerning the custody of children, and on the treatment of juvenile offenders. (The district children's inspector draws up a social report for the court.) The district also has to fulfil its role in the hierarchy of government. It responds to circulars from above and prepares twice-yearly reports from the republican ministry, and supervises village soviets' welfare activity or supplements it where necessary. The districts executive committee recruits staff of professional and 'social' children's inspectors to perform these functions.

The child care section of the Vyborg district education department structure is shown in Figure 7.3. There is one deputy head who is responsible for administrative and financial affairs. The child care inspectorate is responsible directly to the head of the education

Figure 7.3   *An example of the organisation of child care services under the education department at district level: Vyborg district, Leningrad*

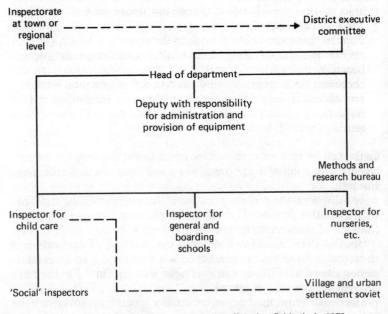

Source: Interviews with departmental staff during field trip in 1972.

department. The child care inspector in a good department such as the Vyborg department will supervise about seven 'social' inspectors, but there could be a far greater ratio of 'social' to professional inspectors. In some departments there may not be an inspector with this specialised function. In such departments a 'social' inspector may be relied upon to perform the role, or it may be subsumed under the functions of another inspector. The district inspector also supervises the work at village and urban settlement level.

Residential care of school-age children in boarding schools is the responsibility of the general schools inspector. Some boarding schools, however, notably the boarding schools for difficult children, are the city or regional inspector's responsibility. The Leningrad city department has one special school for difficult boys which takes referrals from all over the republic. Pre-school children's homes appear to be the responsibility of the inspector for pre-school institutions.

THE 'SOCIAL' AGENCIES

'Social service' is an important element in Soviet public administration. According to the Soviet concept of democracy, the interests of the populace must be expressed not only through paid officials and elected government ('representative democracy'), but also through citizen participation in the affairs and administration of government ('direct democracy').

> Popular participation is cherished because it is held to provide checks against the development of bureaucratic practices and because it enables the size of the bureaucracy to be limited. It is also cherished because unless there is a spectacular increase in popular non-official participation in the immediate future the objective of replacing the socialist state by Communist self-administration must remain a pipe-dream. (Churchward, 1968, p. 265)

In the late 1960s, while there were over 2 million deputies to the local soviets, there were around 4 million 'social' workers assisting in the business of government, and outside the soviet structure itself there were over 9,700,000 'social' workers in 966,412 'social' organisations such as trade union groups, people's courts and residents' committees (*ZhEKi*) (Churchward, 1968, p. 270).

'Social service' in child care expresses itself in many ways. Much of the actual case-work with the child is done by 'social' inspectors under professional supervision. As indicated above, when I visited the Vyborg district of Leningrad in 1972, the average ratio of 'social' to professional inspectors was seven to one. But 'social' work with children takes a variety of other forms.

'Social service' is organised in the workplace by the trade unions. Members are appointed to act in a 'social' capacity, caring for enterprise workers and their families. Trade union members are not likely to have had any formal social work training. They are organised by paid union officials who may have attended one of the trade union-run courses concerned amongst other things with teaching the fundamental principles of 'social' work. The organiser provides loose supervision and advice for the volunteer. Such volunteers may visit individuals at home or in hospital, they may take part in activities such as the People's Militia, the People's Court, or act as 'social' inspectors. Trade union volunteers form a safety net intended to prevent the problem worsening to the extent that a professional is needed. Their role is limited to this, and they must refer the case to professional services when action rather than advice is required.

Like the trade union, the Komsomol has a general welfare function. Its members are delegated to perform a wide range of 'social' work, with a particular concern for young people. Komsomol members help organise summer camps attended by Soviet children in general. They also help by taking 'difficult' children and adolescents on holiday, either as part of a general camp, or as part of a camp run particularly for the children at special boarding schools for difficult children. Or they may take a group of difficult children on a separate holiday. The ratio of Komsomol members to difficult children is normally high and the scheme is intended to lead to close friendships between the participants. The Komsomol encourages its members to 'adopt' a difficult child. Such 'adoption' (*shefstvo*) means that the Komsomol member keeps in close touch with the family, helps the child with homework and general schoolwork, and takes him or her out on excursions and on holiday. I met Komsomol members who had 'adopted' a difficult child in their early teens, had kept contact through the child's schooling and early adulthood, and had achieved a semi-familial relationship. The Komsomol member, normally a student, is nearer the child's age than is the children's inspector or the other 'social' workers who are usually pensioners, and is considered able to provide a more natural reference point or model for the child.

'Social service' at the place of residence is organised through the residents' committees (*ZhEKi*). These committees are made up primarily of residents, but specific agencies are also represented. There is a co-ordinating committee normally headed by the President of the Commission for Work among the Population who is usually a member of the Party committee of the local enterprise. The deputy head of the co-ordinating committee of the *ZhEK* is usually the director of the local secondary school. Other interests represented include the local education department; the soviet is also represented by the delegates' group. Most members of the *ZhEK* are unpaid, but some specialists are employed from the *ZhEK* 'social' work budget. In Leningrad, each *ZhEK* has a paid worker, 'the instructor for sport and mass work', who is often a student working in the evenings. In addition, most *ZhEKi* have a children's room, usually run by a pensioner under militia supervision. In Leningrad in 1972, there were between twenty and thirty rooms manned by about 100 people. These rooms deal particularly with 'difficult' children. Nurseries, clubs and other communal facilities are organised by the *ZhEK* with the co-operation of the local enterprise which provides help both materially and by seconding staff. The workers of the *ZhEK* do preventative work with families of 'difficult' children. When more intensive action is needed, however, the case is referred either to the children's inspector or to the Commission for the Affairs of Minors. Referral is facilitated by the fact that the commission and the education department work closely with the *ZhEK* and are usually represented on it. Some *ZhEKi* also have 'social' Commissions for the Affairs of Minors.

Around the *ZhEK* operate a wide network of preventative and 'social' organisations. The 'social' law and order agencies such as the People's Courts and People's Militia deal with minor offences by or against children and may intervene in cases such as cruelty against children or repeated truancy from school. Matters concerning the appointment of guardians or adoption, or issues of property rights are outside their jurisdiction, however, and would be dealt with by the State Court. Cases may be referred to the courts through a variety of channels, but the People's Militia are the most likely regular source of referrals. It assists the regular militia, most particularly in cases of social problems such as family disputes or youthful offenders. It has special contact with the children's rooms attached to the militia stations and *ZhEKi*.

THE LOCAL COMMISSIONS AND THE LINK BETWEEN 'SOCIAL' AGENCIES AND THE LOCAL SOVIET

The work of the wide range of 'social' organisations needs to be linked and organised together with that of the local soviet departments. The number of agencies involved is considerable, and the manpower they deploy large and varied in skill. Overall planning of 'social' service in child care is performed by two commissions. Information on both commissions comes from interviews in 1972 with a director of a Commission for the Affairs of Minors and a senior instructor of the soviet in Leningrad.

The Standing Commission for Culture, Education, Work with Youth and Socialist Legality

This commission (*Postoyannaya komissiya*) has a wide brief and is responsible for advising the soviet on all matters concerning the social, educational, welfare and legal aspects of the life of the population in its area. It is also responsible for planning professional and 'social' activity in these fields. The commission is elected from the members of the local soviet and meets twice a month. During February each year, the commission draws up a plan with the help of the trade unions, the militia, the Komsomol, the education department, the *ZhEKi* and the Commission for the Affairs of Minors. This plan is checked quarterly, the most important check being in December. The commission also organises meetings of all agencies involved, and sometimes of selected groups.

An example of the sort of meetings arranged by the commission took place in the October district in Leningrad during my visit in 1972. A letter went out in the name of the secretary of the executive committee to the delegates of the soviet, inviting them to a meeting on 11 May in the House of Culture to discuss the theme 'Organising upbringing work among children and adolescents from problem families and among those with a tendency towards delinquency'. The meeting was opened by the District Procurator, the 'social' Secretary of the Commission for the Affairs of Minors, and the Inspector for the Protection of Children. The aim of such meetings is to share and disseminate ideas about all aspects of 'social' and cultural activity, and they try to fill the gap left by lack of formal training of the administrators and officials involved in work such as child welfare. All the 'social' agencies run courses like this. The aim is to inform their workers and maintain their commitment.

The standing commission is made up of soviet delegates and is responsible for advice and administration of a wide range of sociocultural activity. It relies on other organisations working closer to the ground, such as the Commission for the Affairs of Minors, to conduct much of the 'agitation' work and to co-ordinate the work of the agencies involved.

The Commission for the Affairs of Minors

This commission (*Komissiya po delam nesovershennoletnikh*) is concerned with the most problematic aspects of child welfare, child neglect and delinquency, rather than mainstream child welfare problems. Its brief was outlined in a regulation of the RSFSR Supreme Soviet in 1967 ('Polozhenie . . .', 1967). It has an advisory, coordinative and educational role and it has power to place children in special schools for 'difficult' children. The membership of the commission includes soviet deputies, trade union and Komsomol presidents, workers in the education, health and social welfare departments, militia and others (Evteev and Kirin, 1970, p. 6). The Leningrad commission is made up of fifteen members elected every two years from the 'social' organisations (the trade unions and the Komsomol) and from the soviet and the education department; it includes the inspector for child care, a doctor and school teachers. The president is the secretary of the local executive committee who has a more or less formal role, depending on personal inclination. There is a 'social' secretary (*obshchestvennyi sekretar'*) appointed by the local executive committee who takes the more active role. I interviewed the 'social' secretary of the Leningrad City Commission and the secretary of the October District Commission. They both fulfilled several roles, the former being a senior instructor of the Leningrad City Soviet, concerned with special schools for 'difficult' children and with special labour schools (*spets PTU*). She was also a deputy head of the Commission for Work with the Population. The secretary of the October District Commission was also the president of the local trade union committee and had been a Party member for two years. From interviews, however, I could find little difference between the day-to-day work of the two secretaries, except that the latter was more committed to the commission's work as she had no other full-time commitments besides running the commission.

The commission acts as the interface between the state apparatus and the 'social' apparatus. Issues arise in the community at various points: the *ZhEKi*, the youth clubs, the brigades of volunteers and the children's rooms. Problems which cannot be resolved at these points are referred, either through the militia, or directly to the commission. The commission deals with referrals in a variety of ways depending on the nature of the case. Some cases go to the courts, some to the children's inspector or the juvenile section of the procuracy concerned with legal affairs of minors, and some children will be referred to a reception centre (*priemnik*) for assessment. The commission's approval is necessary for a child to be admitted to a special school for 'difficult' children. The commission can also decide to put a child on probation (*uslovnoe nakazanie*). It has the power to do this on its own, or it may seek help from the court. The referral structure is summarised in Figure 7.4. The commission also runs educational seminars and courses for various groups on child welfare issues. Seminars of this type may be run jointly with the cultural department of the local soviet. It draws up a yearly plan in February. The plan for the October district for 1972 set tasks, gave a period for their execution, allocated responsibility to a named person, named that person's superior and stated the times at which the programme would be checked, as well as who would be the checkers. It was entitled 'Plan for measures to prevent crime and to strengthen the social order in the district to be taken by the Party and state (soviet) administrative organs and the "social" organisations'. The third section of the plan, 'Measures for the prevention of crime among minors and youth' included proposals

Figure 7.4   *Referral pattern of child with problems*

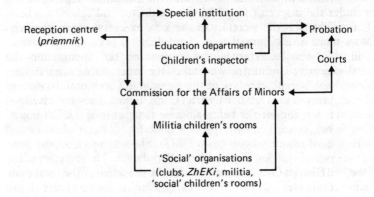

to establish new clubs, circles, children's rooms and sports groups for the young people of the district.

The soviet penetrates local 'social' activity in two further ways: first, through the Commission for Work with the Population and, secondly, through the delegates' groups in the *ZhEK*.

The Commission for Work with the Population
This commission (*Komissiya po rabote s naseleniem*) exists at all levels of local government and it is represented on the *ZhEK* as well. Each *ZhEK* has a co-ordinating Commission for Work with the Population which has a section concerned with children. Soviet delegate members come from the cultural committee, the education committee, and others who are interested. The commission draws its other members from among the local people and the workers of the local enterprise, and the president is normally one of the latter. The enterprise patronises its local commission, providing for material needs, offering its facilities for the leisure activities of residents, seconding its personnel to help out in a variety of ways, most typically in running clubs.

This commission co-ordinates 'social' activity at the place of residence, ensures that adequate resources are available and draws up a plan for each year's work. The planning time-table is simultaneous with that of the plans of the Commission for the Affairs of Minors and of the Standing Commission for Culture, Education, Work with Youth and Socialist Legality. The plan of the Commission for Work with the Population at soviet level directs the plan of each of the *ZhEK* commissions. The kinds of activities organised by the commission may be illustrated by the following extract from the plan for the commission of the October district for 1972. The section quoted concerns the organisation of methodological work.

i. To conduct sociological research in a 'micro-area' (*mikroraion*) (*ZhEKi* nos 4 and 12) to establish the social structure of the residents.

ii. The developmental characteristics of adolescence. Meetings with a sociologist.

iii. To run an experimental seminar on the theme: 'On the co-operation of workers in the Department of Internal Affairs (OVD) and the 'social' workers of the Admiral factory in preventative work with 'difficult' adolescents and children from 'deprived' (*neblagopoluchnye*) families in *ZhEKi* nos 9, 10, 20.

iv. To run a seminar for the population called: 'Life is not a personal private affair.'

v. To run seminars three times a month for the presidents of the Commissions for Work with the Population attached to the *ZhEKi*.

From this excerpt it will be seen that the commission conducts very serious work of professional calibre, which covers research, training and political activity, and co-ordination of the commissions of the *ZhEKi*.

Delegates' Groups
A further way in which the soviet penetrates the *ZhEK* is by means of the delegates' groups. This mechanism was established in Leningrad at least by the early 1960s (Busko, 1963). In each *ZhEK* there are groups of soviet delegates who ensure that the interests of the *ZhEK* are represented in discussions of local policy. These delegates are responsible for helping to feed the responses of their neighbourhoods into the soviet decision-making structure. They are a form of public consultation.

CONCLUSIONS

'Social service' provides much of the manpower required to run the welfare services, and the Soviet state harnesses this source of labour systematically. Paid workers are as much supervisors of their 'social' workers as they are case-workers.

Despite the obvious advantages of 'social service', Soviet commentators recognise that there are attendant disadvantages. First, rather than being a means to decrease bureaucratisation, 'social' work may, on the contrary, increase bureaucratisation by duplicating the state apparatus. Mitskevich (1959) has criticised the use of volunteers in the law and order agencies because 'it only leads to unnecessary parallelism in the work of the "social" and state organs of order. It does not lead to habits of self-administration but only to the replacement of one coercive apparatus by another.' Self-administration (*samoobsluzhivanie*) is a twin concept of *obshchestvennost'*. It denotes the administration of local affairs by the local population itself and is a necessary pre-condition to achieving communism.

A second problem is that, in the interests of economy, 'social' workers may be used when professional staff are needed. The Soviet professional welfare workers I interviewed did not all subscribe uncritically to the practice of employing 'social' workers. There are various means of control over the latters' work, but nevertheless in areas where there are no professional children's inspectors, such as a rural village soviet, such control is of necessity weakened. Even where it is possible for the professional workers to exert the necessary control this puts a heavy extra burden on them, since they also have the administrative and court functions normally associated with a welfare worker's job.

What might the British learn from Soviet child care administration? First, the Soviet Union makes fuller use than we do of the expertise available in the community through 'social service'. From Soviet practice we might learn to make better use of voluntary effort; but we might also learn that volunteers must be systematically recruited, trained, managed and rewarded. The system relies on a considerable administration to do this. The second lesson is that child care and education services might be more fully linked. This is made easier in the Soviet structure where both responsibilities are fulfilled in one department and sometimes by one worker.

BIBLIOGRAPHY

Busko, L. S., *Deputatskie gruppy* (Leningrad, 1963).

Churchyard, L. G. *Contemporary Soviet Government* (London: Routledge & Kegan Paul, 1968).

Ershova, M. M., *Opeka i popechitel'stvo nad nesovershennoletnimi* (Moscow, 1959).

Evteev, M. P. and Kirin, V. A., *Zakonodatel' stvo ob otvetstvennosti nesovershennoletnikh* (Moscow, 1970).

'Instruktivno-metodicheskie ukazaniya dlya rabotnikov narodnogo prosveshcheniya; Ministerstvo prosveshcheniya RSFSR, 8 maya 1950', *Spravochnik po voprosam okhrany detstva* (Moscow, 1956), p. 7.

'Kodeks o brake i sem'e RSFSR' *Vedomosti Verkhovnogo Soveta RSFSR*, 1969, no. 32, art. 1,086.

'Kodeks zakonov ob Aktakh grazhdanskogo sostoyaniya, Brachnom, Semeinom i Opekunskom prave', *Sobranie uzakonenii i rasporyazhenii rabochego i krest' yanskogo pravitel'stva*, 1918, nos 76–77, section I, art. 818.

Madison, B. Q., *Social Welfare in the Soviet Union* (Stanford, Cal.: Stanford University Press, 1968).

Mitskevich, A. V., 'Rasshirenie roli obshchestvennykh organizatsii v period razvernutogo stroitel'stva sotsializma', *Sovetskoe gosudarstvo i pravo*, 1959, no. 9, pp. 24–33.

'Ob iz"yatii opeki iz vedeniya Narodnogo Komissariata sotsial'nogo obespecheniya', *Sobranie uzakonenii i rasporyazhenii rabochego i krest'yanskogo pravitel'stva*, 1920, no. 93, section I, art. 506.

Pashkov, A. S., Dmitriev, A. V. and Mezhevich, A. M., 'Nekotorye voprosy sotsial'nogo planirovaniya v gorodskom administrativnom raione', *Chelovek i obshchestvo*, vol. 10, 1972, pp. 31–9.

'Polozhenie o komissiyakh po delam nesovershennoletnikh', *Vedomosti Verkhovnogo Soveta RSFSR*, 1967, no. 23, art. 536.

'Polozhenie ob organakh opeki i popechitel'stva', *Sobranie uzakonenii i rasporyazhenii rabochego i krest'yanskogo pravitel'stva RSFSR*, 1928, no. 75, section I, art. 524.

Povarova, A., Godubov, A. and Khvostov, G., 'V glubinke', *Uchitel'skaya gazeta*, 28 October 1969.

8

Backward Children in the USSR: An Unfamiliar Approach to a Familiar Problem

ANDREW SUTTON

INTRODUCTION

In recent years the Soviet Union has participated widely at the institutional level in the general international concern for the special educational needs of handicapped children, and Soviet special educationists (for example, Vlasova and Lubovskii, 1976) have written with considerable pride of the advances made in special education in their country and its close relationship with scientific research.

At a superficial level, the organisation of Soviet provision in this field forms a 'network' (*set*) that might seem very familiar to British educationists. Overall responsibility for the education and training of the handicapped rests with three ministries, the largest involvement being that of the Ministries of Education of the Union Republics. The Ministries of Education run special kindergartens for the deaf and for the blind, special schools for the various categories of handicap at school age, and special evening schools and correspondence courses for young adults with defects of hearing and vision. The Ministries of Social Security of the Union Republics run children's homes for more seriously mentally handicapped young people, and workshops for adults with the same grades of defect. The Ministries of Health provide clinics and sanatorium schools for mentally disturbed children, clinical services for children with speech disorders, and general speech therapy services through the local polyclinics. They may also provide for the lifelong care of the profoundly handicapped in hospitals for the chronically infirm. The services provided by the ministries are supplemented at the 'middle' (*srednii*) level of education by the All-Russian societies for the blind and the deaf, which provide training-production workshops (*uchebno-proizvodstvennye masterskie*). The overall network of special educational facilities (*set' uchebno-vospitatel'nykh uchrezhdenii*) is summarised in Figure 8.1 (D'yachkov, 1970, pp. 243–4, 386–8).

But the superficial structural similarities to British provision mark fundamental differences in conceptualisation and practice, most particularly in the definition and education of children who have been variously described in English as subnormal, retarded, backward, mentally defective and mentally deficient, feebleminded, even 'developmentally young'. On more detailed examination these differences preclude direct identification of special education (and educational psychology) in the Soviet Union with the equivalent bodies of theory and practice in the English-speaking world in general, and perhaps in Britain in particular. Attempts by English-speaking delegations and study tours, for example, to make such a comparison have resulted in uncomprehending and confused accounts. Visiting English-speaking educators and psychologists, failing to comprehend the very different goals and theoretical background of their Soviet colleagues, have tended to dismiss or discount what they do. Such 'travellers' tales' are not restricted to British visitors, nor to the distant past (for example, Dunn and Kirk, 1963; Segal, 1966; Shennan, 1978).

The principal basis for the misunderstandings of the Soviet approach to the identification and education of mentally handicapped children lies in the vastly different philosophical and psychological bases for the provisions made.

THE HISTORICAL BACKGROUND

Soviet developmental psychology is mainly Russian in origin. There is a small school of Georgian psychology, the psychology of 'set' (*ustanovka*), that coexists with it in a general Marxist–Leninist framework, but it has no general bearing on the conceptualisation of special education and will not be considered further here.

One of the first measures of the new Soviet government after the Revolution was the abolition of all charitable and philanthropic bodies and the transfer to the state of all their establishments for the upbringing and education of children. In December 1917, a sub-department for defective children was created within Narkompros (The People's Commissariat for Education) and during the years up to 1923 the state formulated the principles that would guide its policy on handicapped children (Zamskii, 1974, pp. 325, 341). These were:

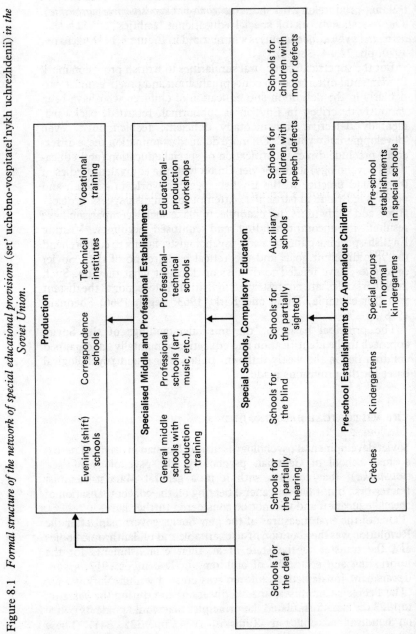

Figure 8.1 *Formal structure of the network of special educational provisions (set' uchebno-vospitatel'nykh uchrezhdenii) in the Soviet Union.*

Production

Evening (shift) schools   Correspondence schools   Technical institutes   Vocational training

Specialised Middle and Professional Establishments

General middle schools with production training   Professional schools (art, music, etc.)   Professional–technical schools   Educational–production workshops

Special Schools, Compulsory Education

Schools for the partially hearing   Schools for the blind   Schools for the partially sighted   Auxiliary schools   Schools for children with speech defects   Schools for children with motor defects

Schools for the deaf

Pre-school Establishments for Anomalous Children

Crèches   Kindergartens   Special groups in normal kindergartens   Pre-school establishments in special schools

(1) public concern for 'anomalous' (*anomal'nye*) children;
(2) a guarantee of whatever educational circumstances might be necessary to enable them to become full citizens;
(3) the provision of general education even to anomalous children.

Yet, by the beginning of 1924, there were only sixty-five establishments of various kinds for mentally deficient children in the whole of the RSFSR, accommodating only 3,442 children. Twenty-seven of the establishments (1,450 children) were in Moscow and its surrounding district and eight in Leningrad (1,880 children), about two-thirds of the total provision therefore being centred in the two metropolitan areas. Many outlying districts had no provision at all. Altogether there were 532 teachers working in these establishments (Zamskii, 1974, p. 343).

The above figures represent a modern recalculation of data presented in tabular form, which did not quite add up. They had been published as an appendix to a small collection of articles addressed to the question of what would constitute the dialectical materialist approach to the education of the handicapped. Its editor was a young psychologist from Gomel', L. S. Vygotskii, who placed especial emphasis on the dialectical nature of handicap, neither solely physical nor solely mental but essentially social in nature.

> Each bodily inadequacy – be it blindness, deafness or congenital feeblemindedness – not only changes man's relationship to the world, but above all tells on his relationship with people. The organic defect or flaw is realised as asocial, non-normal behaviour. (Vygotskii, 1924, p. 3).

The establishment of a developmental psychology that was compatible with the requirements of Marxism–Leninism involved intensive ideological and methodological struggle over the course of the 1920s and early 1930s, with first idealist and then mechanistic approaches being discounted. To a large degree this involved the rejection of movements in psychology that were then current in the West (Freud's views being an example of an idealist approach, behaviourism, a mechanistic one), but the indigenous heritage of the physiologist Pavlov (still at that time an active worker in the field) lent important support to those who sought to 'physiologise' psychology (see Bauer, 1952).

In the 1920s there emerged an influential movement, 'pædology' (*pedologiya*), an apparent synthesis which claimed to be a 'unified Marxist science of childhood'. Intended as a multidisciplinary approach to the whole of children's education and development, pædology was enormously influential for a short time in the everyday running of education. Pinkevitch considered that:

The utilisation and pedagogical evaluation of the facts of pedology [*sic*] provide the science basis for the work of every teacher who deals with children of preschool and school age . . . This science is concerned with the psychological and physical development of the child from birth to maturity. It studies the biology and psychology of human growth. Pedagogy takes the findings of pedology and utilises them in the organisation of methods for promoting the desired physical and mental development of the child. (Pinkevitch, 1929, pp. 6–7)

Beatrice King, treating 'pedologue' and 'child psychologist' as synonymous, reported that 'in the bigger schools are organised method committees from members of the staff, which include a mistress of methods and a child psychologist' (1936, p. 219).

But by the time that King's book was published in England, pædology had come under unceasing attack in the Soviet Union. At a theoretical level, it had failed to make a real synthesis of the biological and environmental in explaining the origins of human intelligence and personality, and thus remained a 'two-factor' theory unable to explain the inter-relationship of its component disciplines. At a practical level, its involvement in psychological testing brought it into considerable disrepute. Intelligence testing had been widely espoused in the Soviet Union. Bowen (1962) has reported that by 1926 Blonskii had tested the intelligence of 10,000 children in Moscow, and that in 1926/7 he organised a programme to measure the intelligence of every child entering school in two out of the six of Moscow's educational districts (what we would now term 'screening'). Particularly, intelligence testing became associated with the admission of children to schools for 'difficult children'.

This increasing dissatisfaction culminated in the decree of the Central Committee of the CPSU, 'On Pædological Perversions' ('O pedologicheskikh . . .', 1936). This decree complained that the People's Commissariat of Education had tolerated the widespread influx of pædologists into the schools where they had assumed a broad range of organisational responsibilities, including class placement, determining the reasons for pupils' failure to achieve (*neuspevaemost'*), and removal of non-achievers from the normal school system. The decree devoted especial attention to the particular activities of the pædologists relating to the disposal of backward children.

The practice of the pædologists, conducted completely separately from the pedagogue and the activities of the school, have amounted basically to pseudo-scientific experiments and the administration amongst pupils and their parents of an innumerable quantity of surveys in the form of meaningless and harmful questionnaires, tests, etc. long condemned by the Party. These would-be scientific surveys, conducted amongst a large number of pupils and their parents, were directed mainly against backward (*neuspevayushchie*) pupils or those who do not fit in to the school regime, and have as their aim to prove, from the would-be 'scientific, bio-social' viewpoint of contemporary pædology, the hereditary and social conditioning of the pupils' backwardness or individual defects of behaviour, to find the maximum of negative influences and pathological perversions in the pupil, his family, kin and social environment, and thus to find a reason for removal of pupils from the normal school collective.

To the same end there has operated a widespread system of investigating pupils' mental development and endowment (*odarennost'*), uncritically transplanted into Soviet soil from bourgeois class pædology, a sheer mockery of the pupils and a contradiction of the tasks of the Soviet school and of common sense. Children of 6 or 7 years were asked standard casuistic questions, after which were worked out their so-called 'pædological age' and the level of their intellectual endowment.

All this has led to greater and greater numbers of children being counted in the company of the mentally deficient, defective and 'difficult'.

Having ascribed the pupils subject to pædological 'study' to one of the categories indicated, the paedologists determined the children liable to removal from normal school to 'special' schools and classes for 'difficult' children, for the mentally deficient, for psycho-neurotics, etc.

The Central Committee finds that as a result of the pædologists' harmful activity the filling of 'special' schools has been conducted on a broad and ever-increasing scale. Contrary to the direct instruction of the Central Committee and the Council of People's Commissars on setting up two or three schools for deficient and disruptive pupils, the Narkompros of the RSFSR has established a large number of special schools under various designations, in which the huge majority of pupils are completely normal children eligible for return to normal schools. In these schools, alongside defective children, there study talented and (normally) endowed children groundlessly assigned by the pædologists to the category of 'difficult' on the basis of pseudo-scientific theories.

The decree resolved to restore the supremacy of pedagogy and teachers in education, to liquidate the pædological units in the schools, to withdraw pædological methods and abolish all teaching of pædology, and to recommend to the Narkompros of the Soviet republics that they should review their schools for 'hard to rear' (*trudnovospituemye*) children and transfer the greater part of their pupils back into normal schools.

Vygotskii had died in 1934. In the ten years that he had worked as a psychologist his interest in the education of backward children had led him into a concern to understand the nature of child development generally, and he had become involved in the disputes over the nature of what constituted a true dialectical-materialistic psychology. He based his approach directly on Engels (Petrovskii, 1973, p. 13), not only on his dialectical method, but also upon his ideas on the role of labour in man's adaption to nature, and the transformation of natural forces with the help of tools in the process of production. He advanced the idea that labour and activity with tools led to a change in the nature of man's behaviour and to the qualitative differences between man and the animals. This difference depends therefore on the mediated character of human activity. He also owed a heavy and conscious debt to Marx.

> I don't want to discover the nature of mind by patching together a lot of quotations. I want to find out how science has to be built, to approach the study of the mind having learned the whole of Marx's *method* . . .. In order to create such an enabling theory-method in the generally accepted scientific manner, it is necessary to discover the essence of the given area of phenomena, the laws according to which they change, their qualitative and quantitative characteristics, their causes. It is necessary to formulate the categories and concepts that are specifically relevant to them – in other words to create one's own *Capital*. (From an unpublished notebook, quoted in English translation by Cole and Scribner, 1978, p. 9)

Vygotskii's works were withdrawn from publication shortly after his death, perhaps in part because of his apparent tinkering with the classics of Marxism. He had also been guilty of an earlier association with the pædologists (which he had later repudiated). But, though his theory of child development has been subject to certain ideological criticism (see Leont'ev and Luriya, 1956), his overall formulation of what constitutes the nature of the human mind, and how this phenomenon is brought about over the course of our childhood, remains the basis of Soviet development psychology and has particular relevance to the identification and differential education of backward children.

SOVIET DEVELOPMENTAL PSYCHOLOGY

Two major editions of Vygotskii's writings (Vygotskii, 1956, 1960) have been published in the Soviet Union. Vygotskii himself was not a clear writer, and especially in his later works devoted little attention to ordering and systematising his material. The brief introduction to his 'socio-historical theory' (*obshchestvenno-istoricheskaya teoriya*) that follows represents a considerable rendering down of expositions that were often repetitious and sometimes obscure, and restricts itself to certain cardinal points essential for an understanding of present-day Soviet defectology.

The Socio-Historical Theory

Vygotskii's socio-historical theory of human mental development insists that there is an essential distinction to be made between, on the one hand, the learning and thinking of humans and, on the other, the learning and thinking of all other species. They are *qualitatively different phenomena*.

The behaviour of animals depends on two kinds of experience. First, there is the inherited, biologically fixed experience, consolidated in the conditional reflexes. In content it is the experience of the species. Secondly, there are the individual creature's own experiences, acquired ontogenetically as the result of the formation of conditional reflexes.

Man, of course, shares these lower-order influences. He enters life with a repertoire of hereditarily consolidated species-experiences. And his behaviour, like that of the lower animals, is influenced by his concrete experiences over the course of his life. But in man these experiences include a special kind of experience that is unique in life on this planet, the individual transmission from adult to child of the generalised historical experience of society (its culture), primarily, of course, through the medium of speech, in the *active* mutual interaction of adult and child. The child never experiences his physical world alone: his connections with it are always mediated by his relationship with adults, and in a particular way by the mediation of speech. His behaviour is therefore a product not solely of the actual properties of the surrounding world, its propensities and relationships (the first-signal system of conditional responses, such as animals are dependent on to modify their behaviour), but upon such properties and relationships *detached from the actual objects* (i.e. on meaning). This, the second-signal system of reality, expressed primarily in speech, not only permits the accumulation and transmission of knowledge and skills gained from practical human experience from one generation to the next, it also transforms the whole nature of individual mental development over the course of the individual's childhood (ontogenesis). This transformation not only affects the way that hereditarily transmitted experience acts to preform behaviour, but also introduces a decisive change in the way that the child learns from his immediate experience (his first-signal learning). Both kinds of learning, the first- and the second-signalling systems, are part of the child's development, and they interact one with the other. But it is the unique higher-order, second-signal learning that assumes the leading role, that changes, develops and perfects actions, and *creates* specifically human kinds of behaviour (for example, operations with tools, speech activities and ultimately verbal thinking itself).

The behaviour and thinking of the modern human adult are, therefore, the end-product of two separate processes of development:

(1)   the biological evolution which over the course of millions of years resulted in the emergence of *homo sapiens*;
(2)   the historical development that over a much shorter period has transformed primitive man into modern cultured man, with no corresponding structural or biological change in his brain.

Soviet psychology denies a direct relationship between brain physiology and mental functioning in human development, asserting instead that this relationship is always mediated by cultural factors, with especial reference to the role of speech in human mental development (see, for example, Luriya and Yudovich, 1959). It recognises, even affirms, that there are differences in brain functioning between one individual and another *at the physiological level* and that these differences may be genetically determined, but asserts that these differences on the physiological plane may be wholly over-ridden on the mental plane by subsequent learning conducted in a process of sociogenesis. Leont'ev (1963) has used the term 'new functional organs' to describe the formation in the brain of stable reflex systems dependent upon verbal stimuli, new 'tools of mental production'. It is the formation of these functional organs that will determine the intelligence of a given individual, and these are ontogenetical developments formed by the child's experience of acting on his surrounding world in interaction with adults. Soviet psychologists are not, therefore, obliged (as often seems assumed in the West) to regard all humans as 'equal', since different personal circumstances will lead to these functional organs being variously formed, or even not being formed at all. Indeed, there is an active branch of Soviet psychology working to encourage variability in human development. But the acceptance by Soviet psychologists and educators of individual variability, and their work to encourage emerging individual talents and interests are to be seen against a view of what constitutes human *potential* which is very unfamiliar to that of their British equivalents. Potential depends not upon what a child brings into the world, but upon what society makes of him.

Present-day Soviet psychology distinguishes itself both from its own earlier days and from many current Western writings and assumptions on intelligence mainly by its emphasis on a 'third factor'. Vygotskii cut across the argument of whether intelligence is primarily due to inheritance or to environment by separating out from the 'environment' category those aspects relating to the child's purposeful interactions with adults (*obshchenie*), especially 'teaching' (*obuchenie*). After this 'partitioning of the environment' the three factors determining mental development are:

(1) heredity,
(2) environment,
(3) social interaction (especially *obuchenie*),

with the third of these potentially able to override the influence of the other two, thus permitting the unique malleability and potentiality of human mental development. The role of adults in children's development is not therefore to help children 'fulfil their potential'. Rather it is to create the very mental abilities that they need to master the world.

Though Vygotskii is now acknowledged as the founder of Soviet developmental psychology, he is regarded as having been at fault in his discussion of *obuchenie*, in emphasis though not in substance. In partitioning the adult–child interaction from the wider universe of environmental influences acting upon the child, one must be very careful to avoid the implication that this describes solely the processes of adults' acting upon the child (teaching him, playing with him, showing him things, etc.) and the child's inner experience of this interaction (his learning). What is essential is that there is not just an *interaction*, but that the concept of *obuchenie* involves equally *the child's own active participation* in real practical activities. Vygotskii is not regarded as having been sufficiently alert to this. In Soviet terms, his failure in this respect opened the door to idealism, by suggesting that human consciousness might arise solely from the interaction between subject and subject. But that would be dialectics without the materialism, in our terms simply 'interactionism' or 'intersubjectivity'. To be material the child's development also has to involve the child's active participation in the real world, consciousness arising therefore from the interaction of subject and object (Leont'ev and Luriya, 1956).

It should be noted, too, that the Russian word *obuchenie* does not admit to a direct English translation. It means both teaching and learning, both sides of the two-way process, and is therefore well suited to a dialectical view of a phenomenon made up of mutually interpenetrating opposites. Its frequent conventional translation simply as 'learning' therefore renders much Russian work in English translation wholly meaningless, particularly the intense Soviet interest in the relationship between *obuchenie* and development. It should be recalled that the verb 'to develop' is transitive as well as intransitive, and that the dialectical viewpoint will therefore include a different view of the concept of 'development'. Not only do children develop, but we adults develop them. On balance, Soviet developmental psychology is a psychology of teaching and teaching difficulties, as much as ours is one of learning and learning difficulties.

The Zone of Next Development

Vygotskii differentiated between two means of acquiring concepts:

(1) 'everyday' (*zhitel'nye*) or spontaneous concepts are those that a child forms for himself out of his day-to-day experiences;

(2) 'scientific' (*nauchnye*) or taught concepts are those passed on to him ready-formed by the speech of adults.

An essential feature of the scientific concept is its already established existence within the culture in systematic relationship with other concepts. As the child acquires the scientific concept, he also acquires this relationship, enabling him to systematise his spontaneous concepts and handle them too as scientific ones, in a conscious fashion. Any given concept may be acquired either 'spontaneously' or 'scientifically'.

The distinction between scientific and spontaneous concepts opens the way for an important conceptual tool for educational research and for clinical investigation, and 'zone of next development' (*zona blizhayushchego razvitiya*). Vygotskii described two levels of intellectual development existing simultaneously in the developing child:

(1) the 'actual' or 'present' (*aktual'nyi*) level of development, manifest in what the child can do on his own, without the help of an adult;

(2) the 'potential' (*potentsial'nyi*) level of development, demonstrated by what the child can do 'in co-operation' with an adult, with the maximal, optimal help, guidance, explanation, demonstration, etc. that the adult can give.

Vygostkii termed the gap between the two levels the zone of next development. It indicates the level of task that the child is ready to undertake on the basis of what he can already do as long as he receives the best help possible from an adult. In defining and evaluating potential, therefore, attention focuses not on whether a child can solve a problem on the basis of what he already knows and the skills that he has already formed (as in the interpretation so often put upon the results of standardised intelligence tests), but rather upon his zone of next development. Vygotskii held that the child's greater or lesser ability to transfer from what he can do on his own to what he can do with help, proves to be the most sensitive symptom that characterises the dynamics of the child's development and success ('success' here meaning school achievement). Consequently in evaluating a child's educational potential, attention should focus not on whether he can solve a problem on his own, but rather on his zone of next development, i.e. upon whether he can solve harder problems with the adult help best suited to his needs, then having mastered the process taught him to go on to use his new 'mental tool' to solve analogous problems on his own. Assessment in a dialectical and materialist psychology is, therefore, concerned as much with the teacher and the means of teaching as it is with the learner, as much with the process of teaching and of learning as with their products, and as much with the child's practical action as with his understanding.

The psychology founded by Vygotskii maintains that to teach a child at the level determined by the use of intelligence tests (i.e. at his level of actual or present development) does nothing to accelerate the process of his development, but rather impedes it, by reinforcing his present level and failing to provide him with new tools of mental production. In contrast to this, the zone of next development provides an indication of the upper limits of the child's teachability (*obuchae-most'*) and permits teaching to be regulated to create maximal growth and development. Vygotskii (1956, pp. 278, 277, Vygotskii's emphasis) held that *'the only good teaching is that which stays ahead of development'*, and that maximal mental progress can only be ensured by teaching directed towards the upper end of the child's zone of next development, *'pedagogy must be oriented not towards the yesterday of development but towards its tomorrow'*.

Stages not Ages

Characteristically, despite the ideas and influence of Western developmental psychologists – especially, in recent years, the formulations of Piaget – practice in our own educational system has been predicated on the general background assumption that mental development is some sort of continuous process, a continuum. In psychology this has been traditionally expressed formally in learning 'curves', covering the whole span of childhood, and in mental ages, language ages, etc., that record the course of development in equal-size units along single dimensions. More recently, there has been some reaction against formal psychometric examinations and these have been replaced, particularly in the fields of pre-school and handicapped provision, by a host of 'developmental check lists' which, despite their general eschewel of normative data, adhere to the same general linear model. Such continuous models of normal child development have been reflected in the idea of a continuum of ability, intelligence, potential, etc., within a given age-group, with 'normal' gradually fading through 'borderline' and on into 'subnormal'.

The particular relationship between theory and practice in Soviet psychology, however, has made very explicit demands that educators at all levels should be very aware that child development is not a continuous process, but that it is broken by changes in kind. This means that the child not only 'grows' in his mental skills, but that there are developments, changes in quality, that fundamentally change both his own mental operations and how he relates to those around him and to his practical activities (Petrovskii, 1973).

Thus for a protracted period, the child maintains the same basic mental characteristics, the same relationship to his surrounding world (demanding both actions and interactions). But these periods of relatively slow progressive change (growth) are interrupted by periods of enormously sharper, more spasmodic changes (development) in which quite new mental characteristics emerge. These new characteristics not only rearrange the child's already existing structures, but also his relationships with his outside world (including his social world), demanding in turn that the adults around him also introduce new ways of behaving towards him to ensure activities and interactions best suited to a new range of needs. There is a clear parallel between this model and that of the contradictions between the forces and relations of production in historical materialism. These sudden changes in the child's mental and social operations, 'developmental crises', are not brought about by biological maturation. Normal children living in broadly similar social circumstances will enter these crises at roughly the same age. Children whose circumstances differ markedly one from another in important respects will differ in the ages at which stage-change occurs, and if their circumstances are particularly unfelicitous may fail to progress right through the system appropriate to children in their society. But there will also be a few children who, because of defects in vital aspects of their own physical structure, might develop 'anomalously', again failing to achieve normal stage-changes at the ages that most children do. Thus, at a given age, a population of children will show a range of stage attainment, different stages indicating different kinds of development and different kinds of developmental needs, as well as differences in the amount that each child can do. And amongst the least advanced, some children will be behind because of differences in their experience of teaching and social interaction, whilst others will be developing anomalously because of physical problems.

The child's interactions with his outside world account for his growth within a particular stage of development. They do not, however, explain his development from one stage to another. This stems from 'contradictions' within the child himself. At a given stage, the relationship that it involves with his outside world initially facilitates the growth and extension of his abilities, his knowledge, his skills, etc. But as they increase this ceases to be an advantage; his expanding abilities render such kinds of activities and inter-relationships obsolete, he senses new abilities and loses interest in activities that at one time attracted him; he strives for change. The adults around him might perceive this striving in the form of 'problems' (obstinacy, negativism, etc.,) and how great such difficulties are, will depend significantly on the adults' response to them. They must recognise that the child is trying to change, to develop, and above all they must change their own relationship towards him, identifying his new abilities and giving shape to new kinds of activity in which they can be realised.

In Soviet psychology, it is these contradictions that arise in the course of mental development that provides its essential driving force. Without such contradictions it would not be possible to develop from one stage to another, the child would remain at a given stage with no stimulus to move on to the next.

Since the overall theoretical framework holds that mental abilities do not arise out of themselves, but are formed in the course of upbringing and *obuchenie*, it is not possible within it to define a stage of development without taking into account the influence of these factors. Children at different stages of mental development differ between themselves not in the psychological qualities that they already possess but in that, given certain circumstances of upbringing and *obuchenie*, certain mental qualities can be formed within them. A stage, therefore, is defined by the potentialities generated by achievements, rather than by the achievements themselves.

It is apparent from the Soviet literature that there is continuing active debate about which precise changes in the course of children's mental development comprise the most important developmental crises. But consideration of Soviet formulations of retardation depend upon areas which do find general agreement: that the period before the first acquisition of speech (on average about twelve months) must be separated from what comes after; that the period before about three years ('nursery age') is to be distinguished from the period after it ('the pre-school age'), and that the pre-school age is to be distinguished from the 'school age'. (Though whether the pre-school age runs on average from 3 to 5 or from 3 to 7 years is far from clear.)

For the educator, the importance of an individual child's stage (defined, remember, in terms of potential) lies in the 'leading' activity required to maximalise that child's development. Very briefly, before the onset of speech the characteristic need is for emotional links with the adult; at nursery age it is for teaching concerned with concrete objects, actions, etc.; at pre-school age it is 'play' (defined in a certain way, see Vygotskii, 1966), and at school age it is the teaching of rules or principles via scientific concepts.

The dialectical principle of qualitative leaps, manifest in the discontinuities of normal mental development over the course of childhood, is reflected in discontinuities within the range of intellectual potential when children of a given age are compared one with another. In thinking, therefore, about what English-speaking educational psychology and child psychiatry term 'the lower end of the ability range', Soviet psychology looks for differences in kind.

DEFECTOLOGY

Defectology (*defektologiya*) is the study of the laws of development, the upbringing and education of children with physical and mental inadequacies. It includes branches of medicine, psychology and education. A 'defectologist' (*defektolog*) is a five-year trained special educator.

Soviet defectology insists that a child who is failing to develop and progress can only be understood and helped to the full on the basis of an appreciation of the 'structure of the defect' (*struktura defekta*), that is of the peculiar relationships that have developed in that child between various aspects of mental functioning (memory, attention, perception, thinking, speech, emotional aspects, etc.). Those peculiarities can only be properly understood by an analysis of their genesis, of how they were formed, and this demands the inclusion in the analysis of both the biological and social bases of the child's development. Given an understanding of the structure of a child's defect, then it is hoped that as early as possible in the cause of development differential corrective and educational measures can be applied, according to the particular goals that the child's defect determines in the light of present knowledge.

Where a child has a physical defect affecting mechanisms essential to the course of development, the nature of this defect will interact with the conditions of his education and upbringing to direct his development into a particular anomalous course.

Defectology is concerned then, both in assessment and provision, with careful qualitative distinctions.

Anomalous Children
Anomalous children (*anomal'nye deti*) comprise the deaf, the partially hearing and the late-deafened, the blind and the partially sighted, children with severe speech defects, children with motor disabilities, and the mentally deficient.

The Mentally Deficient

A Soviet child may be deemed mentally deficient (*umstvenno otstalyi*) only when his failure to progress in school has been shown to result from damage to the brain of such a nature and degree as to lead to a distortion of the higher mental processes (voluntary memory, attention, perception, verbal thinking, etc.). Though physiologically based and expressed the concept focuses attention upon the course of the subsequent, systemic, psychological damage to the child's mental and personal development. It is a qualitative as much as it is a quantitative differentiation that is made between the deficient and the non-deficient child.

It should not, of course, be understood from this that central nervous system damage = mental deficiency = central nervous system damage. Cerebral palsy, epilepsy, specific defects and other conditions do not necessarily imply mental deficiency (though in some cases they clearly do overlap with it). On the other hand, a child cannot properly be diagnosed mentally deficient in the Soviet Union without the understanding that he has central nervous system damage.

Grades of defect. There are three grades (*stepeni*) of mentally deficient children, 'idiots', 'imbeciles' and 'debiles', their relative prevalence reported to be similar to the ratio of 5:20:75 in the classic studies of Lewis and Jarvis (Gintsberg, 1971, p. 64). The grades are distinguished one from another according to criteria that are again qualitative as well as quantitative. Idiots (*idioty*), the profoundest grade, do not master speech (or at best only a few words), with corresponding effects on every aspect of their development. Their education is under the control of the Ministry of Social Security, or in certain cases they are placed in 'colonies' (hospitals for the chronically ill) under the Ministry of Health. Imbeciles (*imbetsily*) attain speech, though it may remain agrammatical, limited in vocabulary and poorly articulated. They are capable of learning simple skills of production and independence, and are educated mainly in establishments run by the Ministry of Social Security and staffed by teachers from the Ministry of Education. Debiles (*debil'tsy*), the highest grade of defect, attend special 'auxiliary' (*vspomogatel'nye*) schools under the Ministry of Education, where with special help they should attain the equivalent of Grade IV education (an 11-year-old standard). As adults they will live and work in the community, though they are exempted from compulsory military service. Vlasova (1967, p. 2) has reported that debiles comprised about 0·6 to 0·8 per cent of the school population, the overwhelming majority in auxiliary schools.

Oligophrenia and dementia. Within the mentally defective group a distinction is made between 'oligophrenia' and 'dementia'.

Oligophrenia (*oligofreniya*) is mental deficiency arising as a result of damage to the central nervous system during or before the early period of life (including at birth or before). The physical damage is non-progressive. Subsequent mental damage (not, of course, solely to how much the child learns, but also to the way in which his mental structures develop and inter-relate) will indeed be cumulative, and will be the worse for failure to apply corrective educational measures.

Dementia (*dementsiya*) is mental deficiency stemming from a disease or trauma that occurs after a period of normal development. The unfamiliar developmental differentiation made between oligophrenia and dementia is analogous to the more familiar distinction of the congenitally and adventitiously deaf. Dements comprise only a small proportion of mentally deficient children.

Various authors (for example, Pevzner, 1959; Luriya, 1960; Isaev, 1971; Freierov, 1964) have advanced systems for qualitative differentiations within oligophrenia, but general agreement has not been met. There is universal agreement, however, on the major distinction that has to be made between oligophrenia and a variety of non-'anomalous' conditions that might be confused with it, and this is no longer considered a major research problem except for the continual need to improve technique.

Pseudo-oligophrenia.   Most children who fall behind academically in Soviet schools are not mentally deficient. It is official policy that no such child should be placed in an auxiliary school and receive the sort of education suited to the oligophrenic, though it is recognised that an exact differentiation may be very difficult in certain cases and that mistakes do happen. Backwardness in children who are not mentally deficient is ascribable to a variety of factors, which share the common feature that they do not involve an irremediable defect of the central nervous system. To varying degrees their causation is peripheral.

Factors wholly outside the child include growing up in a deprived or different cultural milieu, and 'pedagogic neglect' (*pedagogicheskaya zapushchennost'*) either in the home or at school. Peripheral mechanisms within the child himself (peripheral, that is, to the central nervous system) include most notably the secondary systemic effects of chronic middle-ear hearing loss upon the development of speech and the mental structures and personal attributes dependent upon it.

Such environmental and constitutional factors in children's mental underdevelopment are not, of course, unfamiliar to Western practitioners. Particularly Soviet, however, is the emphasis in Soviet methodological texts (for example, Dul'nev and Luriya, 1973; Pevzner, 1959; Zabramnaya, 1971) on the immense importance of ensuring that children with such 'pseudo-oligophrenias' should not be educated as anomalous, but instead be catered for by whatever combination of provisions – social, medical and educational – best meets their individual problems.

One subgroup of pseudo-oligophrenias is, however, wholly unfamiliar to Western practice, though it has been subject to increasing attention in Soviet defectology over the last decade (see Vlasova and Pevzner, 1971, 1973). Children with 'temporary delays in development' (*vremennye zaderzhki razvitiya*) have a retardation or impediment of function which is general, and may even involve the operation of the child's brain at a physiological level. It does not, however, affect the fundamental processes of abstraction and generalisation and, however intractable it may appear to be, the child's retardation is to be treated as potentially remediable. Two diagnostic groups comprise the 'temporary delays'. Children with 'psychophysical infantilism' (*psikhofizicheskii infantilizm*) show an overall delay in their mental and physical development and are characterised by the retention of features of an earlier stage of development. Children with a chronic 'asthenic' (*astenicheskii*) condition are characterised by a neural and mental weakness arising as a result of infectious somatic illness, or earlier traumatic damage to the brain. The latter would not have been of the degree or nature to cause oligophrenia if the child were suffering solely from a temporary delay, but oligophrenic children might also be asthenic, thus greatly complicating the problem of differential diagnosis. At the psychological level asthenic children might be highly fatiguable or distractable, with a much lowered 'capacity for work' (*rabotosposobnost'*).

The prevalence of backwardness is of necessity dependent upon arbitrary criteria of what is regarded as school failure. Pevzner (1971) has reported that 39 pupils out of 317 (12 per cent) were selected by their teachers as backward (*neuspevayushchii*) in one Moscow mass school. Ages, sex, criteria, etc., were not reported. In a more recent report the same author (Pevzner, 1977) has described a much wider study in which she found that 'amongst backward pupils about half are children with delays in mental development'. Again, precise criteria were not reported. She did report, however, on two experimental special schools set up especially for children with severe temporary delays. It was found that the majority of such children could, after a three- to four-year programme of individualised help and teaching, return successfully to the mass school. In the severest cases of all, however, especially those complicated by emotional disturbance, the special school placement had to last throughout their school days.

The diagnostic and educational taxonomy of these differing conditions is summarised in Figure 8.2.

Figure 8.2 *A taxonomy of difficulties of learning/teaching (zatrudneniya obucheniya) in Soviet defectology*

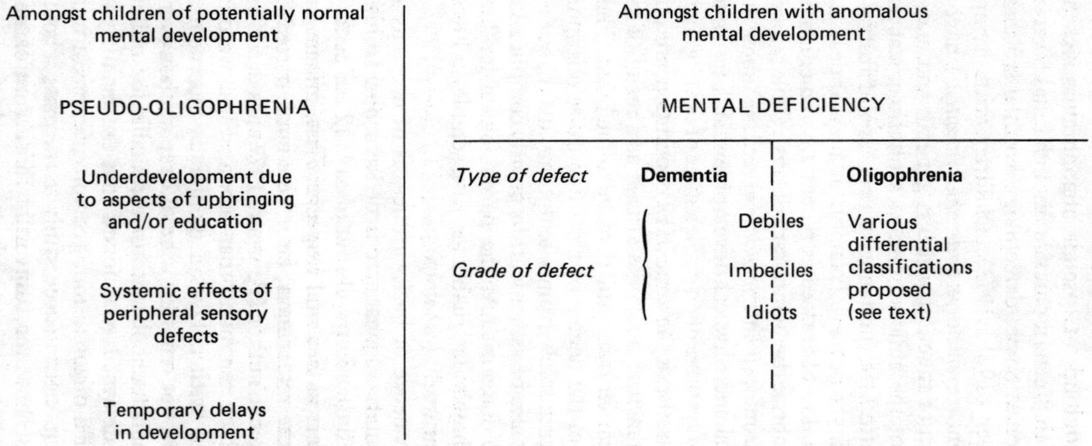

Amongst children with anomalous mental development

MENTAL DEFICIENCY

Type of defect: Dementia | Oligophrenia

Grade of defect: Idiots / Imbeciles / Debiles

Oligophrenia — Various differential classifications proposed (see text)

Amongst children of potentially normal mental development

PSEUDO-OLIGOPHRENIA

Underdevelopment due to aspects of upbringing and/or education

Systemic effects of peripheral sensory defects

Temporary delays in development

Differential Education

Oligophrenic children (*deti-oligofreny*) follow an education with defined goals, as do children with other handicaps. They are prepared for lives as handicapped adults, unable to do certain of the things that normal adults do. Given the limitations imposed by their defects, their development is maximalised through corrective education to make the best possible adaptation to their handicap. The particular handicap in oligophrenia blocks the spontaneous learning of many basic cognitive skills, grossly affecting not just the amount that the child learns but the very formation of essential higher mental functions. The child will require teaching that is structured and systematic, requiring what we would term 'overlearning', with less hope of generalising what has been taught than would be expected in the normal child. That does not, however, imply a retreat into simple, non-verbal training, since the child may still be able to make significant development if taught, as 'scientific concepts', basic cognitive and educational skills that the normal child acquires spontaneously.

> The concept of the zone of next development is particularly relevant to teaching anomalous children. Having determined what the child can do independently and what he can do in imitation or in collaboration with an adult, then one translates his zone of next development progressively and consistently into his zone of present development and prepares for a new zone of next development. The correction and compensation of the child's anomalous development is only possible by taking the zone of next development into account and continually developing it. (D'yachkov, 1970, pp. 121–2)

The pseudo-oligophrenic may, according to his reasons for being retarded, have a range of needs but they will differ from those of the oligophrenic in two vital respects. First, in many cases, the original basis for the retardation, be it biological or social, may be open to intervention. A central nervous system defect is not. Secondly, the educational goal is not to compensate for a continuing defect, but to provide the intellectual skills previously denied, and once provided to use them as the basis for normal development and education.

It is considered that misplacement is harmful for children from both groups since it denies them help specific to their needs. The unidentified oligophrenic, given an effective education system, will not go unnoticed for ever; the non-oligophrenic misplaced in an auxiliary school is probably in greater danger of 'vanishing', learning to adapt to a handicap that he does not have.

Diagnosis

The determination of a child's need for special education (or not, as the case may be) is a question decided at local level by a special 'medico-pedagogical commission' (*mediko-pedagogicheskaya komissiya*) comprising a 'psychoneurologist' (*psikhonevrolog*), a teacher-defectologist and a speech pathologist (*logoped*). The determination of oligophrenia is a medical diagnosis, of which an essential indicator or symptom is the child's teachability.

The diagnostic importance of the zone of next development in arriving at such a decision had been first formulated by Vygotskii in the early 1930s.

> When we define the level of present development we use problems that require the child to solve them on his own and which are indicative only of functions that have already matured and taken shape. But let us try a new method. Let us suppose that we have determined the mental age of two children and that for both of them it is 8 years. If we do not stop there, but try to show how both children solve problems which are meant for children of the next age level and which they are in no position to solve on their own, if help comes to them in the form of demonstration, a leading question, the start of the solution, etc., then it turns out that one of them, with help, with co-operation and under instruction, solves tasks up to the 12-year-old level – the other to the 9-year-old level. This discrepancy between the mental age, or the level of present development, which is determined by problems that the child has solved on his own, and the level of problem-solving that the child achieves when he is not working on his own but in co-operation, defines the zone of next development. In our example, the zone of next development is defined by the figure four in one child, by the figure one in the other. Can we then consider that both children stand at an identical mental level, that the state of their development is the same? Clearly we cannot. As investigation shows that there prove to be far greater differences between these two children at school caused by the discrepancy between their zones of next development than there are similarities arising from the identical level of their present development. Above all, this tells of the dynamics of their mental development in the course of teaching and of their relative school achievement. Investigation shows that the *zone of next development has more direct significance for the dynamics of mental development and school achievement than does the present level of children's development*. (Vygotskii, 1956, pp. 273–4, emphasis in original)

It should be remembered that the differences to be looked for are qualitative as well as quantitative.

The mentally defective child differs fundamentally from the normal, not in that the one solves the problems set him correctly and the other solves them incorrectly, but in that the child with normal mental development uses the help rendered him markedly better. Interpreting the instructions that have been given to him in a more generalised manner, the normal child consequently uses them easily and correctly in performing a new task. If the child can perform a set task with a certain amount of help from the teacher, this means that it lies within the bounds of his abilities and that he will soon learn to perform it independently. The teacher must therefore always direct his attention to how much the child's work improves with his help; only this help must not be incidental but systematic, well thought out and appropriate to the child's level of development and accomplishments. (Dul'nev and Luriya, 1973, p. 161).

Psychological testing was abolished in the Soviet Union by the decree on pædological perversions. Probabilistic statistics have now been rehabilitated (Artem'eva and Martynov, 1975), familiar Western intelligence tests such as the WISC (Wechsler Intelligence Scale for Children) and the Stanford-Binet have been used for survey purposes (Isaev and Lychagina, 1971; Panasyuk, 1971), and even Eysenck's *Know Your Own IQ* has been published in Russian translation (Eysenck, 1972), but standardised intelligence testing is not part of the procedures for establishing a child's individual needs. The deliberations of the medico-pedagogical commissions focus on a qualitative analysis of the child and his circumstances, aiming to base a formulation of his needs upon an understanding of the causation of his problem. Dul'nev and Luriya have offered two contrasting cases as types of children under examination by such a commission.

A decision on a child to be placed in an auxiliary school
Yura F, 9½ years, referred from Grade I with the complaint that he was backward.
History. Child of fifth pregnancy. Mother fell at eighth month as a result of which she began haemorrhaging. Boy born in deep asphyxia. Marked delays in early development: teeth, towards 1 year of age; walking towards the end of the second; first words from 3 years. At 4½ years placed in kindergarten where the staff soon noticed his inadequate vocabulary and inexact pronunciation. The boy did not know how to play with other children, he was clumsy, poorly co-ordinated, he did not understand stories and could not learn rhymes. At 8 years, Yura started at normal school where he fell behind in all subjects, repeated the year, and was referred to the medico-pedagogical commission.
Data from investigation. The boy is somewhat behind his age in

physical development. There is a diffuse, defective symptomatology of the nervous system, a right-sided hemisyndrome. It was shown in investigation of his school achievements and skills that he does not know a single letter. He can count to five, but cannot count backwards. When counting a row of objects he comes to a different result at each attempt. His vocabulary is inadequate. He can only retell a story read to him from a book if helped with questions; he cannot explain the contents of a picture that tells a story, being only able to give a list of unrelated objects and actions. Special investigation by means of visual material demonstrates significant underdevelopment of abstraction and generalisation. He does not manage to classify pictures, as he does not understand the goal of sorting pictures into groups. In conversation one notices his inadequate orientation to his environment. Yura underestimates situations and neither realises nor worries about his difficulties in learning (*obuchenie*). Investigation showed the absence of mental changes within the bounds of the various analysors. Yura does not make use of demonstration and explanation, and cannot transfer (what he has learnt) to new material.

Diagnosis. Oligophrenia at the debile grade. The above data testify to the severe inadequacy of the child's cognitive activity. This particular underdevelopment arose from the earliest period of childhood as a result of having suffered traumatic damage to the central nervous system in the intra-uterine period (haemorrhage of the womb in the eighth month of pregnancy). The severity and diffuseness of the underdevelopment of cognitive activity and of the overall personality, the learning difficulty (*zatrudnenie v obuchenii*) that arose on the basis of this, and the child's inability to use help, allow one to speak of oligophrenia and of placement of the child in an auxiliary school.

A decision on a child not to be placed in an auxiliary school.
Serezha Kh, 8½ years, referred from Grade I of normal school where he was unsuccessfully repeating the year.
History.   Child of second pregnancy. Born in mild asphyxia. At 1½ years suffered severe influenza with meningeal manifestations. Began to walk at 2 years, first words at 3 years. Preferred to play with younger children. Started school at 7 years. Could not at first get used to demands of school. Attended to lessons for only first ten to fifteen minutes. Tired quickly. Would sometimes get up during lessons and walk around the class. Often unable to do the tasks set him as he had not listened to the teacher's explanation, and used the teaching material as toys. Had attained almost no school skills by the end of the first year. Stayed down for a second year. At the beginning of the second year he gradually participated more and more

in school work, but he could not progress in class. Various parts of the syllabus remained unmastered. The boy coped badly with the written work of the class. For the most part he did not complete his homework. In the middle of the second term he was referred for examination for not coping with the normal school syllabus.

Data from investigation. The boy is somewhat behind his age in physical development. There are no changes in his nervous system. In the investigation of his school skills it was shown that Serezha knows the letters but reads badly, guessing words on the basis of a single letter. There are reversals when he writes letters and figures. He can count up to ten but cannot count backwards, he can add with visual materials but cannot subtract. When undertaking tasks with teaching materials Serezha quickly becomes tired, listless and passive. In play activity he is active and shows initiative. It is possible to interest him in conditions of one-to-one teaching. When he was shown completed addition sums Serezha quickly understood them and solved them correctly. In the same way, in a situation specially created for him, he learned to understand and apply a method of subtraction with concrete materials. In investigation of his cognitive activity it was shown that he can understand stories read to him and retell them with the help of leading questions. He understands the contents of pictures. He finds it easy to classify pictures, though it is hard for him to complete the task independently. The boy's orientation to his environment is adequate. At the same time his conversation reveals an inadequate awareness of his difficulties in learning (*obuchenie*).

Diagnosis. A temporary delay in the child's development, after suffering an illness of the central nervous system. As the data from the investigation show, Serezha's level of cognitive development is quite adequate for mastering the syllabus of Grade I. Evidence that the boy's backwardness was not due to an underdevelopment of cognitive activity is further provided by his ability to use the help given to him. At the basis of the retardation in learning (*obuchenie*) lies a delay in the development which was manifest in early childhood in delays in walking and speech, and on attaining school age in a certain difficulty in mastering school knowledge and skills. He was erratic, became quickly fatigued and did not progress in class. As the effect of not having been offered the necessary help in his studies from the very outset of teaching (*obuchenie*) he soon became a backward pupil. This backwardness increased the more with the complexity of the syllabus. The boy must remain in normal school, where for the first time he will have call on a teacher's individual help. (Dul'nev and Luriya, 1973, pp. 215–17)

This passage again illustrates the insuperable problem of translating *obuchenie* into English. Both 'learning' and 'teaching' have been used to suit the expectations of the English reader, but the additional nuance that derives from their interchangeability emphasises the very different approach of Soviet psychology. This, with its, to us, unfamiliar concept of 'potential', is essential to an understanding of why Serezha (however backward he had been shown to be in his year-and-a-half in the first grade) is considered even so in the investigation to have a level of cognitive development 'quite adequate for mastering the syllabus of Grade I'. This level refers to his potential rather than his present level of ability, and this potential will be created and achieved as long as the teacher is able to make the special allowances that this particular pupil requires.

The Teaching Experiment

The investigation of children's zone of next development has in recent years been formalised into an experimental means of evaluating teachability and generalisation, known as the 'teaching experiment' (*obuchayushchii eksperiment*). Initially the investigation of potential seems to have been evaluated by *ad hoc* procedures, such as the example suggested by Vygotskii involving the two children both with mental ages of 8, or the informal teaching of school materials such as suggested by Dul'nev and Luriya's example. Additionally, there was the much longer 'natural experiment' which involved trying to initiate change in the child by manipulation of his everyday living environment, a classic example of which is well known in the English-language child development literature (Luriya and Yudovich, 1959). In the early 1960s a new technique was developed for use with both normal and anomalous children, the 'teaching experiment'. This represents a basic principle of experimental change that can be used to modify a range of already existing assessment and teaching procedures, as well as be adapted to original material. Soviet psychologists appear to regard it as the first major advance in psychological evaluation since Binet developed his scales of intelligence.

The teaching experiment has abandoned the mental-age approach suggested by Vygotskii, and has been adapted to a variety of tasks and contexts. Kalmykova (1968) has reported that with normal children it has been found most effective when utilising academic teaching material. Egorova (1971) reported a teaching experiment in which the final stage was conducted in group administration to ensure that 'the experimental conditions approximate the usual conditions of education'.

Rozanova and Yashkova (1971) have reported the successful adaptation of the teaching experiment to the needs of the deaf. For investigating oligophrenic and temporarily retarded children at least two major models have been used for constructing such experiments. In Ivanova's (1970) approach the child is set a task that will be too difficult for him to complete unaided, but help is meted out by the experimenter from the outset. His teachability is evaluated by the amount and kind of help that he needs to master this problem, and his ability to generalise by whether he can then transfer what he has been taught to an analogous task. In Egorova's (1973) approach the child also begins with a task that is too hard for him. He is then taught how to solve an analogous problem, after which he is reset the original task to trace the changes that have taken place in his thinking under the influence of teaching.

The teaching experiment is intended to encapsulate the fundamental questions that for the rest of their lives will separate oligophrenic from pseudo-oligophrenic children, both in formal education and in their everyday lives. Are they capable of taking the knowledge that others can provide for them and use it creatively in new and unfamiliar contexts, and by what means and to what level can this knowledge be provided? In Ivanova's teaching experiment the oligophrenic child characteristically makes an unproductive orientation to the task set him, requires repeated explanation backed up with demonstration before the basic task is completed, and then makes at best only a limited transfer of what he has been taught. The pseudo-oligophrenic tends to orientate to new learning with ease, to grasp the principles of the task when the adult explains them, and then to adapt those principles to use elsewhere.

TOWARDS AN EVALUATION

The Soviet Union is a society in some ways very like our own, European, post-Christian, mainly urban and highly industrialised, and the superficialities of its formal educational system, its schools and their organisation, might easily trap us into mistaken identifications of how the Soviet Union brings up and educates its children with how we do. In taking a cross-cultural or comparative educational look at special education in a different society we must be continually aware that an educational system as a whole has significance only when related to its own culture. We must also recognise that whatever concrete human universals (faulty vision, impaired hearing, a defective brain, etc.) lie at the basis of a given handicap, handicap itself is a social construct, socially developed and socially defined. If children with particular developmental needs are to benefit fully from a scientific approach to their problems, then part of this scientific approach must include a critical appraisal of different models. The extent to which our two models differ is summarised in Figure 8.3. There are as yet, however, only the beginnings of a comparative special education in the English-language literature (see Goldberg, 1968; Sutton, 1977).

Figure 8.3 *A comparison between the respective topologies of the linear, quantitative model of mental retardation (Western psychometrics) and a discontinuous, qualitative model (Soviet defectology)*

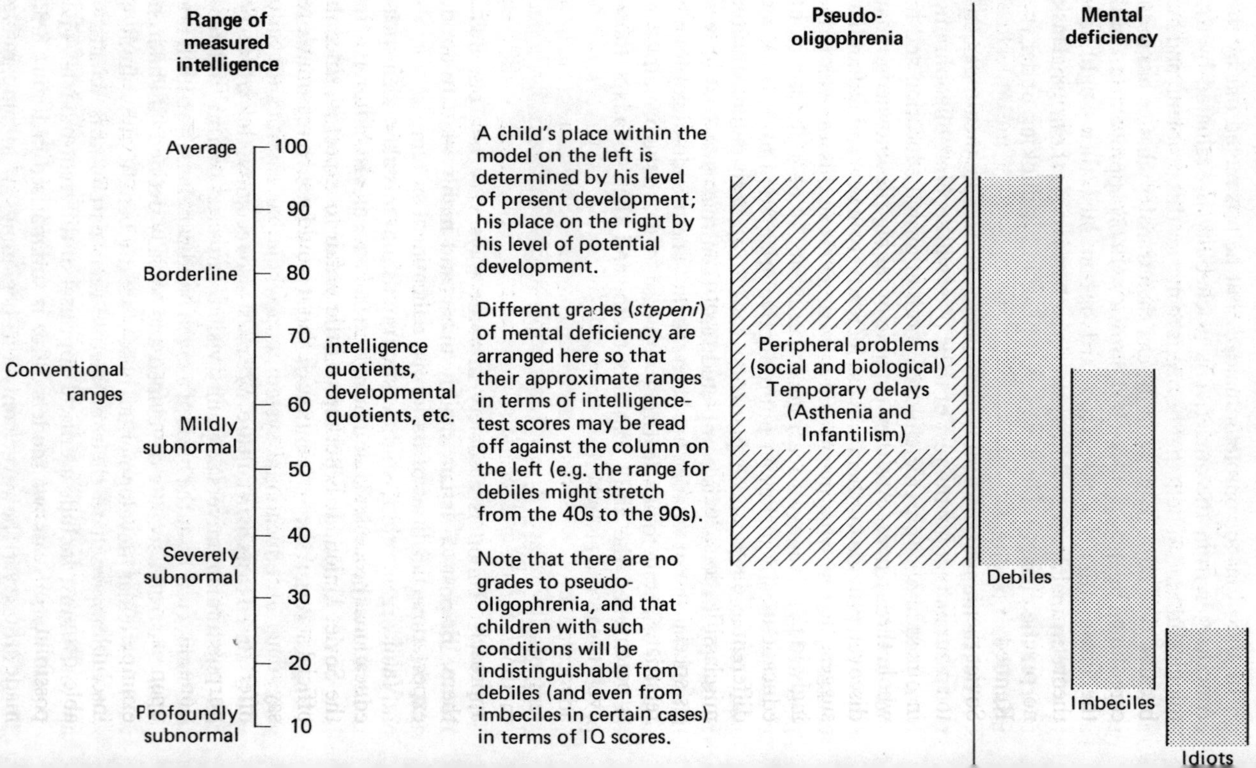

Range of measured intelligence		Mental deficiency	Pseudo-oligophrenia

Range of measured intelligence:

- 100 — Average
- 90
- 80 — Borderline
- 70 — Mildly subnormal
- 60
- 50
- 40 — Severely subnormal
- 30
- 20 — Profoundly subnormal
- 10

Conventional ranges: intelligence quotients, developmental quotients, etc.

Mental deficiency: Debiles, Imbeciles, Idiots

Pseudo-oligophrenia: Peripheral problems (social and biological) Temporary delays (Asthenia and Infantilism)

A child's place within the model on the left is determined by his level of present development; his place on the right by his level of potential development.

Different grades (*stepeni*) of mental deficiency are arranged here so that their approximate ranges in terms of intelligence-test scores may be read off against the column on the left (e.g. the range for debiles might stretch from the 40s to the 90s).

Note that there are no grades to pseudo-oligophrenia, and that children with such conditions will be indistinguishable from debiles (and even from imbeciles in certain cases) in terms of IQ scores.

In the absence of a proper comparative approach, British and American visitors' accounts of Soviet special education and defectological research have tended to dismiss the Soviet work as poor because different. They have spoken highly of the quality of human care shown by special school staff for their charges, but have criticised the formality and structure of the education as 'Victorian'. The theoretical differences have either not been noticed, or dismissed as of no practical effect. Dunn and Kirk (1963), reporting to President Kennedy's Panel on Mental Retardation, wholly misunderstood Soviet theory and the means of diagnosis, and concluded from a visit to an auxiliary school that 'to us, the children enrolled typified pupils in our special classes for educable retardates'. From their visit as a whole they concluded that in general 'we did not find any startling discoveries in diagnosis or education that we could use'. They did not suggest that any further evaluation be made. It remains an exceedingly important question, however, to determine whether the Soviet educational system, with all its pretence to a scientific approach to differential diagnosis of the retarded, and its strong urgings against misclassification, does in fact end up with the same sort of children in its special provision for debiles as the Americans place as educable retardates, and we ascertain as educational subnormals. The question is potentially important for the education of backward children all over the world; for the division of the retarded population, as advocated by Soviet defectologists, into the permanently and the temporarily retarded, with correspondingly different goals and methods for their education, represents a fundamentally different approach to the provisions that their societies will have to make for them. 'Backward' here refers, of course, to a level relative to normal expectations in the advanced industrial countries.

Validation of the Soviet taxonomy as a basis for the differential educational processes that derive from it is not available from within the Soviet Union. It is perhaps a little unfair to expect it, since the official status of the system is such that it would not be reasonable to, say, deny a diagnosed oligophrenic a place in an auxiliary school or offer to a temporarily retarded child such a place, solely for the purposes of controlled trials. Nor could validation of the differentiations, and the claims for a better special-education system founded upon it, be made by comparative studies between pupils in, for example, the English and the Russian education systems. Countless insoluble problems interpose. For example, given the lack of comparable diagnostic groups at the mildly ESN/debile level there is no possibility of matched groups. Even if a study of this nature were made, the results would be uninterpretable because of the host of other, non-educational variables that would differ in the lives of the two groups of pupils. Just one of those factors, the sheer consistency of Soviet provision for its members, would introduce an influence into the life of the Soviet retarded child, his family, his school, his social and medical care, that would be wholly absent in the life of an analogous British child.

The only meaningful trial of the Soviet approach to backwardness would be to adapt some of the Soviet techniques for one's own society and to utilise them within the theoretical framework in which they originated. O'Connor and Hermalin (1963) and the present author (Douglas and Sutton, 1978; Sutton, 1979a) have done this, and achieved results consistent with Soviet predictions, but these personal endeavours have been small against the bulk of the problem, and there remains negligible general interest in this country in what Soviet defectologists may have done.

For their part, Soviet defectologists, educators and psychologists have in recent years taken a keen interest in Western work. Soviet journal articles and monographs show evidence of widespread reading of the Western literature, whilst the methodology of Soviet investigations reported in the scientific press now shows an experimental repertoire comparable to Western work. Soviet psychologists are very aware of the possibly deleterious effects of their long estrangement from experimental method, and even as influential a paradigm as the development of verbal regulation must now have its basic experimental work redone according to more acceptable standards of statistical demonstration (Lubovskii, 1978, pp. 29–30).

The statistical and mathematical treatment of data involving the zone of next development and possible qualitative, as well as quantitative, differences between children will probably present problems of measurement quite unfamiliar in Western psychometrics (Sutton, 1979b).

As a final point of reference it should be noted by the English reader that Soviet defectology, with its underlying assumptions of discontinuity and qualitative differences, is not necessarily a deviant that has to account for itself in a way that our own special education does not. There are three major psychologies of childhood in the modern industrial world, the Anglophone (mainly American), the Russophone, and the Francophone. French-speaking psychology shares with Soviet psychology longstanding intense interest in qualitative stages in development (see Association de Psychologie Scientifique de Langue Française, 1956), and differentiations between different kinds of backwardness with different kinds of educational needs and prognosis closely parallel those of Soviet defectology, both in the school of Piaget (Inhelder, 1943) and in modern French practice (Moor, 1973). French- and Russian-speaking approaches to the problem share a common emphasis on qualities rather than quantities, on processes rather than products, in respect of which it is our own

Anglo-Saxon conceptualisation of backwardness that is the deviant.

The Soviet Union has the largest system of special education in the world, operating according to the most elaborated structure of theory and metatheory. The theoretical basis for this system (and presumably much of the practice related to it) differs substantially from our own society's way of tackling analogous problems. Special education in the Soviet Union proceeds according to prescribed methods, towards prescribed goals. Special education in our own country is not so encumbered. The two societies provide special help for their backward children against two very different educational and social backgrounds. At one level of analysis, therefore, it might be possible to dismiss the question of their differences as merely different ways of doing things for different social ends, without introducing the question of whether one system is 'better', 'more effective', etc., at bringing up and educating backward children. But the wider social issues cannot mask the existence of possible technical differences of immense human importance. In the adjacent area of education for the deaf, the oral method of teaching has been a long and fervently held article of faith in British special education, with the insistence of Soviet defectologists that deaf children should learn sign-language being regarded as, at best, a marked oddity. Now there has been a revolution in our thinking in the West, and early introduction to signing is recognised as of potentially enormous value to the intellectual and personal development of the deaf child. A proper comparative educational view must recognise not only that different societies do things differently, but also that other societies might do things better.

BIBLIOGRAPHY

Artem'eva, E. Yu. and Martynov, E. M., *Veroyatnostnye metody dlya psikhologov* (Moscow, 1975).

Association de Psychologie Scientifique de Langue Française, *Le Problème des stades en psychologie* (Paris: Presses Universitaires de France, 1956).

Bauer, R. A., *The New Man in Soviet Psychology* (Cambridge, Mass.: Harvard University Press, 1952).

Bowen, J., *Soviet Education: Anton Makarenko and the Years of Experiment* (Madison, Wis.: University of Wisconsin Press, 1962).

Cole, M. and Scribner, S., 'Introduction . . .', in L. S. Vygotskii, *Mind in Society: the Development of Higher Psychological Processes* (Cambridge, Mass.: Harvard University Press, 1978), pp. 1–14.

Douglas, J. E. and Sutton, A., 'The development of speech and mental processes in a pair of twins: a case study', *Journal of Child Psychology and Psychiatry*, vol. 19 (1978), pp. 49–56.

Dul'nev, G. M. and Luriya, A. R. (eds.), *Printsipy otbora detei vo vspomogatel'nye shkoly*, 3rd edn (Moscow, 1973).

Dunn, L. M. and Kirk, S. A., 'Impressions of Soviet psycho-educational service and research in mental retardation', *Exceptional Children*, vol. 29 (1963), pp. 299–311.

D'yachkov, A. I., *Defektologicheskii slovar'*, 2nd edn (Moscow, 1970).

Egorova, T. V., 'Nekotorye osobennosti umstvennogo razvitiya neuspevayushchikh mladshikh shkol'nikov', in *Deti s vremennymi zaderzhkami v razvitii*, ed. T. A. Vlasova and M. S. Pevzner (Moscow, 1971), pp. 157–63.

Egorova, T. V., *Osobennosti pamyati i myshlenii shkol'nikov otstalykh v razvitii* (Moscow, 1973).

Eysenck, H. J., *Prover'te svoi sposobennosti* (Moscow, 1972).

Freierov, O. E., *Legkie stepeni oligofrenii* (Moscow, 1964).

Gintsberg, V. L., 'K voprosu o patologii beremennosti i rodov v anamneze detei-oligofrenov', *Trudy Leningradskogo pediatricheskogo meditsinskogo instituta*, vol. 57, 1971, pp. 63–6.

Goldberg, I. I., 'Comparative special education for the mentally handicapped', in *Proceedings of the First International Conference for the Scientific Study of Mental Deficiency* (Reigate, Surrey: Jackson, 1968), pp. 147–54.

Inhelder, B., *Le diagnostic du raisonnement chez les débiles mentaux* (Neuchâtel: Delachaux et Niestlé, 1943).

Isaev, D. N., 'Dinamika sostoyaniya psikhicheskogo nedorazvitiya', *Trudy Leningradskogo pediatricheskogo meditsinskogo instituta*, vol. 54, 1971, pp. 33–43.

Isaev, D. N. and Lychagina, L. I., 'Psikhologicheskie osobennosti detei s raznymi formami oligofrenii po rezul'tatam issledovaniya metodikoi Vekslera', *Trudy Leningradskogo pediatricheskogo meditsinskogo instituta*, vol. 57, 1971, pp. 67–77.

Ivanova, A. Ya., 'Obuchayushchii eksperiment', in *Psikhologiya umstvenno otstalogo rebenka*, ed. S. Ya. Rubinshtein (Moscow, 1970), pp. 71–81.

Kalmykova, Z. I., 'K voprosu o metodakh diagnostiki obuchaemosti shkol'nikov', *Voprosy psikhologii*, 1968, no. 6, pp. 127–32.

King, B., *Changing Man: the Education System of the USSR* (London: Gollancz, 1936).

Leont'ev, A. N., 'Principles of mental development and the problem of intellectual backwardness', in *Educational Psychology in the USSR*, ed. B. and J. Simon (London: Routledge & Kegan Paul, 1963), pp. 68–82.

Leont'ev, A. N. and Luriya, A. R., 'Psikhologicheskie vozzreniya L. S. Vygotskogo', in L. S. Vygotskii, *Izbrannye psikhologicheskie issledovaniya* (Moscow, 1956), pp. 4–36.

Lubovskii, V. I., *Razvitie slovesnoi regulyatsii deistvii u detei* (Moscow, 1978).

Luriya, A. R., *Umstvenno otstalyi rebenok* (Moscow, 1960).

Luriya, A. R. and Yudovich, F. Ya., *Speech and the Development of Mental Processes in the Child* (London: Staples, 1959).

Moor, L., *La Practique des tests mentaux en psychiatrie de l'enfant*, 3rd edn (Paris: Masson, 1973).

'O pedologicheskikh izvrashcheniyakh v sisteme Narkomprosov; postanovlenie TsK VKP(b)', *Pravda*, 5 July 1936.

O'Connor, N. and Hermalin, B., *Speech and Thought in Severe Subnormality: an Experimental Study* (Oxford: Pergamon, 1963).

Panasyuk, A. Yu., 'K issledovaniyu umstvennoi otstalosti detei revizovannoi shkaloi Stenford-Bine', *Trudy Leningradskogo pediatricheskogo meditsinskogo instituta*, vol. 57, 1971, pp. 78–82.

Petrovskii, A. V., *Vozrastnaya i pedagogicheskaya psikhologiya* (Moscow, 1973).

Pevzner, M. S., *Deti-oligofreny* (Moscow, 1959).

Pevzner, M. S., 'Klinicheskaya kharakteristika detei s narusheniem tempa psikhicheskogo razvitiya', in *Deti s vremennymi zaderzhkami v razvitii*, ed. T. A. Vlasova and M. S. Pevzner (Moscow, 1971), pp. 15–20.

Pevzner, M. S., 'S osoboi zabotoi', *Uchitel'skaya gazeta*, 16 August 1977.

Pinkevitch, A. P., *The New Education in the Soviet Republic* (New York: John Day, 1929).

Rozanova, T. V. and Yashkova, N. V., 'Metody psikhologicheskogo izucheniya glukhikh detei', in *Psikhologiya glukhikh detei*, ed. I. M. Solov'eva (Moscow, 1971), pp. 31–5.

Segal, S. S., *Backward Children in the USSR* (Leeds: E. J. Arnold, 1966).

Shennan, V., *Russian Education for the Retarded: a Report of a Study Tour* (London: National Society for Mentally Handicapped Children, 1978).

Sutton, A., 'Acupuncture and deaf-mutism: an essay in cross-cultural defectology', *Educational Studies*, vol. 3 (1977), pp. 1–10.

Sutton, A., 'The moderately educationally subnormal: a contradiction and a possible resolution', *Collected Original Resources in Education (CORE)*, 1979*a*, fiche 20.

Sutton, A., 'Measures and models in developmental psychology', in *Rehabilitating Psychometrics* (London: SSRC, 1979*b*).

Vlasova, T. A., 'Système d'instruction et d'éducation des enfants mentallement arriérés en l'URSS', in *Reports by Members of the Institute of Defectology of the APN USSR to the First Congress of the International Association for the Scientific Study of Mental Deficiency* (Moscow, 1967).

Vlasova, T. A. and Lubovskii, V. I., 'The Union of Soviet Socialist Republics', in *The Present Situation and Trends in Research in the Fields of Special Education* (Paris: UNESCO, 1976), pp. 105–46.

Vlasova, T. A. and Pevzner, M. S. (eds), *Deti s vremennymi zaderzhkami v razvitii* (Moscow, 1971).

Vlasova, T. A. and Pevzner, M. S., *O detyakh s otkloneniyami v razvitii*, 2nd edn (Moscow, 1973).

Vygotskii, L. S. (ed.), *Voprosy vospitaniya slepykh, glukhonemykh i umstvenno otstalykh detei* (Moscow, 1924).

Vgotskii, L. S., *Izbrannye psikhologicheskie issledovaniya* (Moscow, 1956).

Vygotskii, L. S., *Razvitie vysshikh psikhicheskikh funktsii* (Moscow, 1960).

Vygotskii, L. S., 'Igra i ee rol' v psikhicheskom razvitii rebenka', *Voprosy psikhologii*, 1966, no. 6, pp. 62–76.

Zabramnaya, S. D. (ed.), *Otbor detei vo vspomogatel'nye shkoly; opyt raboty po komplektovaniyu vspomogatel'nykh shkol* (Moscow, 1971).

Zamskii, Kh. S., *Istoriya oligofrenopedagogiki* (Moscow, 1974).

Part Three

Recreation

9

Achievements and Problems in Soviet Recreational Planning

DENIS J. B. SHAW

INTRODUCTION

A few years ago an official report by a House of Lords Select Committee discussed the provision of recreational facilities in Britain in the 1970s and current problems of recreational planning. 'Urgent action must be taken', said the report, 'to meet the heavy pressure which is building up on the countryside, on water space and on sports facilities, or the well-being of the community and the conservation of the countryside will suffer . . . The Committee are sure that there must be deliberate and coordinated planning of facilities' (House of Lords, 1973, p. 1). The problems of developing recreational facilities and of controlling land use in an era of mass leisure are now facing many countries in the West. It is probably true to say that no country has yet found a fully satisfactory answer to the wide range of issues involved.

Parallel with such developments in the West, the socialist countries of Eastern Europe have been facing their own leisure boom. In the case of the Soviet Union, the upsurge in demand for recreational facilities has occurred in the 1960s and 1970s at a time when the government has been striving to achieve a marked increase in living standards. As in the West, the Soviet literature has been characterised both by plans for future development, and by concern at trends now under way. Part of this chapter will focus on current recreational developments and on the achievements to date of Soviet recreational planning. But perhaps the most unusual and interesting feature of Soviet recreational planning from the Western viewpoint is the fact that it occurs in the context of a centrally planned economy in which all the major means of production, including the land, are owned by the state. This chapter will thus also be concerned with examining how recreational planning works in this system. The problems to which the system gives rise will necessarily be emphasised. By implication, some light may also be thrown on the extent to which the Soviet system has managed to avoid recreational planning problems characteristic of Western societies.

Recreation and leisure are very broad terms which are used in a variety of senses and are the subjects of varying aspects of academic inquiry. The present discussion is concerned with those aspects of recreation which are commonly the concern of town and country planners in the West. The focus will therefore be on open-air recreation, including the provision of recreational open space, sports facilities, recreational accommodation and related aspects of tourism.

THE CONTEXT OF SOVIET RECREATIONAL DEVELOPMENT

Environment, culture and history all have some influence on patterns of recreational activity. In the case of the Soviet Union, these factors have sometimes had unexpected effects, especially when viewed from the standpoint of Western Europe and North America. Before examining recreational developments in detail, therefore, it is necessary to say something about the context in which they have arisen.

Environmentally, the Soviet Union possesses many advantages by comparison with Western Europe and even (though to a much lesser extent) with large parts of North America. The sheer size of the territory with which Soviet planners have to deal provides a marked contrast with the situation in overcrowded countries such as Britain. The USSR, with its 22,400,000 square kilometres, is almost ninety times the size of the UK, and two and a half times that of the USA. The population density – only eleven people per square kilometre on average – is well below Western norms. Moreover, the vast territory of the USSR possesses a wide variety of natural environments which could potentially offer a very considerable diversity of recreational experience. In addition to the relatively well-developed beaches of the Baltic and the Black Sea, and many inland water bodies, there are the mountains of the Caucasus, the Altai, the Pamirs, and others, where alpinism is as yet at an initial stage. The immense forests of the taiga and of the mixed forest zone, where hunting and other activities await development – a fifth or more of the world's area of forest belongs to the Soviet Union (Vasilyev, 1971, p. 188) – many natural wetlands, and remoter areas such as the tundra and the deserts also have marked tourist potential. The Soviet Union, then, unlike many other lands, can hardly be said to lack space for many kinds of recreational development.

The water body is of particular importance for recreation, and here the endowment of the Soviet Union is very great. For example, the USSR possesses 150,000 rivers of over 10 kilometres in length and a total length of 3 million kilometres, and 270,000 lakes of above 0·01 square kilometres in area. The country has four of the world's eighteen largest lakes, all with areas over 10,000 square kilometres (Mil'kov and Gvozdetskii, 1969, pp. 76, 83). In addition to this there are many artificial reservoirs. The combined surface area of lakes and reservoirs greater than ten hectares exceeds 330,000 hectares (Kuznetsov and Lvovich, 1971, p. 19).

The environmental advantages of the Soviet Union in the recreational field can, however, be exaggerated. The extreme continentality of the climate, for example, deters many types of recreational activity, especially in the harsh Siberian winter. Many of the rivers, lakes and reservoirs, large parts of the forest, and much of the 60,000 kilometres of coastline, lie in remote areas, far from the major centres of population and in regions with severe climatic conditions. In reality, therefore, their recreational potential may be restricted. In fact about half of the Soviet population is concentrated in only 7·5 per cent of the territory, and in these areas recreational pressures on the environment can sometimes be as severe as in the most heavily populated parts of Western Europe. Soviet planners, for example, complain of the deleterious consequences of visitor pressure on forests and lakes around Moscow, the former tsarist estates near Leningrad, and the popular beaches of the Baltic and the Black Sea (Khromov, 1973). Even an area as comparatively remote as the Braslav lakes region in north-eastern Belorussia merits mention in *Izvestiya*, in view of the harm caused to the delicate natural environment by a rash of visitors and tourists (Shimansky, 1975). Such problems are increasingly highlighted in the press. Despite the fact of space, therefore, the Soviet Union does face the problem of considerable local pressures from visitors and tourists. However, the very fact of space may also provide the planners with opportunities not available to planners in smaller countries.

The environment itself naturally plays an important role in influencing the particular types of recreational activity favoured by a country's citizens. In contrast with Britain, for example, where beach tourism was for a long time the traditional holiday activity, in much of the USSR an analogous role was played by the forest. The closeness of the forest to many of the country's large cities meant that it formed the obvious goal for the day trip, the weekend, and the longer holiday. The lure of the forest was enhanced by its important role in Russian history, literature and folk-lore. Recently, because of this environmental context, Soviet recreational patterns have begun to assume forms similar to those of the USA and Canada. Thus there is much emphasis on weekending, camping, hunting and the 'wilderness' experience. Perhaps the most remarkable aspect of this situation is the fact that, unlike North America, the Soviet Union is even now not an automobile society. Thus the Soviet citizen has adopted something of the life-style of his North American peer without the advantages conveyed by the motor car. Soviet writers have suggested that on summer weekends about a third of the population of Moscow and Leningrad forsake their cities for the peace and quiet of the forest (Khromov, 1972, p. 29). Such large migrations will obviously have major implications for recreational planners.

In addition to the environment, numerous special cultural, historical and sociological influences are discernible in the recreational patterns characteristic of Soviet society. One cultural feature which perhaps merits particular mention is the central European spa and sanatorium tradition. This tradition, underlining the close connection between leisure and the restoration of health, was once important throughout much of Europe but has now largely lapsed. In the USSR, however, the tradition continues to thrive and has led in recent years to the development of many new spas and sanatoria (Azar, 1972, pp. 31ff; Pinneker, 1977). Although simple pleasure-seeking has always been a characteristic of such places, in the USSR, at least, the purely medical aspects cannot be overlooked. However, the poverty of alternative forms of holiday accommodation also helps to account for the continuing popularity of sanatoria in many places.

Recreational planning in the USSR, therefore, takes place against the background of a particular set of environmental conditions and in the context of a particular grouping of cultural traits. Two other features are, however, important in explaining the recreational situation as it exists in the USSR today. The first of these is ideology. Ideology in Soviet thinking refers to that special body of doctrine which is regarded as providing the guiding basis for the whole of life, including the practice of planning. But the actual role of ideology in planning is difficult to define. Not least amongst the reasons for this is the fact that the relationship between the Marxist–Leninist ideology, on the one hand, and planning decisions affecting the use or distribution of space on the other, has never been strictly defined. In the field of recreational planning, as in many other aspects of Soviet life, ideology is often invoked as a rationalisation for actions seemingly taken on totally unrelated grounds. Whether ideology has a more positive role is a matter for some controversy. What can be said is that spatial planning has always been a fruitful field for debate amongst Soviet theoreticians. It may be, however, that in such matters as its favouring of group rather than individual forms of holiday accommodation, its emphasis upon children, and its encouragement of sport, the Soviet government has been moved, at least in part, by ideology in its approach to recreational questions.

Undoubtedly more important than ideology in its influence upon present-day recreational patterns has been the USSR's peculiar history of recreational development. After 1917, Russia's numerous resorts, spas and sanatoria were nationalised by the socialist state for the use of the working classes. However, despite many proclamations stressing the importance of leisure and health facilities in the new society, recreation in actuality long played a minor role in Soviet thinking. The available capital was needed for industrialisation, defence and other purposes, whilst recreation, forming part of the consumer sector of the economy, attracted little in the way of investment. In a centrally managed economy, moreover, what was not encouraged by the state did not arise of its own accord. More recently, however, the situation has begun to change. As the Soviet consumer has won a greater measure of consideration by the authorities, the rise in standards of living coupled with a decrease in working hours have greatly increased the level of demand amongst citizens for recreational facilities of all types. The result has been enormous pressure on available resources and the spontaneous development of recreational activities, frequently in a manner contrary to the wishes of the planners. In response to this situation, the authorities have often acted in haste and careful planning considerations have sometimes ceased to operate. At the same time, recreational considerations even now often rank low on the list of priorities and the overall achievements to date are relatively modest. It is this situation which has resulted in the current concern in the press and the planning literature about the need for a more effective system of recreational planning.

THE RECREATIONAL PLANNING INFRASTRUCTURE

The Soviet Union is one of the few countries in the world in which all recreational space is centrally owned and controlled. All land was nationalised after the 1917 Revolution. Since that time only the right to use land, rather than its ownership, has been granted by the state to its own agencies or to other users, and the state naturally has the right to resume land so alienated. Later legislation on land has divided it into a number of legal categories: agricultural land, land occupied by populated settlements, industrial and associated land (including the land of health resorts), state forest land, state water-resources land and state reserve land (Surganov, 1969). Machinery exists for the transfer of land from one category to another. In principle, therefore, because of the absence of private land ownership, the political structure ought to allow for a far more flexible policy of land-use planning than is the case in the West. For example, the category of state water-resources land, first promulgated in 1968, should allow for much greater freedom in the development of water-based recreation within a unified planning structure.

In practice, however, the land-use planning system is by no means entirely smooth in its functioning. First, it will be noted from the above that, apart from health-resort land, there exists no legal category of recreational land. In view of the vagueness of the term 'recreation', and the close relationship that exists between the various aspects of recreation and other functions of society, often involving the multiple use of land, this situation is probably unavoidable. Nevertheless, it does mean that recreation must frequently compete in its use of land with many other activities. The responsibility for allocating land lies with the local city, provincial or district soviets which undertake this task under the supervision of republican governments ('Uniform . . .', 1975). In view of the political power of industrial ministries and other agencies, however, the actual allocation of land may not proceed in the interests of recreational development, or indeed of other aspects of local planning. The real power of local soviets over the field of physical planning is often restricted, especially in medium or small cities (Taubman, 1973, pp. 30–40; Bater, 1977, p. 187). And once land has been allocated to another user, there can be no guarantee that that user will always utilise his land in the interests of recreation or other needs. Industrial users, for example, are frequently accused of hoarding land and of refusing to release it for agricultural or other purposes. Likewise, forestry bodies often appear unsympathetic to recreational requirements (Grishayev, 1976).

In terms of land use, therefore, recreation often falls foul of the classic conflict between sectoral and spatial planning in the USSR which has been analysed by a number of Soviet and Western writers (Taubman, 1973; Kochetkov, 1975). There are additionally many problems with regard to the provision of recreational facilities deriving from the bureaucratic structure. As in most Western countries, no one body in the Soviet Union is responsible for the overall control of recreational development. General physical planning, which includes the planning of recreational facilities and control over recreational land use, lies within the competence of the local soviets. The soviets also provide many forms of recreational accommodation, as well as parks, gardens, sports facilities and other recreational forms. In this they are guided by appropriate national or republican institutions, such as the State Committee of Physical Culture and Sport, and the Ministries of Culture, Health, Communal Economy, etc. But a major role in the provision of recreational accommodation, sports facilities and similar services is also played by other institutions, such as the industrial ministries and their enterprises, the trade unions, collective and state farms, and many other public bodies. Their discretion in such matters is frequently considerable. After the 1965 economic reforms, industrial enterprises were permitted to retain a certain proportion of their profits for the construction of services, including those of a recreational type. Their role in recreational provision has thus recently increased.

Outside the cities, major water bodies, national parks and reserves often fall under the control of the republican governments and their agencies, or even of the All-Union government, which therefore assume responsibility for recreational development in these areas. Finally, tourism falls under the aegis of numerous bodies at both national and local level, perhaps the most important of which is the Central Council of Trade Unions which runs many of the country's sanatoria and plays a major role in resort development. Other bodies important for promoting tourism, including the provision of hotels and other facilities, are the travel agencies Intourist and Sputnik.

Whilst planning control within their areas is exercised by the local soviets, the physical plans for cities and regions are drawn up by the soviets' architecture-planning departments, together with such national bodies as the State Committee on Construction (*Gosstroi*) and the State Committee on Civil Construction (*Gosgrazhdanstroi*), or appropriate republican authorities. The actual level of participation in plan construction by the higher bodies will depend upon the size and importance of the place. This reliance on central control derives both from the lack of trained physical planners at the local level, and also from the desire to make local physical planning conform to nationally approved norms. At the national level, an important role in recreational planning is played by the various research bodies which specialise in various aspects of physical planning. For recreational planning amongst the most important bodies are the Central Scientific Research Institute for Town Planning (*TsNIIP gradostroitel'stva*) and analogous institutes for trading establishments and tourist complexes, for spectator and sports establishments, and for health and cure facilities. These institutes are frequently involved in local planning at the most detailed level. In this task they are regularly aided by academic personnel working in departments of universities and in various institutes of the Academy of Sciences.

In spite of the absence of private ownership of the means of production in the USSR, therefore, the planning and provision of recreational land uses and facilities is a complex affair. Control over land use and general physical planning come under both national and local authorities, with the national bodies playing a larger role than that normal in the West. The provision of recreational facilities, on the other hand, is the function not only of local soviets, but also of a whole range of other public bodies. As shall be seen, co-ordination between these various institutions and also with the physical planning machinery is not always easy to achieve. Physical planning is itself a complex and somewhat difficult activity within the Soviet centrally planned economy. In the field of recreation, this complexity is enhanced by the very breadth and diversity of the processes it covers.

Having outlined the context in which Soviet recreational development has occurred, and explained something of the infrastructure responsible for that development, it is now necessary to describe some of the achievements and problems of that development in urban and rural areas and in the field of tourism.

RECREATION IN THE CITY

Both before and after 1917, those in Russia who debated the future of cities were generally agreed on the necessity of avoiding the unhealthy conditions and the overcrowding which characterised the capitalist city. Although the radical sentiments of the de-urbanist school were eventually discarded by Stalin (Starr, 1976, pp. 235–7), many notions deriving from the English 'garden city' movement came to be incorporated in the theory and practice of Soviet city planning. In particular, the provision of adequate open space, for reasons both of health and of recreation, became a basic aim of urban planning. From the late 1920s, Soviet cities began to develop the so-called 'parks of culture and rest', which were multi-functional in character and possessed both a recreational and an educational purpose. In Moscow's pioneering city plan of 1935 these ideas were taken much further, for the capital was to be provided with a series of green wedges penetrating the urban fabric and connecting the inner suburbs with the surrounding countryside (Parkins, 1953, pp. 30–47). Similar notions were applied to other cities and reappeared most markedly in the second generation of city plans which were drawn up in the 1960s. Since then the principle of the 'greenification' (*ozelenenie*) of the city has become a standard concept. Planners now generally talk in terms of a hierarchy of parks and gardens to be provided in the Soviet city, allowing for specialisation of purpose. The hierarchy ranges from the so-called 'micro-parks' or neighbourhood parks within the neighbourhood unit (*mikroraion*), through suburban and city-wide parks, to the large, natural forest parks on the edge of the built-up area.

It is perhaps hardly surprising that actual open-space provision in Soviet cities is well below the norms considered desirable by the specialists. The urban population of the USSR has increased from 18 per cent of the total population in 1914 to over 60 per cent today, and this rapid rate of urbanisation produced numerous crises in the cities, especially in housing and service provision. In the era of rapid industrialisation and urbanisation, the development of urban open space was naturally not seen as an urgent necessity. Worst off in this respect are the newer industrial cities of the interwar and immediate postwar period where until recently there was little time to devote to the niceties of city planning. In the case of older cities, such as Moscow and Leningrad, the situation was somewhat better because of the heritage of the pre-revolutionary period. In the mid-1970s Moscow had 8·02 square metres of public open space per person, Leningrad 9·3, Kiev over 18, and Novosibirsk only 7·3. These figures can be compared with that for the old LCC area of London where there were 10·5 square metres of public open space per person in the early 1970s. Plans for the expansion of open space in Soviet cities are ambitious. Thus the ultimate aim for Moscow is 19 square metres (Bakhtina, 1975, p. 51), and planners consider 15 square metres to be the desirable norm, at least in the short term, for the large cities (Tosunova, 1975, p. 61). However, open-space provision also varies steeply within the built-up areas of the cities. In Moscow, for example, open space has been provided in the outer suburbs at a rate of 30–50 square metres per person. In the city centre, by contrast, there is less than 2 square metres.

There is some evidence to suggest that the shortage of open space in many Soviet cities may not be ameliorated quickly. In recent years, increasing concern has been expressed in the press and the planning literature at the expansion of urban areas, the propensity to build in the green belts, and the high cost of providing infrastructure in big cities (for example, Grishayev, 1976; Kabakova and Segedinov, 1976). The latest wisdom is thus to build at higher densities, which means that pressure on urban space is increased. There is also evidence to suggest that open-space provision still enjoys a fairly low priority in the minds of land-use planners. Bakhtina (1975, pp. 56–7) complains that the open-space requirements laid down in Moscow's general plan are currently being met at a rate which will only satisfy 22–25 per cent of its norms. Much land in the mid-1970s was being allocated to residential, industrial or service uses, despite its designation in the plan as public open space, and there are many complaints of the lack of capital and infrastructure for the maintenance and improvement of city parks both in Moscow and in other cities (Bursanovskii, 1972, pp. 15–16; Bakhtina, 1975, p. 57; Lyubchenko, 1977). Many of these problems are the result of official priorities and also of the power struggle between city soviets and other users of land.

One important function of urban open space is to provide for the sporting needs of Soviet citizens. Since the early days of Soviet power, sport has been encouraged as contributing to personal health, productivity and military preparedness. Particularly important since the 1930s has been the emphasis placed upon specialist sport as contributing both to the development of spectator interest and to Soviet prestige in the international arena. Facilities in the USSR for specialist sports activity have been amongst the finest in the world. In the public sphere, much of the initiative in the provision of sports facilities has rested with the industrial enterprises, trade unions, and such organisations as the Young Communist League (Komsomol) and the Pioneer movement amongst schoolchildren (Riordan, 1977, pp. 260ff.). City soviets, by contrast, have often been slow in this matter, although neighbourhood 'houses of culture' have an important role to play. The result has been that facilities at the neighbourhood level have often been lacking, and sports participation in the outer suburbs of large cities has all too often been negligible (Khromov, 1972, pp. 29–30). The preparations in Moscow for the 1980 Olympics are designed to combat this problem by providing facilities which might eventually be used by the citizens at large.

Moscow's general scheme for the development of physical culture and sport is a specialist plan which attempts to translate into reality the recreational provisions of the city's general plan (Dobrokhotova and Gudkova, 1975, p. 58). It contains numerous provisions which are likely to be followed in many other cities. Amongst its major priorities are the aim to bring the area devoted to sport in Moscow from its present 1 square metre per person much closer to the general plan's norm of 3·5; to found a hierarchy of sports centres and sports areas in public parks which will fit in with Moscow's evolving hierarchical suburban structure (Hamilton, 1976, pp. 45–8); and to allow for about 55 per cent of the population to become regular sports participants. The aim is that about 37 per cent of the city's population will participate regularly in sports groups in sports centres, and 18 per cent will participate in unorganised sport in city and neighbourhood parks close to their homes. One interesting aspect of this plan is the desire to save on open space by building multi-storey sports complexes and by contructing the sports centres as close as possible to the green belt. It is hoped that through this plan the present discrepancy in sports provision between the city centre and the suburbs will be removed, and that every Muscovite will find adequate sports facilities close to home – ever more important in view of lengthening leisure hours. Its successful fulfilment will clearly depend upon adequate capital provision and the careful co-ordination of city planning and construction. (For a fuller analysis of recreation in the city, see Shaw, 1979.)

RECREATION IN THE COUNTRYSIDE

Recreation is only one of many demands made upon the countryside. In an urbanised society such as that of the USSR, however, it is an important one. Since the prewar period, Soviet planners have attempted to cater for such demands by designating particular parts of the countryside as suitable for recreational development. Most large Soviet cities are now surrounded by official green belts whose functions include recreation. Moscow, for example, has a green belt or forest park zone of 172,000 hectares, about half of which is occupied by forests and by open space not devoted to agriculture (Gorbatov, 1972, p. 25). Likewise, Leningrad has a zone of 280,000 hectares (Shaw, 1978, p. 197). A primary aim of official planning policy is to designate so-called forest parks within these zones, usually centred upon forest massifs, which can be utilised for recreational purposes. In these parks, access and tourist routes can be laid out, suitable accommodation provided, and various kinds of recreational activity developed. Moscow is more fortunate than many Soviet cities in having actual administrative jurisdiction over its forest parks. A special arm of Moscow's executive committee manages some 70,000 hectares of forest situated within the forest park zone. At the present time a land-use cadastre is being compiled of the lands in the Moscow region, partially with the aim of recreational development. It is planned that agriculture should in time be phased out of all those areas designated as forest parks (Bozhko, *et al.*, 1975, pp. 16ff.).

The relatively low population density of many rural areas in the Soviet Union, coupled with the comparative immobility of the majority of the population, means that planners can pay particular attention to zonation. Of the seven forest parks to be developed in Moscow's green belt, for example, each is to be devoted to a different type of recreational activity. The spaciousness of many of these areas also means that it is possible to define networks of roads and pathways in and through the forests so as to provide nodes of attraction for the many, and seclusion for those desiring it (Rodoman, 1972). Similar principles have been applied to accommodation and holiday provision, plans specifying specific zones for day visitors, weekenders, and longer-term holidaymakers (Shaw, 1979, pp. 132–3). Zones catering primarily for holidaymakers on a week's vacation or longer would be situated farther away from the central city.

Official plans therefore envisage the Soviet city surrounded by carefully designated zones of recreation, each zone specified according to approved purposes. Within these zones, in which the conservation of the natural environment would be a high priority, accommodation would be provided by soviets, ministries, enterprises and other public bodies, usually in the form of tourist camps, rest homes, sanatoria and similar facilities. Many camps and sports bases would be devoted to specialist activities, such as hunting and fishing. And particular attention would be paid to the provision of camps for children. Around many cities, special zones are now being designated for the development of children's camps and sports facilities, often provided by the 'Pioneer' organisation or the Komsomol (Ushakova,

1972). The importance of these developments is revealed by an article in *Literaturnaya gazeta* in July 1975 which stated that 70 per cent of Moscow's children spend up to twenty-six days each summer in such camps and 40 per cent up to forty-five days (Kuznetsova, 1975).

The available evidence would seem to indicate that reality frequently falls short of the planners' dreams. Official concern at the tendency for some cities to sprawl into their green belts, at unauthorised construction and land-use practices, and at the need to develop agricultural output and conserve agricultural land, would seem to imply that in practice recreational development may often be sacrificed to other needs. As already indicated, bureaucratic attitudes may mean difficulties in changing established land uses. Years of neglect in the recreational field may also mean that recreational patterns have become entrenched which conflict with the planners' carefully considered principles of zonation.

A most interesting example of the way in which theory and practice may conflict, leading in time to changes in the theory, is the Soviet attitude towards individual forms of recreation. Despite official emphasis upon the development of parks and public forms of accommodation, much of the overnight accommodation close to Soviet cities has been in the form of individually owned or rented dachas or cottages (a form of second home) or of renting rooms from local collective farmers. In the early 1970s, for example, over 90 per cent of overnight accommodation in the Leningrad city region was in this form (Lobanov, 1973, p. 13), and, despite official restrictions, settlements of dachas continue to develop around such cities as Moscow (Vedenin, *et al.*, 1976). For years, planners have criticised dachas as unsightly, badly planned, wasteful of land, and expensive to service. Observers are also worried about their ideologically dubious status in a society which does not encourage private property, and about profiteering amongst those who rent out dachas and rooms to visitors from the city. A more socialist variant, the so-called 'summer garden cottage', a small chalet with associated garden plot on a co-operative garden, has been seen by some as an acceptable alternative but for many years was virtually ignored in the planning literature (Shaw, 1979, pp. 129–31).

From the mid-1970s, however, attitudes towards the dacha and the co-operative garden have seemingly begun to change. Recognising the fact that the state will not be in a position to provide alternative forms of accommodation for many years, and that individual communion with nature should have a place even in a socialist society, pleas have appeared in the press that official recognition be granted this form of recreation and that more information be provided as to the range and form of accommodation on offer (Dorofeyev, 1973; Kuznetsova, 1975). Moreover, official concern at the unsatisfactory nature of the city-dweller's diet has led to complaints of neglect of the garden co-operatives and the failure to manufacture garden tools and materials for the construction of garden chalets. From 1978, credits are available for chalet construction and more tools and other materials are to be manufactured (Kozhevnikova, 1977; Denisov, 1978; Viktorov, 1978). In this way the Soviet government seems to be recognising reality for what it is and is now beginning to make use of that situation for its own ends.

Visitor pressure upon numerous areas in the vicinity of populated regions has led in recent years to an interest in the possibility of developing countryside and national parks in remoter spots, where visitors can be channelled and contained. At present this movement is only at an initial stage. In Estonia, for example, the first national park was opened only in the mid-1970s, centred upon two old dacha communities and with regulations carefully controlling building, land use, and other activities (Kaera, 1975). Elsewhere, however, the situation is much less advanced. In the Shatsk lakes area in northwestern Ukraine, for instance, over forty organisations are involved in developing facilities for visitors and tourists, and these organisations are accused of polluting the lakes and of building unauthorised wharves on their banks. *Literaturnaya gazeta* complains of the bureaucratic difficulties in creating a national park in this area (Grigoryev and Khandros, 1975). An overall conservation plan for Lake Baikal, on the other hand, does contain provision for the creation of national parks and nature reserves in specialised zones. The delay in implementation, however, causes considerable concern in view of the rapidly expanding tourist industry and its associated pollution (Monchinsky, 1973; Veretennikov, 1977).

Bureaucratic barriers, deriving from mixed priorities and divided responsibilities, are therefore particular problems for the careful development of recreational land uses. Delay and indifference in turn lead to other problems. *Pravda* in May 1976, for example, complained of the unplanned construction of piers and makeshift marinas on many water bodies resulting from the local authorities' lack of interest in water recreation (Mazuruk, 1976). Likewise, official indifference and the lack of tourist provision leads to unauthorised invasion of nature reserves by tourists and even to unauthorised building in reserves by public bodies. In June 1977, *Pravda* pleaded for a single authority to be made responsible for the designation and protection of nature reserves (Krasnitsky, 1977).

Although the available evidence is limited, it seems beyond dispute that the present recreational situation in rural villages in the USSR is much inferior to that enjoyed by urban dwellers. For one thing, the average hours of leisure available to farmers are significantly fewer than those available to urbanites (Zaslavskaya and Ryvkina, 1975;

Rebrin, 1978; Kapelyush, 1978). The seasonality of labour on the farm, coupled with time spent on the private plot, seriously erodes leisure time during the most favourable period of the year. Moreover, the physically exhausting nature of much farmwork reduces the propensity to engage in active forms of recreation. In terms of the provision of facilities, with the longstanding Soviet emphasis upon the cities, rural areas have suffered a lack of services of all kinds, including recreational facilities. The work in sports and recreational provision which has been done in the cities by the trade unions has not been parallelled in the countryside. These problems have been compounded by the underdeveloped nature of the rural construction industry, and the lack of capital on the farms. The 1960s and 1970s have, however, witnessed a gradual improvement in the situation, with more collective and state farms providing sports and ancillary facilities (Riordan, 1977, pp. 295–305). Nevertheless, progress remains slow and the situation is spatially extremely uneven.

TOURISM

Russia has a long history of tourism which dates back to at least the early nineteenth century, and since the late 1950s a concerted effort has been made to develop it, especially by the three major travel agencies – Intourist, Sputnik and the Central Council of Trade Unions. Both foreign and domestic tourism have been encouraged, and four major foci have been identified: (1) the most important cities such as Moscow, Leningrad and Kiev; (2) the 'golden ring' of ancient capitals near Moscow and other historic towns such as the ancient cities of Central Asia; (3) the resort areas such as the Southern Crimea, the Baltic and Black Sea littorals, and the Caucasian spas; and (4) ethnically and socially distinctive areas such as the Baltic States and the Transcaucasus. More recently, attention has begun to focus upon wider vistas for tourists, such as mountaineering in the Caucasus or the Altai, winter sports, hunting in the taiga, excursions to Siberia, and the development of a tourist industry on inland seas and lakes such as Lake Baikal and the Caspian (Lebedev, 1972). The trend is encouraged by the growing body of information available to the intending tourist.

In spite of the awakening official interest in tourism, however, this activity encounters many of the problems of Soviet recreational planning in general. Long neglect and insufficient forward planning have led both to overcrowding and to environmental deterioration. Moscow, Leningrad and other cities continue to lack adequate hotel accommodation and the highly valued foreign tourism is threatened in consequence. In Yalta on the Black Sea, *Izvestiya* claims that only business people or conference delegates are able to stay in hotels

(Gukasov, 1975). Others must either stay in sanatoria, largely pro-vided by the trade unions (and this is possible only for the fortunate minority) or shift for themselves. In 1975, 25,000 people in Yalta rented out accommodation to tourists. *Izvestiya* complains that this has led to needless profiteering in many cases – over 7 million roubles, much of it tax-free, thus being made by enterprising locals. In July 1976, *Pravda* complained at the slow pace and poor standards of hotel construction in the USSR (Dergachev, 1976). The norm, of 5 rooms per 1,000 population, is far from being reached and is not expected to be achieved before the late 1980s. The newspaper lamented the loss of revenue resulting from this situation, though more investment is now being poured into resort development (Perevedentsev, 1978).

The popularity of the established resorts such as Yalta and Sochi has led to plans for their further expansion, but in such a way as to preserve their better features. The implementation of such plans, however, faces numerous difficulties. At Sochi, for example, accord-ing to a report in *Izvestiya* in 1975 (Giller, 1975), the construction of the hotels and other facilities is in the hands of the Chief Sochi Special Construction Agency, whose plan is drawn up by the USSR Ministry of Industrial Construction in Moscow. There is no participation in the development of this plan either by the local planning agencies or by the city government itself. The result has been numerous problems, such as the building of hotels without at the same time providing the housing necessary for the service personnel. Certain aspects of Sochi's development, moreover, have been in the hands of other agencies, to the detriment of the city as a whole. By-pass facilities, for example, are the responsibility of the Ministry of Transport Construction which, in spite of urgent need, has failed to provide them. Likewise, the city government has itself been unable to provide sufficient funds for coastal defence, nor has it been able to extract them from other responsible bodies, such as the Sochi Territorial Council for the Administration of Trade Union Health Resorts, the Special Con-struction Agency, or Intourist. The writer notes that many central ministries, though provided with funds for the provision of housing and services for their employees in Sochi, consistently fail to build them. The city government can do very little about this.

Plans are now afoot to develop new centres of tourism along the popular Black Sea coast – for example, at Odessa, on the Sea of Azov, and in the Western Transcaucasus (Ionov, 1972). Other centres to attract people away from the Black Sea are to be created on the Caspian. Plans for spreading tourism, however, are themselves run-ning into problems. On Lake Baikal not all observers are satisfied that the expansion of tourist facilities will not spoil the Lake's delicate ecological balance (Veretennikov, 1977). Elsewhere, environmental damage is caused by unregulated development of tourism in new districts. And tourism frequently falls foul of the many vagaries of the Soviet economy. For example, on Lake Issyk-Kul in Kirgizia, the inefficient construction industry could only accept 3·1 million of the 16·2 roubles allocated to it for tourist development in the ninth Five-Year Plan. In the end only 2·3 million roubles were actually put to use (Abakirov, 1976). This area, like others, suffers seriously from uncoordinated development (Veretennikov and Kozlov, 1978).

Despite the great popularity of group excursions in the Soviet Union, individual tourism – often referred to in the press as 'unplanned' tourism – is now very significant, and it is likely to become increasingly so. Larisa Kuznetsova, writing in *Literaturnaya gazeta*, has estimated that only 10–12 per cent of the demand in Moscow *oblast'* for holidays in excursions or groups can now be met (Kuznetsova, 1975). Again, over 700,000 people per year holiday on an individual basis on the Sea of Azov alone (Shaulsky, 1975). This development, however, poses new challenges to Soviet planners, since up to now the tourist industry has been geared very largely to the group. Numerous articles in the press lament the lack of provision for the individual tourist and especially the lack of accommodation for the roving tourist ('Recreation . . .', 1973; Gavrilenko, 1978; Shilnikov, 1978). The poor level of provision for the motorist also attracts unfavourable comment. *Izvestiya*, for example, has criticised the low standard of facilities on motorists' camp sites in many parts of the country (Ovchinnikova, 1975). Problems of this kind are naturally all too common in Western countries also, but in the USSR they are compounded by the sudden increase in individual tourism. It remains to be seen whether the absence of a market mechanism will prove a hindrance in catering for this group.

In recent years, various Eastern European countries have pioneered foreign tourism in their need to import hard currencies. Their example is being followed by the Soviet Union which now offers a wide variety of tourist excursions to foreigners. Unlike some of her competitors, however, the USSR has so far proved unwilling to develop this traffic further by relaxing many of the more stringent visa and travel regulations. Political considerations allowing, this may eventually happen. Nevertheless, in the short term such activities as beach tourism, mountaineering and hunting will continue to receive official encouragement as a means of attracting foreign visitors.

CONCLUSIONS

A central argument of this chapter has been the fact that the sudden rise in the importance of recreational activity and tourism in the 1960s and 1970s has posed many problems for the Soviet authorities. Although plans for encouraging recreation and for controlling its development were already laid in the 1920s and 1930s, in practice it received little attention from the government. Today, with the impetus given to recreation by lengthening leisure hours and higher standards of living, the planners can no longer afford to ignore this area. Already, however, they are planning behind demand. The great pressure upon facilities produces numerous environmental problems, and a spontaneity in recreational development that sometimes seems difficult to control. The result has been a significant and possibly widening gap between paper ideals and concrete reality. That gap is enhanced by the government's own policies, which still rank recreation low by comparison with other priorities, and by various shortcomings in the country's economy. The tendency in the later 1970s seems to be the adoption of an increasingly pragmatic attitude by the government and a recognition that some earlier policies will now be difficult to achieve.

None of these problems is entirely unknown in the Western context. Perhaps the main difference lies in the longer history of provision of recreational facilities in the West and thus the avoidance of some of the pressures currently being experienced in the USSR. Even in the West, however, changing patterns of demand and technological developments are now producing grave new challenges for the planners. At the beginning of this chapter, the question was posed whether such challenges can be better met in a centrally planned system of the Soviet type. While no definitive answer can yet be made to this question, the present situation gives no cause for complacency. The USSR, with its heavy dependence upon sectoral planning, has yet to come firmly to grips with the problems and requirements of good spatial planning. To do so will undoubtedly require the devolution of some authority and power from higher to lower planning bodies and authorities. Given the Soviet political structure, this may well prove difficult. On the other hand, during the 1960s and 1970s, the Soviet system has on occasion proved itself sufficiently flexible to find new answers to situations of this sort.

Soviet experience to date, therefore, forces us to the conclusion that central ownership and control of the means of production, including the land, will not of itself provide an easy solution to recreational problems, nor guarantee good and rational planning. To do so the system needs to find new priorities and to evolve new infrastructures. It is this necessity which now exercises the Soviet authorities.

BIBLIOGRAPHY

Abakirov, E., 'Setting for Issyk-Kul' (*Pravda*, 11 May 1976), *Current Digest of the Soviet Press*, vol. 28, no. 19 (1976), p. 26.
Azar, V. I., *Ekonomika i organizatsiya turizma* (Moscow, 1972).

Bakhtina, I. K., 'General'naya skhema ozeleneniya Moskvy', in *Praktika razrabotki i realizatsii general'nykh planov gorodov* (Kiev, 1975), pp. 51–7.

Bater, J. H., 'Soviet town planning: theory and practice in the 1970s', *Progress in Human Geography*, vol. 1, no. 2 (1977), pp. 177–207.

Bozhko, M. G., *et al.*, 'Rekreatsionnaya otsenka prirodnykh kompleksov v raionnykh planirovkakh', in *Geograficheskie problemy organizatsii turizma i otdykha*, vol. 2, 1975, pp. 13–21.

Bursanovskii, S. G., 'Lesoparki trebuyut zaboty', *Gorodskoe khozyaistvo Moskvy*, 1972, no. 8, pp. 15–16.

Denisov, A., 'Personal auxiliary farming' (*Ekonomika sel'skogo khozyaistva*, 1978, no. 4), *Current Digest of the Soviet Press*, vol. 30, no. 32 (1978), pp. 7–8.

Dergachev, N., 'How do you find a hotel?' (*Pravda*, 13 July 1976), *Current Digest of the Soviet Press*, vol. 28, no. 28 (1976), pp. 21–2.

Dobrokhotova, S. N. and Gudkova, A. P. 'General'naya skhema razvitiya fizicheskoi kul'tury i sporta v Moskve', in *Praktika razrabotki i realizatsii general'nykh planov gorodov* (Kiev, 1975), pp. 57–61.

Dorofeyev, V. 'Echo of the tourist explosion' (*Literaturnaya gazeta*, 18 July 1973), *Current Digest of the Soviet Press*, vol. 25, no. 30 (1973), pp. 16, 29.

Gavrilenko, V. 'A resort and its surroundings' (*Pravda*, 7 September 1978), *Current Digest of the Soviet Press*, vol. 30, no. 36 (1978), pp. 5–6.

Giller, M., 'The resort city could be more beautiful' (*Izvestiya*, 2 November 1975), *Current Digest of the Soviet Press*, vol. 27, no. 44 (1975), pp. 5–6.

Gorbatov, V. I., 'Lesoparkovyi zashchitnyi poyas stolitsy', *Gorodskoe khozyaistvo Moskvy*, 1972, no. 6, pp. 24–8.

Grigoryev, K. and Khandros, B., 'The wonder of Shatsk' (*Literaturnaya gazeta*, 26 February 1975), *Current Digest of the Soviet Press*, vol. 27, no. 32 (1975), p. 13.

Grishayev, M., 'Conserve and restore' (*Ekonomicheskaya gazeta*, 1976, no. 39), *Current Digest of the Soviet Press*, vol. 28, no. 39 (1976), pp. 9–10.

Gukasov, G., 'Vacationing by the sea' (*Izvestiya*, 11 October 1975), *Current Digest of the Soviet Press*, vol. 27, no. 41 (1975), p. 30.

Hamilton, F. E. I., *The Moscow City Region* (Oxford: OUP, 1976).

House of Lords, *Second Report from the Select Committee of the House of Lords on Sport and Leisure* (London: HMSO, 1973).

Ionov, I., 'Problemy razvitiya kurortov na Chernomorskom poberezh'e', *Arkhitektura SSSR*, 1972, no. 6, pp. 38–42.

Kabakova, S. I. and Segedinov, A. A., 'Make more efficient use of land designated for construction' (*Ekonomika i organizatsiya promyshlennogo proizvodstva*, 1976, no. 3), *Current Digest of the Soviet Press*, vol. 28, no. 28 (1976), pp. 8–9.

Kaera, R., 'Land of bays' (*Literaturnaya gazeta*, 26 February 1975), *Current Digest of the Soviet Press*, vol. 27, no. 32 (1975), pp. 13, 22.

Kapelyush, Ya., 'Is Misha Kuchkin typical?' (*Literaturnaya gazeta*, 28 June 1978), *Current Digest of the Soviet Press*, vol. 30, no. 32 (1978), p. 14.

Khromov, Yu. B., 'Ob usloviyakh otdykha naseleniya', *Zhilishchnoe stroitel'stvo*, 1972, no. 1, pp. 28–31.

Khromov, Yu. B., 'Razvitie primorskikh-rekreatsionnykh tsentrov v grup-povykh sistemakh rasseleniya', in *Zony otdykha i ozelenenie gorodov*, ed. Yu. B. Khromov (Moscow, 1973), pp. 1–20.

Kochetkov, A., 'Sotsial'no-ekonomicheskie aspekty gradostroitel'stva', *Voprosy ekonomiki*, 1975, no. 10, pp. 23–34.

Kozhevnikova, K., 'Do garden plots need a manager?' (*Literaturnaya gazeta*, 26 January 1977), *Current Digest of the Soviet Press*, vol. 29, no. 5 (1977), pp. 17–18.

Krasnitsky, A., 'Who should work in a nature reserve?' (*Pravda*, 6 May 1977), *Current Digest of the Soviet Press*, vol. 29, no. 18 (1977), pp. 22–3.

Kuznetsov, L. I. and Lvovich, M. I., 'Multiple use and conservation of water resources', in *Natural Resources of the Soviet Union: their Use and Renewal*, ed. I. P. Gerasimov, *et al.* (San Francisco: W. H. Freeman, 1971), pp. 11–39.

Kuznetsova, L., 'I'll take the dacha!' (*Literaturnaya gazeta*, 2 July 1975), *Current Digest of the Soviet Press*, vol. 28, no. 16 (1976), pp. 24–5.

Lebedev, G., 'Kurorty Urala, Sibiri i Dal'nego Vostoka', *Arkhitektura SSSR*, 1972, no. 6, pp. 52–3.

Lobanov, Yu. N., 'Otdykh i krov; nekotorye voprosy organizatsii kratko-vremennogo otdykha naseleniya Leningrada', *Stroitel'stvo i arkhitektura Leningrada*, 1973, no. 5, pp. 13–15.

Lyubchenko, O., 'Restore parks' beauty' (*Pravda*, 8 May 1977), *Current Digest of the Soviet Press*, vol. 29, no. 19 (1977), p. 19.

Mazuruk, I., 'Without docks or enforcement' (*Pravda*, 13 May 1976), *Current Digest of the Soviet Press*, vol. 28, no. 19 (1976), pp. 26–7.

Mil'kov, F. N. and Gvozdetskii, N. A., *Fizicheskaya geografiya SSSR* (Moscow, 1969).

Monchinsky, L., 'Baikal: problems and hopes' (*Ogonek*, 1973, no. 35), *Current Digest of the Soviet Press*, vol. 25, no. 43 (1973), pp. 13–14.

Ovchinnikova, I., 'Should one say "thank you" ' (*Izvestiya*, 7 September 1975), *Current Digest of the Soviet Press*, vol. 27, no. 36 (1975), pp. 26–7.

Parkins, M. F., *City Planning in Soviet Russia* (Chicago, Ill.: University of Chicago Press, 1953).

Perevedentsev, V., 'Who'll pay for summer jaunts?' (*Literaturnaya gazeta*, 30 August 1978), *Current Digest of the Soviet Press*, vol. 30, no. 36 (1978), p. 5.

Pinneker, Ye., 'Siberian mineral waters' (*Pravda*, 14 October 1977), *Current Digest of the Soviet Press*, vol. 29, no. 41 (1977), pp. 26–7.

Rebrin, P., 'Country youngsters' (*Literaturnaya gazeta*, 8 February 1978), *Current Digest of the Soviet Press*, vol. 30, no. 8 (1978), p. 14.

'Recreation for everyone' (*Pravda*, 3 June 1973), *Current Digest of the Soviet Press*, vol. 25, no. 22 (1973), p. 22.

Riordan, J., *Sport in Soviet Society* (Cambridge: CUP, 1977).

Rodoman, B. B., 'Gorod, priroda, turizm v Podmoskov'e', *Vestnik Moskovskogo universiteta, seriya geograficheskaya*, 1972, no. 3, pp. 87–90.

Shaulsky, N., 'By sunny estuaries' (*Pravda*, 11 October 1975), *Current Digest of the Soviet Press*, vol. 27, no. 41 (1975), pp. 30–1.

Shaw, D. J. B., 'Planning Leningrad', *Geographical Review*, vol. 68, no. 2 (1978), pp. 183–200.

Shaw, D. J. B., 'Recreation and the Soviet city', in *The Socialist City – Spatial Structure and Urban Policy*, ed. R. A. French and F. E. I. Hamilton (Chichester, Sussex: Wiley, 1979), pp. 119–43.

Shilnikov, V., 'The Karelian ring' (*Pravda*, 10 September 1978), *Current Digest of the Soviet Press*, vol. 30, no. 36 (1978), p. 6.

Shimansky, M., 'I gaze at blue lakes' (*Izvestiya*, 7 October 1975), *Current Digest of the Soviet Press*, vol. 27, no. 40 (1975), p. 26.

Starr, S. F., 'The revival and schism of urban planning in twentieth century Russia', in *The City in Russian History*, ed. M. F. Hamm (Lexington: University of Kentucky Press, 1976), pp. 222–42.

Surganov, F. A., 'Text of the land legislation principles as adopted' (*Pravda*, 14 December 1969), *Current Digest of the Soviet Press*, vol. 21, no. 1 (1969), pp. 12–20.

Taubman, W., *Governing Soviet Cities* (New York: Praeger, 1973).

Tosunova, M. I., *Planirovka gorodov i naselennykh mest* (Moscow, 1975).

'Uniform deed granting the right to use land' (*Izvestiya*, 9 April 1975), *Current Digest of the Soviet Press*, vol. 27, no. 14 (1975), pp. 10, 28.

Ushakova, I. F., 'Roshchino i Ushkovo – spetsializirovannye zony detskogo otdykha', *Stroitel'stvo i arkhitektura Leningrada*, 1972, no. 11, pp. 2–5.

Vasilyev, I. V., 'Forest resources and forest economy', in *Natural Resources of the Soviet Union: their Use and Renewal*, ed. I. P. Gerasimov *et al.* (San Francisco, Cal.: W. H. Freeman, 1971), pp. 187–215.

Vedenin, Yu. A. *et al.*, 'Formirovanie dachnykh poselkov i sadovykh kooperativov na territorii Moskovskoi aglomeratsii', *Izvestiya Akademii nauk, seriya geograficheskaya*, 1976, no. 3, pp. 72–9.

Veretennikov, A., 'Preserve the Siberian pearl' (*Ekonomicheskaya gazeta*, 1977, no. 4), *Current Digest of the Soviet Press*, vol. 29, no. 5 (1977), p. 15.

Veretennikov, A. and Kozlov, Ye., 'The Issyk-Kul is an All-Union health resort' (*Ekonomicheskaya gazeta*, 1978, no. 36), *Current Digest of the Soviet Press*, vol. 30, no. 37 (1978), p. 17.

Viktorov, A., 'The collective garden' (*Trud*, 25 August 1978), *Current Digest of the Soviet Press*, vol. 30, no. 34 (1978), pp. 13–14.

Zaslavskaya, T. and Ryvkina, R., 'Proponents of the city – how are they right?' (*Pravda*, 19 May 1975), *Current Digest of the Soviet Press*, vol. 27, no. 20 (1975), pp. 25–6.

10

Sport in Soviet Society: Fetish or Free Play?

JAMES RIORDAN

INTRODUCTION

Should sport exist at all in a communist society? After all, sports as we know them today, competitive and disciplined, were almost entirely developed and shaped by the industrial bourgeoisie during the last century. 'Most of the games that are now played across the world and which command such earnest attention from kings and presidents were invented by a few hundred wealthy young Victorian Englishmen' (Goodhart and Chattaway, 1968, p. 22). These sports grew up not as general leisure pursuits but as specific subjects at public schools for the training of the bodies and minds of wealthy young men; their principal purpose was quite explicitly to prepare the new industrial ruling class for future careers in *laissez-faire* capitalism and colonialism, as captains of industry and of the Empire. As both Tawney (1948, pp. 230–1) and McIntosh (1966, p. 107) remind us, the moral code of the builder of capitalism and the British Empire applied equally to and was reinforced by the Business House, the Church (enshrined in its Protestant Ethic) and the playing field.

With economic change, rising living standards and the beginnings of leisure for wider sections of the community, many sports were extended to the urban populace, some being taken over almost completely by them. The process was uneven and incomplete: several 'middle-class' sports (for example, in Britain golf, tennis, squash, sailing, badminton and, in some parts of the country, rugby) are still confined by convention or design to private clubs and associations and controlled by their committees. In the course of these changes, many sports became commercialised and adapted for mass consumption and diversion, dominated by the profit motive and emasculated by the needs of a sports industry.

That is not to say that all the sporting activities engaged in by all sections of the community are invariably commercially or politically manipulated – or shaped solely by the ethic of the ruling class. More or

less autonomous popular pursuits exist (pigeon-fancying, whippet-
and greyhound-racing, darts, snooker, fell walking, coarse fishing,
crown green bowling) – games often based on co-operation and
solidarity rather than on society's dominant values of individualism
and competition. The authorities would not wish to, nor indeed could
they, control all popular leisure pursuits. This notwithstanding, the
dominant pattern of sport in Western society would seem to be a
microcosm of that society: sport is a source of profit, something to
package up and sell (a medium for football pools, betting shops,
cigarette advertising and the booming sportswear and equipment
industry), as well as being a distraction for the populace, an opiate of
the people – all of a piece with the Hollywood dream factory, pop
music and the sex–scandal–sport tittle-tattle of much of the mass
media.

To explain why this should be so – and clarify the question posed in
the title to this chapter – it will be necessary to examine the place of
sport within society in the Marxist terms current in the USSR. Since,
for the Marxist, 'the ideas of the ruling class are, in every age, the
ruling ideas' (Marx and Engels, 1965, p. 35), in Western society based
on private ownership of the means of production, it will be the
ideology of the possessing class that permeates every area of society,
including sport – indeed, every area where ideas are held about what is
necessary or desirable, what is the natural and proper way to do
things. In sport, there are some games right and proper for boys, and
some for girls. And we have an ideology of leisure that regards it as
something distinct from work and something that has to be earned; it
is the proper recompense for having done an honest day's work.
Marxism argues for the need to probe these 'self-evident' beliefs, the
ideology surrounding sports activities in Western society. Similarly,
the need exists to probe beneath the phenomenal forms of sport in
state socialist societies, as we attempt to do later.

However, it is not enough to perceive dominant ideas as nothing
more than the ideal expression of dominant material relationships; it
is necessary to comprehend both the use to which the ideology is put
and its limitations.

Bourgeois ideology, ever since Adam Smith, could only tackle the
problem of education and leisure in a narrowly utilitarian
framework: as 'amusement of the mind', destined partly to restore
the worker's energies for the next day's soulless routine, and partly
to keep him away from wasteful 'debauchery'. The conception of
'free time' as the vehicle of transcending the opposition between
mental labour and physical labour, between theory and practice,
had to remain far beyond the bourgeois horizon. (Mészáros, 1972,
p. 306)

To the Marxist, further, sporting activities that are subordinated to the needs of capitalism in general, and the leisure industry in particular, cannot be either free or spontaneous; they merely serve to mitigate the sense of meaninglessness which people experience in their relationships with one another. Why does this situation arise?

Marxists argue that the answer to this question must be sought in laws that govern human relations under capitalism, which develop according to the principles of commodity exchange. People's life chances, their area of freedom depend on their relationships to commodities. They themselves, for a major part of their lives, become little more than the labour-power which is all they have to sell; they become appendages of the machine they serve. The system of production thereby reduces them to mere adjuncts of commodities deprived of self-control and operated on by external and impersonal economic forces. Thus, members of the modern industrial working class, alienated from the means of production, lack all control over their working lives and feel their lives lack meaning. The human being is reduced to the status of a thing: relations, in other words, become reified. Or as the Hungarian Marxist Georg Lukács put it,

a man's own activity, his own labour, becomes something objective and independent of him, something that controls him by virtue of an autonomy alien to man. There is both an objective and a subjective side to this phenomenon. *Objectively* a world of objects and relations springs into being (the world of commodities and their movements on the market). The laws governing these objects are indeed gradually discovered by man, but even so they confront him as invisible forces that generate their own power. The individual can use his knowledge of these laws to his own advantage, but he is not able to modify the process by his own activity. [This is reification.] *Subjectively* – where the market economy has been fully developed – a man's activity becomes estranged from himself, it turns into a commodity which, subject to the non-human objectivity of the natural laws of society, must go its own way independently of man just like any consumer article. [This is alienation.] (Lukács, 1971, pp. 86–7)

The rationale of capitalist production based on commodity exchange, therefore, reduces individuality in a mass society to a quantitative abstraction. It organises and controls people and objects, not only in their work but also in their leisure. Under capitalism, the commodity becomes a fetish, 'the universal category of society as a whole' (Lukács, 1971, p. 86). The logic of the market thus permeates all aspects of individual and social life.

The products of the culture industry are part of a system of mass-produced behaviour patterns and manipulated consumer habits. The end-result of this cultural 'brainwashing' is that ideology deposits itself as a sort of objective mind in the debased personality structure. It appears

> in the unconsciousness rather than the consciousness of the masses. A world of mass-produced artefacts shapes and ossifies the conscious and unconscious mind of those who consume them. Along with its products, the production apparatus sells the social system as a whole. Home furnishings, cars, clothes and films create attitudes which are declared normal and result in mental and emotional behaviour that binds the consumer to the corporation and hence to the whole social system. (Vinnai, 1973, pp. 113–4)

Sport, too, in capitalist society must, of necessity, be seen in the same light by the Marxist. It is, after all, part of the system of mass culture designed to keep the victims of the alienated industrial apparatus under close control. It works, like other manifestations of the culture industry, to identify people with existing values and with the social conditions that lie behind them.

The establishment makes a fetish of sport, drawing a veil over the realities of the manipulation of people's imaginations and making opaque what would be clearly seen as intolerable if social relations were transparent. Sport is singularly suitable for such application on a mass scale since, unlike more cerebral cultural forms, it is most commonly incompatible with a highly critical consciousness.

By 'sport' is meant here the vastly publicised, big-league, competitive commercial *simulacra* of play that so effectively take precedence in the mass consciousness over the real events and processes that actually shape the lives of ordinary people. A society in which the popular media supply the public with enough pabulum of pseudo-events and plastic personalities in the field of phoney sport (and depersonalised sex) can dispense with an official censor of news and comment in a government office and rely on the censor in the worker's head; it can operate by consensus, helping to ensure conformity with the consensual *status quo*.

It was the less sophisticated forerunner of this sport, the public relations-created non-event, that Anatolii Lunacharskii, the early Soviet political leader, litterateur and educationist, declared unsuitable to the new socialist state: 'Bourgeois sport has a clearly defined class character . . . It cannot have far-reaching social significance, in so far as it leads to a fetishism of sport and sheer commercialism' (Lunacharskii, 1929, p. 5).

How can sport, a patently unfree activity under capitalism (and even at the lower stages of communism) become a free activity under complete communism? According to Marx, under complete communism, once human activities ceased to be regulated on the basis of private ownership the social character of labour would manifest itself directly, without the alienating mediation of the enforced division of labour:

> Modern industry compels society, under penalty of death, to replace the detail-worker of today, crippled by life-long repetition of one and the same trivial operation, and thus reduced to the mere fragment of a man, by the fully developed individual, fit for a variety of labours, ready to face any change of production, and to whom the different social functions he performs are but so many modes of giving free scope to his own natural and acquired powers. (Marx, 1961a, p. 488)

Marx, therefore, expected that individuals, liberated from the fetishism of commodity exchange, from reified relationships and abstract labour, would have every opportunity for self-fulfilment in free and spontaneous activity.

The concept of the possibility of the maturation and full development of the individual's inclinations and abilities (for Marxists, a process conceivable only in a social framework freed from the paralysing requirements of commodity production which represses the human need in favour of the commercial demand) implies that the activities of the individual must have meaning and purpose. It is in the meaningfulness of human action in the society of the future – its liberation from the condition of being a mere means to an alienated end – that the crux of the Marxist vision (and prediction) of free human activity resides.

Play at the higher stage of communist society, conceived as a meaningful and self-justifying activity, would not be one speciality among many, reserved for professionals or for a leisured élite, but an essential dimension of human life in general:

> In communist society, where nobody has one exclusive sphere of activity but each can become accomplished in any branch he wishes, society regulates the general production and thus makes it possible for me to do one thing today and another tomorrow, to hunt in the morning, fish in the afternoon, rear cattle in the evening, criticise after dinner, just as I have a mind, without ever becoming a hunter, fisherman, shepherd or critic. (Marx and Engels, 1965, p. 295)

The point here is that sport, in so far as it is a product of the division of labour, must come to be superseded. It would no longer be a manifestation of man's alienation from control over his own play. Once liberated from the iron laws of capitalist economics and once they ceased to be necessities performed under the pressure of making a living, such activities as hunting and fishing (or running, jumping, playing) would have their quality and connotation transformed. Precisely what forms playful activity would take under complete communism Marxists have not attempted to predict; all that is clear is that these forms would be freely chosen by the individual, and pursued for their inherent pleasure rather than as instrumentalities in the prosecution of some external goal.

During the Renaissance the bourgeoisie developed a substantially new pattern of sport imbued with their own values, usurping the more casual field sports of the feudal aristocracy, and changed the entire mode of playing games. In the same way, it was thought perfectly natural by some after the Russian Revolution that a fundamentally new pattern of recreation would emerge, reflecting the requirements and values of the working class and the new socialist state.

And so it was. In the development of Soviet society, sport became state-controlled, encouraged and shaped by specific utilitarian and ideological designs – primarily for labour and military training and the all-round education of an ideal citizen and, additionally since the last war, for international prestige. This state-centralised control of sport has prevented commercial exploitation of mass spectator sports for private profit and the playing of particular sports in which actual or simulated violence predominates, and has inhibited the extremes of hooliganism, corruption and commercialism associated with a number of sports in the West.

All the same, there are today features of organised sport strikingly common to both Soviet and Western societies. There are, of course, the very sports themselves. Together with these sports goes an elaborate system of government sports departments, giant amphitheatres, officials, trainers, semi- and full-time professional players, sports journalists, and so on – even gambling establishments (for horse racing, for example). A similar sports ideology in East and West cultivates irrational loyalties and ascribes similar prominence to the winning of victories, the setting of records and the collecting of trophies. Indeed, the modern Olympic motto *citius, altius, fortius* ('faster, higher, stronger') (*Avery Brundage Collection*, 1977, p. 75) has probably nowhere such an elaborate supporting system as in the USSR for spotting, nurturing and rewarding sports talent, with the aim of establishing world sporting superiority.

The following is an attempt to examine the extent to which the forms of recreation which have developed in Soviet society have coincided with the predictions of Marxist writers about playful activities in the society of the future, and to assess the reasons for any divergence between the ideals and the practice, the free play and the fetish.

SPORT IN SOVIET DEVELOPMENT

The Immediate Post-Revolution Debate on 'Sport' in Society

It was against the background of world and civil war, economic and political breakdown that the Bolsheviks had to introduce a new system of sport after 1917. The first steps to be taken were by no means obvious, for there was no pattern to follow; the change-over from criticism of capitalist institutions and the sports structure of industrial states to practical action in an 80 per cent peasant, illiterate society presented immense problems and dilemmas: What of the past was valid and useful? Were the schools of gymnastics inherited from Germany, Scandinavia and what are now the Czech lands, and the organised sports of Britain utterly bourgeois and unworthy of a place in the new proletarian order?

Could use be made of the *Sokol* gymnastics and sports movement, which had been given government backing before the Revolution? The Scout Movement, introduced into Russia in 1909, had a membership of about 50,000 girls and boys by 1917 – could it be adapted? (Pantyukhov, 1969, pp. 19–20). Was the bourgeois legacy a cancer that had to be cut from the Russian body to make it healthy? Or could the best of bourgeois practice be adapted to serve the needs of the struggling proletarian state? Was there any social value in attempts to achieve top-class results, to break records, and so on? These were the types of questions that were being debated, often furiously, in educational circles immediately after the Revolution. Two of the leading parties to the debate were the 'hygienists' and the 'proletkultists'. (For fuller details of the history of Russian and Soviet sport, see Riordan, 1977*b*.)

The hygienists.　Basically, the 1920s were the years of physical culture rather than sport, the dividing-line between the two being the presence of an element of competition: 'sport begins where the struggle for victory begins' (Ivonin, 1971, p. 1). The strongest proponents of physical culture were known as the hygienists, who were mainly medical people concerned about the need to raise health standards, to eliminate disease and epidemics. The extent of their influence may be judged from their virtual control of the Supreme Council of Physical Culture, the Health Ministry, the institutes of physical culture and the 'sporting' press.

The hygienists sharply contrasted physical culture with competitive sport: to their minds, sport implied competition, games that were potentially injurious to mental and physical health. Such pursuits as weightlifting, boxing and gymnastics were said to be irrational and dangerous, and to encourage individualist rather than collectivist attitudes and values – and, as such, were contrary to the desired socialist ethic. They frowned upon the record-breaking mania of contemporary sport in the West, and they favoured non-commercialised forms of recreation that dispensed with grandstands and spectators. Doubts were cast on the social value of competitive sport – above all, on attempts to attain top-class results. As Kalinin, a future Soviet president, was to put it:

> Sport is a subsidiary affair and should never become an end in itself, a striving to break records . . . Sport should be subordinate to communist education. After all, we are preparing not narrow sportsmen, but citizens of communist society who should possess first and foremost a broad political outlook and organisational ability as well as strong arms and a good digestive system. (Kalinin, 1962, pp. 17)

Opponents of 'sport' charged that it distorted the eternal ideals of physical education, that, instead of being universal, it led to narrow specialisation and was detrimental to health, it encouraged commercialism, demoralisation and professionalism. Competitive sport, it was alleged, diverted attention from the basic aim of providing recreation for the masses; it turned them into passive onlookers.

Not all supporters of the hygienists, however, were opposed to every form of competitive sport. The Chairman of the Supreme Council of Physical Culture, Nikolai Semashko, who was himself a doctor and concurrently also People's Commissar for Health, was opposed to restricting physical education to narrow medical confines and to banning competitive games: 'If you feed the populace on the semolina pudding of hygienic gymnastics, physical culture will never gain wide popularity' (Semashko, 1954, p. 264). Competitive sport was, he believed, 'the open gate to physical culture . . . It not only strengthens the various organs, it helps a person's mental development, teaches him attentiveness, punctuality, precision and grace of movement, it develops the sort of will-power, strength and skill that should distinguish the Soviet people' (Semashko, 1954, p. 265). Moreover, although he wrote the following lines before the full-scale campaign for 'socialist competition' had been launched to accompany the industrialisation drive, he clearly anticipated the regime's support for competition: 'Competition should serve ultimately as a means of involving people in building socialism. That is how I look upon competitive sport and competition generally' (Semashko, 1926, p. 14).

All the same, there were others of the hygienist school who did not share his broadmindedness. Several members of his staff at the Health Commissariat and lecturers at the physical culture institutes, including the Principal of the Moscow State Institute of Physical Culture, A. A. Zigmund, were firmly opposed to a whole number of competitive games. Zigmund (1925*a*) prepared a list of 'approved' sports which included athletics, swimming and rowing (against oneself and the clock, not against opponents); 'non-approved' sports included boxing, wrestling, soccer and fencing – all of which, by their nature, implied competition. Further, he rejected the 'use of physical exercise as spectacles for mercenary ends, narrow specialisation and professional *rekordsmenstvo* [indulgence in record-setting and record-breaking]'. These views were fully in keeping with those of the father of Russian physical education, P. F. Lesgaft (1837–1909) (Riordan, 1977*a*).

Since Zigmund was also Chairman of the Scientific and Technical Committee attached to the Supreme Council of Physical Culture, his views carried considerable weight. The committee was also responsible for PE syllabuses in schools: as a specific subject PE was excluded from most schools, in as much as it was felt that it should be 'an integral part of the educational process and not something tacked on to the curriculum artificially' (Zigmund, 1925*a*). In the periodical *Vestnik fizicheskoi kul'tury*, Zigmund (1925*b*) asserted that 'the existence of PE teachers is a sign of pedagogical illiteracy'.

One result of pressure from the hygienists was the reduction in the number of sports contests that took place in the first half of the 1920s and the exclusion from those contests that did take place of certain harmful sports. The First Trade Union Games, in 1925, excluded soccer, boxing, weightlifting and gymnastics from its programme, even though these were four of the most popular sporting pursuits in the country at the time. Boxing was outlawed in the same year by order of the Leningrad Physical Culture Council.

A change in the fortunes of the hygienist school came with the Party intervention in the controversy over physical culture and sport in an elaborate declaration in 1925 (see below) which effectively rejected the hygienists. Their downfall was partly caused by the shifting political climate in the mid-1920s and the alleged connection of some of their leading exponents with Trotskii – whose star had been on the wane since 1924. Thus, in the witch-hunt of Trotskyists that occurred at the end of the decade, Dr Zigmund was labelled a Trotskii-supporter and removed from all his posts (he subsequently vanished in the purges). A more immediate reason for the demotion by the Party of the hygienists may well have been that the former was beginning to see competitive sport (with its record-breaking, individual heroes and spectator-potential) as a useful adjunct to its impending industrialisation drive.

The Proletkultists.   Proletkul't ('Proletarian Cultural and Educational Organisations') was formed in 1917 with the intention of producing a proletarian culture as an indispensable part of a socialist revolution. It became widely influential after the October 1917 Revolution and, until 1919, remained independent of the Party; it was then subordinated to the Commissariat of Education, transferred to the unions in 1925, and eventually abolished in 1932. In the sphere of sport, the proletkultists demanded the complete rejection of competitive sport and all organised sports that derived from bourgeois society, as remnants of the decadent past and emanations of degenerate bourgeois culture. A fresh start had to be made through the revolutionary innovation of proletarian physical culture which would take the form of labour gymnastics and mass displays, pageants and excursions. Gymnasiums and their bourgeois equipment would be replaced by various pieces of apparatus on which young proletarians could practice their labour movements.

The proletkultists, therefore, went much further than the hygienists in condemning all manner of games, sports and gymnastics tainted by bourgeois society. In a book entitled *New Games for New Children* which they had published, the proletkultists advocated such innovatory games as 'Swelling the Ranks of Communist Groups', 'Rescue from the Fascists', 'Agitators', 'Helping the Proletarians' and 'Smuggling Revolutionary Literature Across the Frontier' (Kornil'eva-Radina and Radin, 1927, p. 37).

One such novel proletarian event was staged on Moscow's Sparrow Hills (now the Lenin Hills) in the summer of 1924, with as many as 6,000 participants. The spectacle was called simply 'Indians, British and Reds', the Indians being led by a plumed chieftain, the British by 'Joseph Chamberlain' and the Reds by the 'Chairman of the Revolutionary Military Council' (Trotskii). The plan of events was as follows:

(1)   Life goes on peacefully in all countries, with people engaging in games and sports: Indians in primitive folk games, hunting, dancing and fighting; the British pursuing sports [note the negative connotation – author] and carrying out punitive expeditions; and the Reds simulating factory work, engaging in proletarian recreation and workers' outdoor fetes.

(2)   The British suddenly attack the Indians and conquer them.

(3)   The Reds receive an appeal for help, cross the sea (the Moscow River) and join the struggle.

(4)   The Indians join the Reds and, together, repulse and defeat the British.

(5)   Victory festivals take place in a new communist world. (Starovoitova, 1969, pp. 139–40).

Many such theatrical spectacles were presented and Sparrow Hills became a regular stage for proletarian pageants and mock battles. *Proletkul't*, while accusing others of 'sportisation' and 'militarisation of sport', was itself accused of a 'theatricalisation of sport'.

While the hygienists admitted the possibility of the usefulness of some bourgeois sports, the proletkultists made no such concessions. Thus, the hygienist V. V. Gorinevskii (1924) described the game of lawn tennis as 'ideal from the biological standpoint in enhancing harmonious development; I find it hard to say what organs and muscles are not in use in tennis.' The proletkultist, S. Sysoev (1924), on the other hand, maintained that this game 'for the white-pants brigade and the bourgeoisie exhibits no comradeship or teamwork – the very qualities that the Russian needs. Tennis is also an expensive summer game . . . It should not and cannot receive as much support in the USSR as other, mass games.'

To many proletkultists, the recourse to 'bourgeois' institutions such as sports seemed a compromise, a withdrawal from already conquered positions. They might have exerted more influence over the movement if they had had a better-defined programme of pro-letarian physical culture to take the place of organised sports. As it was, a number of factories introduced production gymnastics (*proiz-vodstvennaya gimnastika*) for their workers and some trade union clubs confined their activities to regenerative exercises, which tended to turn people, especially the young, away from sport and came in for increasing criticism from the Party. Lenin had earlier admonished the *Proletkul't* movement, pointing out the need to draw on the cultural heritage of the past and to base further development on everything valuable that had been accumulated by mankind up to the Revolu-tion: 'What is important is not the *invention* of a new proletarian culture, but the *development* of the best forms, traditions and results of *existing* culture from the viewpoint of Marxist philosophy' (Lenin, 1945, p. 148). Other critics such as Lunacharskii (1929) maintained that there were no such separate entities as bourgeois and proletarian sports; there was, rather, a bourgeois and a proletarian attitude to sport, a bourgeois and a proletarian spirit of competition. Sporting attainments were, he asserted, necessary for inspiring young people to fresh successes in sport – which were, in some way, a measure of the country's cultural and technical development. Lunacharskii called for a careful study of foreign sporting experience and the inclusion of everything worthwhile into Soviet sport; he singled out rugby and boxing as especially worthy of inclusion. Rugby was a gentlemanly battle (*dzhentel'menskii boi*) that encourages courageous qualities and should be widely practised (Lunacharskii, 1930, p. 72). Training for boxing 'develops inventiveness and accuracy, stamina and self-control, fearlessness and courage more than in any other sport. Even the fiercest bout teaches one to regard one's opponent as a comrade with whom one has common cause' (Lunacharskii, 1929, p. 18).

Nevertheless, several proletkultist notions were subsequently taken up on a mass scale with the onset of the First Five-Year Plan and are, today, a distinctive feature of Soviet physical education – though their purpose is more utilitarian than aesthetic, more geared to higher productivity than the proletarian bodily perfection that the proletkultists advocated. Further, the attempted portrayal of proletarian grandeur and a messianic mission in sporting displays, pageants, spartakiads, children's games and even art forms, so favoured by the proletkultists, is as strong today as it ever was.

The years of experimenting and searching in the 1920s reflect a contradiction fundamental to the period: between the subjective desires to shape society according to ideological preconceptions and the objective lack of the material conditions for implementing ideals. There can be little doubt that because they were not based on the reality of Russia's situation some immediate aspirations, including those of the hygienists and proletkultists, were utopian and unrealistic. Even so, the questions they raised are fundamentally important and relevant to any assessment of the place of sport in Soviet (and any socialist) society for, as the actual development of sport showed, sport became geared far more to practical needs than to ideological considerations.

The Actual Development of Sport: 1917–21

Essentially, sport during the first few years came to be subordinated to the needs of the war effort. All the old clubs and their equipment were commandeered and handed over to the military training establishment *Vsevobuch* (*Vseobshchee voennoe obuchenie*), whose main aim was to supply the Red Army with contingents of trained conscripts as quickly as possible. One means of achieving this was to carry out a crash programme of physical fitness for all people of recruitable (18–40 years) and pre-recruitment (16–18 years) age.

In line with the policy of combining military drill and weapon-handling with political and general education in elementary hygiene, it was also decided to co-ordinate the activities of *Vsevobuch* with those of the Commissariats of Education and Health. In the opinion of the head of *Vsevobuch*, Nikolai Podvoiskii, it was impossible to bring the civil war to a successful conclusion or to build socialism without a large-scale campaign to improve physical fitness and health.

A second major consideration, then, was health. Having inherited a country with an inclement climate, whose population was overwhelmingly illiterate, where disease and starvation were common, and where most people had only a rudimentary knowledge of hygiene, the Soviet leaders appreciated that it would take a radical economic and social transformation to alter the situation substantially. But time was short, and able-bodied and disciplined men and women were vital, first for the country's survival, then for its recovery from the ravages of war and revolution, for industrial development, and defence against further possible attacks.

Regular participation in physical exercise was to be one relatively inexpensive but effective means of improving health standards rapidly, and a channel by which to educate people in hygiene, nutrition and exercise. One indication of the health policy being pursued was the campaign during the civil war under the slogans 'Help the Country with a Toothbrush!', 'Help the Country by Washing in Cold Water!' and 'Physical Culture 24 Hours a Day!'. With the influx of masses of peasants into the cities – bringing with them rural habits – the significance of health through physical exercise took on a new dimension.

The ignorance that was the cause of so much disease, starvation and misery – and which hampered both military effectiveness and labour productivity – was to be combatted by a far-reaching programme of physical exercise and sport. And if the material facilities were lacking, then people were urged to make full use of 'the sun, air, water and natural movement – the best proletarian doctors'.

The campaign could catch on, in the view of Podvoiskii (1919, p. 9) only if the emotional attraction of competitive sport were to be utilised to the utmost. Contests began to be organised from the lowest level upwards, culminating in the All-Russia Pre-Olympiads and the First Central Asian Olympics of 1920. Sports were taken from the town to the countryside, from the European metropolis to the Asian interior, as an explicit means of involving as many people as possible in physical exercise and organised sport.

A third explicit function of sport was integration. The significance of the First Central Asian Olympics, held in Tashkent over a period of ten days in early October 1920, may be judged by the fact that this was the first time in history that Uzbeks, Kazakhs, Turkmenians, Kirgiz and other local peoples, as well as Russians and other European races, had competed in any sporting event together (as many as 3,000 participants altogether). As was made clear later, the authorities regarded sport as an important means of integrating the diverse peoples of the old Russian Empire in the new Soviet state:

The integrative functions of sport are very great. This has immense importance for our multinational state. Sports contests, festivals, spartakiads and other types of sports competition have played a major part in cementing the friendship of Soviet peoples. (Prokhorov, 1975, p. 9)

Integrative policies aside, these sporting initiatives should be seen as a highly principled aspect of the general cultural emancipation of what were formerly subject peoples.

Thus, already at the dawn of the Soviet state, three ingredients of the sports policy – for health, defence and integration – were made explicit by the new regime.

The 1920s

It was during the 1920s that the Party made clear its views on physical culture and took it completely under state control. In its famous resolution of 1925, the Party stressed that

> physical culture must be considered not simply from the standpoint of public health and physical education, not only as an aspect of the cultural, economic and military training of young people. It should also be seen as a method of educating the masses (in as much as it develops will-power and teamwork, endurance, resourcefulness and other valuable qualities). It must be regarded, moreover, as a means of rallying the bulk of workers and peasants to the various Party, Soviet and trade union organisations, through which they can be drawn into social and political activity . . . Physical culture must be an inseparable part of overall political and cultural education, and of public health. ('O zadachakh . . .', 1925)

This then was the definitive statement on the role of sport in Soviet society to which all subsequent policy statements were to refer. We have already seen that sport, having become the responsibility of the Health Ministry, was employed as a means of inculcating standards of hygiene and regular exercise in a predominantly socially backward peasant country. Its therapeutic value was, for example, widely advertised in the intermittent three-day anti-tuberculosis campaigns of the late 1920s. It was also not thought incongruous to put out a poster ostensibly advertising sports, yet featuring a young man with a rifle and toothbrush above the slogan 'Clean your Teeth! Clean your Rifle!'.

But sport was not confined to improving physical health; it was regarded as important in combating anti-social and anti-Soviet behaviour in town and country. If urban young people, especially, could be persuaded to take up sport and engage in regular physical exercise, they might develop healthy bodies and minds. Thus the Ukrainian Party Central Committee issued a resolution in 1926 expressing the hope that 'physical culture would become the vehicle of the new life . . . a means of isolating young people from the evil influence of the street, home-made liquor and prostitution' (Landar', 1972, p. 13). The role assigned to sport in the countryside was even more ambitious: it was to play a big part in the campaign against drunkenness and uncivilised behaviour by attracting village youth to more sensible and cultured activities . . . In the fight to transform the village, physical culture is to be a vehicle of the new way of life in all measures undertaken by the Soviet authorities – in the fight against religion and natural calamities. (Landar', 1972, p. 13).

Sport, then, stood for 'clean living', progress, good health and rationality and was regarded by the Party as one of the most suitable and effective instruments for implementing its social policies.

The far-reaching aims envisaged for sport may be illustrated by the early concern that physical culture should make some contribution to the social emancipation of women – in Soviet society generally, and especially in the Muslim areas where women were effectively excluded from all public life. As is made clear, 'In Uzbekistan, as in other Central Asian republics, women's path to sport has been linked with a struggle against religious prejudices and for equal status in society' (Davletshina, 1970, p. 5). The bodily liberation and naked limbs (and faces!) along with the independent, competing image associated with sport (as, for example, personified in the graceful Tartar gymnasts Elvira Saadi and Nelli Kim) have not been accepted without a struggle: 'I would call our first sportswomen real heroines. They accomplished real feats of valour in liberating women from the age-old yoke of religion and the feudal-bey order' (Davletshina, 1970, p. 5). Even in the European areas of the country, the women's emancipation-through-sport policy was presented as both feasible and effective. For example, in a letter to Podvoiskii, the first women graduates from the Central Military School of Workers' Physical Culture wrote: 'You understand how important physical culture is for women and you tried to impress its importance upon us women, among whom there is so much passivity and conservatism, the results of age-old servitude, both economic and social'('Dorogoi . . .', 1922).

To sum up, there existed during the 1920s a widespread idealistic adherence to the notion of a 'healthy mind in a healthy body', a feeling that physical culture could somehow be used, along with other policies, to combat socially and politically undesirable phenomena. Sport meant personal and social health; it was therefore a useful instrument for countering all anti-social and anti-Soviet phenomena, including religion, and for promoting such progressive causes as the emancipation of women.

Sport Against the Background of Industrialisation

By the end of the 1920s, the scene was set for the implementation of an industrialisation programme that was to hurl the whole of the country into a gigantic campaign to 'build socialism', then to lead to the forcible collectivisation of agriculture and to transform the USSR from a backward agrarian into an advanced industrial economy – all on the nation's own resources.

The implications for the sports movement of these economic processes were extremely important, for it was in the 1930s that the pattern of Soviet sport as we know it today was basically formed and its main role and functions set. By the end of the 1930s, the basic organisational pattern had already been established – with its sports societies, sports schools, national fitness programme and the uniform rankings system for individual sports and proficient athletes. The Soviet society of the 1930s differed from that of the preceding period in seeing the flourishing of all manner of competitive sports (soccer, basketball, volleyball) with mass-spectator appeal and the official encouragement of leagues, stadiums, cups, championships, popularity polls, cults of sporting heroes – all the appendages of a subsystem designed to provide general recreation and diversion for the fast-growing urban population.

Millions of people, uprooted from centuries-old traditions, were pitched into new and strange environments; the newcomers to industry joined factory clubs and looked to them for the recreation they had previously enjoyed in an open-air rural setting. Since urban conditions were spartan and deteriorating, sports served many townsfolk as an escape from the drudgery of their domestic and work environments. The many sports contests of the 1930s were intended, too, to create and reinforce a togetherness, to evoke feelings of patriotism, and to demonstrate to people, at home as well as abroad, how happy and carefree life was under socialism. It is significant that sports rallies often accompanied major political events or festivals (May Day, Anniversary of the Revolution Day, Constitution Day). In this way, sport became a means of linking members of the public with politics, the Party and, of course, with their leader.

Furthermore, a relatively close link was re-established in the 1930s between sport and the military. It stemmed partly from the conviction of the need for a state surrounded by unfriendly powers to be strong militarily and constantly on the alert. This conviction became widespread in the 'besieged fortress' atmosphere of the 1930s, encouraged by the rise of fascism in Europe. Sport openly became a means of providing pre-military training and achieving a relatively high standard of national fitness for defence.

Several sports with potential military application – for example, shooting, gliding, skiing and mountaineering – came to be dominated by servicemen. The two largest and most successful sports clubs in the USSR were those run by the armed forces and the security forces: the Central House of the Red Army (today the Central Sports Club of the Army) and Dinamo respectively. And, after 1931, the GTO national fitness programme was expressly intended to train people, through sport, for work and military preparedness – the Russian abbreviation GTO standing for *Gotov k trudu i oborone* (Ready for Labour and Defence).

The Second World War

The war years cannot simply be seen as a wasted interlude that retarded the sports movement. They had certain consequences, some intangible, but none the less far-reaching, whose effect was evident for many years ahead.

The war convinced the authorities that they had been absolutely right to 'functionalise' sport and make countrywide physical fitness a prime target.

It reinforced a belief in a military bias in physical training and sport. After the war, the role of military organisations like the army sports clubs, *Dinamo* and the civil defence organisation DOSAAF was to be enhanced and these institutions made the pillars of the whole sports movement. A national physical-fitness programme was to be the principal goal, and sports with specific military utility were to become compulsory in all educational establishments and sports societies.

Victory in the war gave the Soviet people a sense of pride in their achievements, a feeling that the period of prewar industrialisation and sacrifice had been justified. Now they could take on the world in another – peaceful – form of contest, in sport, and test their potential. But the war had been won at a price: the awful fact that over 20 million Soviet men, women and children had lost their lives in defeating fascism. Many Soviet people felt that they had borne the brunt of German might and had made untold sacrifices to free the world from the blight of fascism. The resultant feelings of patriotism were to be an evident part of the motivation for victory in international sports competition after the war.

Sport since 1945

With the conclusion of the war and the setting of a new national target – to catch up and overtake the most advanced industrial powers (and that included catching up and overtaking in sport) – the Soviet leadership felt it possible to demonstrate the pre-eminence of sport in socialist society. Given the limited opportunities elsewhere, sport seemed to offer a suitable medium for pursuing this goal. This was an area in which the USSR did not have to take second place to the West.

With the central control of sport, it is natural that the pattern of foreign sports competition involving the USSR should follow the course of Soviet foreign policy and display clearly differentiated policies in regard to the geo-political situation of different countries. With the new balance of power after the last war (the creation of a group of socialist states, the emergence of newly independent Afro-Asian countries and the nuclear stalemate), the Soviet leadership assigned to sport such tasks as winning support for the communist system, encouraging friendly, commercial and good-neighbourly relations with the USSR, and achieving unity within the socialist bloc. It evidently considers that sports emissaries can sometimes do more than diplomats to recommend a political philosophy and way of life to the outside world.

Two recent statements regarding sport and foreign policy illustrate the Soviet concern with sport as an important social force in world affairs:

> Sport is an essential element in contemporary international relations; it affects their development, their forms of organisation and their content. Sport effectively helps to break down national barriers, create international associations, and strengthens the international sports movement. It is a great social force helping to establish and promote international contacts between national sports associations of countries with different social systems. (Pavlov, 1971, p. 5)

More recently, in an article entitled 'Emissaries of Peace', a sports monthly, referring to the 'new international tasks defined at the 25th Party Congress', stressed that 'we must consolidate the authority and influence of socialist sport so as to democratise the world sports movement, eliminate racial discrimination, corruption and commercialism in sport, and strengthen friendship and mutual understanding' (Prokhorov, 1976, p. 24).

In terms of winning medals and titles, there can be no doubt that the USSR is the world's most successful Olympic nation: not only has it 'won' every Olympic Games, summer and winter, in which it has taken part (with the sole exception of 1968), it is by far the most versatile nation in the history of the Olympics (winning medals in nineteen of the twenty-one sports in the Montreal 1976 Olympics) and participating in every Olympic event.

Summary

To sum up, the Soviet leaders would seem to have opted for the following in developing forms of sport:

(1) Using sport, specifically, as a means of obtaining the fit, disciplined and co-operative workforce needed for attaining economic and military strength and efficiency – in particular, in order:

    (a) to raise physical and social health standards – and the latter meant not simply educating people in the virtues of bodily hygiene, regular exercise and sound nutrition, but also overcoming unhealthy deviant, anti-social (and therefore anti-Soviet) conduct: drunkenness, delinquency, prostitution – even religiosity and intellectual dissidence.

(b) To socialise the population into the new establishment system of values. Character training, advanced (so the Soviet leaders seem to have believed) by sport, in such values as loyalty, conformity, team spirit, co-operation and discipline, may well have encouraged compliance and co-operation in both work and politics.

(c) To encourage a population, in transition from a rural to an urban way of life, to identify themselves with wider communities – all-embracing social units such as the workplace, the town, the district, the republic and, ultimately, the entire country. By associating sport (like other amenities) organisationally with the workplace, the Party leadership and its agencies could, moreover, better supervise and 'rationalise' the leisure-time activities of employees;

(2) Linking sport ideologically and even organisationally with military preparedness; the reasons for this 'militarisation' of sport must be sought in:

(a) The leadership's fear of war and its conviction of the need to keep the population primed to meet it.

(b) The all-pervasive presence throughout society of the military and security forces, necessitated by the imposition from above, should enthusiasm from below flag, of 'socialist construction' upon a tired public (a state of affairs not so odd-seeming in Russian society, since this military presence had also, if for different reasons, been the norm before the Revolution in sport as elsewhere).

(c) The fact that, in a vast country with problems of communication, lukewarm (at best) popular attitudes towards physical exercise and few sports facilities for most of the Soviet period, the military organisation of sport was actually an efficient method of deploying scarce resources in the most economical way and using methods of direction which were, perhaps, more effective coming from paramilitary than from civilian organisations.

Finally, in a vast multinational land that has witnessed disorientingly rapid change, sport has extended to and united wider sections of the population than probably any other social activity. It has proved to be of peculiar utility by reason of its inherent qualities of being easily understood and enjoyed, being apolitical (at least superficially) and permitting emotional release safely. It has thus had an advantage over drinking, sex, religious ritual and other forms of emotional release and friendship formation by being officially approved and therefore less guilt-inducing, and yet being relatively free of rigid official sanctions. It has had an advantage over literature, theatre and other forms of cultural expression by being more readily comprehensible to the mass public as well as less amenable to direct political control over style and content.

These advantages have been particularly marked in a society which has, in a short span of time, lived through such shattering events as two world wars, three revolutions, a civil war, rapid industrialisation, forced collectivisation of agriculture, purges and mass terror. In this society, hard work, discipline, self-censorship and periodically necessary acute readjustments may well have needed a counterpart in sport, offering as it does a particularly rewarding area of relaxation and recreation.

SPORT AND COMMUNISM: FETISH OR FREE PLAY?

Despite the practice described above, Soviet leaders have consistently affirmed their allegiance to Marxism–Leninism in general, and their adherence to a number of Marxist goals in respect of recreation in particular, emphasising the provision of sport for all and the need specifically inscribed in the Party Programme adopted in 1961 for the new Soviet person, the 'builder of communism', to have every opportunity for harmoniously combining 'spiritual wealth, moral purity and perfect physique' ('Programme of the CPSU', 1961, p. 567). Party affirmations notwithstanding, official practice has diverged substantially from official theory and the forms of recreation which have developed in Soviet society have not coincided with the predictions of Marxist writers about playful activities in the society of the future (see Riordan, 1976).

As far as recreation is concerned, reasons for the divergence between ideals and practice may be assumed to parallel those in other areas of life. In the early post-revolutionary period, genuine efforts were made by certain future-oriented groups to move in the direction foretold by Marx and Lenin, but civil war and national poverty made them impossible to bring to fruition. From the late 1920s, command over the repressive apparatus, disposal of material resources and sources of information were in no real sense under popular control but in the hands of members of the leading group in the ruling party which, in the absence of help from a revolution in the industrial West, was pursuing a policy of building a strong nation-state power base, using these instruments of power.

Some Marxists might argue that the fetishisation of recreation in the form of competitive sport (which, as we have seen, offers vast opportunities for manipulating people's minds) in the USSR is one of a number of temporary 'defects' of a society in transition to communism, 'still stamped with the birth-marks of the old society from whose womb it emerges' (Marx, 1961c, p. 29). Such defects might be regarded as inevitable as long as the individual still remains subordinate to the division of labour, as long as labour is primarily a means of livelihood, as long as the forces of production are at too low a level to permit the all-round development of the individual – i.e., as long as the USSR remains at the first stage of communist society. Accordingly, sporting activities may continue to be an extension of work and serve utilitarian, if no longer commercial, ends. How long this transitional period would last would clearly depend on several factors, objective and subjective. But one would expect that such a society, as it progressed from the lower to the higher stage of communism, as the 'realm of necessity' gave way to the 'realm of freedom' (Marx, 1961b, p. 873), would gradually shorten the working day and increase the time available for the really free development of human potential for its own sake.

We might speculate further on whether given Russia's overall backwardness in 1917, any road to socialism other than that of prolonged bureaucratically enforced development was possible, whether Soviet society is yet ripe for genuinely socialist or communist human relations (including those of free recreation) and whether, indeed, the original social goals can have remained uncontaminated, in the minds of any leaders, by the class or caste differentiation actually involved in the process of bureaucratic state–socialist construction. It is here, perhaps, that we should seek the key to an understanding of the fetishism of sport that developed in the USSR. In Western society, the fetishism of sport was a consequence of this field of human endeavour (like almost all others) offering the possibilities of profit-making – and turning out, characteristically without any conscious purposive intent, to be a highly appropriate means of distracting the populace from class-conscious politicisation. In Soviet society, however, it characteristically resulted from centralised planning and administration designed to subordinate areas of social life, such as sport, to the political and economic tasks of building a strong state. The distinction is important in terms of the potential dynamics of the two systems.

Today, the inheritors of the sports system evolved during the Stalin years must find themselves in a quandary: to what extent should or must they break with the past? How sharply and through what new forms should necessary change be brought about? In the field of culture, and specifically of recreation, how can they dismantle the various by now well-entrenched fetished institutions and values? The task is circumscribed partly by the fact that today sport is evidently regarded as an important weapon in the rivalry between what Soviet leaders see as the two diametrically opposed world systems – capitalism and Soviet socialism. The international situation is just one of a number of objective constraints (that also include domestic, economic, cultural and political factors) on leaders attempting to realise their desires – which are likely to be by no means uniform or clearly perceived. To make two extreme assumptions about the leaders' desires, they may be against fundamental change, or they may be in favour of introducing full communist relations. Whatever course of action is pursued, the subjective will of the leaders is bound to be constrained by the objective possibilities of the situation.

It is hardly surprising, then, that the actions of the leadership should appear contradictory. On the one hand, it reinforces the fetishism of sport by its increasing stress on international success and on the training of even faster, stronger and more skilful professional sportsmen (for example, through sports boarding schools, sports proficiency schools, higher sports proficiency schools, and the like) in an ever-growing range of highly organised and institutionalised sports, while the false consciousness of the mass of people is reinforced through a cultivated obsession with mass-produced, media-oriented spectator sports. On the other hand, the leadership is increasing the amount of free time available to people, providing an ever-wider range of amenities and equipment for people to pursue the recreational activities of their choice, is encouraging people to be active participants rather than passive spectators, and is extending opportunities for individuals to enjoy recreational activities in a non-institutional setting (fishing, hiking, rock-climbing, boating, pot-holing, horse-riding, skin-diving, water-skiing, etc.).

It is too early to prophesy which trend will prevail. There has so far been no obvious sign in the field of recreation of a movement towards transparent, demystified social relationships. At the same time, no fundamental obstacles, such as commercialism, exist to prevent recreational activities in the Soviet Union from being liberated from fetishism and manipulation so that they would become freely chosen and pursued for their inherent pleasure rather than for utilitarian ends. Some Marxists would argue that profound cultural-revolutionary changes of this sort could be brought about, in Soviet conditions, by comparatively minor political changes (new men at the top); others would incline to the view that the present course is more systemic, all possible candidates for the leadership having common class (or quasi-class) relations to the means of production different from the masses and so resulting in a vested interest in the *status quo*.

Whatever the interpretation of past events or the perspectives for future development, there can certainly, however, be no doubt about the absolute positive material gains of the population of the old Russian Empire in the sphere of recreation since 1917. It is also in many ways better off in this respect than the public in the West. Most of the Soviet urban population can today pursue the sport of their choice, using facilities mostly free of charge through their trade union society. Sports are not, as they were before the Revolution, in the hands of foreigners, commercial promoters, circus-entrepreneurs or private clubs with restricted entrance. Unlike some Western sports clubs, Soviet sports societies do not discriminate in regard to membership on the basis of sex, nationality or social background. Even sports involving expensive equipment are open to anyone who shows natural ability and inclination. Lastly, there has been an undeniable consistent aspiration and effort in the USSR to make sport culturally uplifting, aesthetically satisfying and morally reputable which, given all necessary qualifications, has set a tone of altruism and devotion in sport in which there is much which cannot but be admired.

BIBLIOGRAPHY

Avery Brundage Collection, 1908–1975 (Cologne: Bundesinstitut für Sportswissenschaft, 1977).
Davletshina, R. G., 'Zhenshchiny i sport', *Fizkul'tura i sport*, 1970, no. 6, pp. 2–11.
'Dorogoi Nikolai Il'ich!', *Pravda*, 20 July 1922.
Goodhart, P. and Chattaway, C., *War without Weapons* (London: W. H. Allen, 1968).
Gorinevskii, V. V., 'Diskussiya o laun-tennise', *Krasnyi sport*, 21 February 1924.
Ivonin, N. I., 'Sport i fizicheskaya kul'tura', *Fizkul'tura i sport*, 1971, no. 1, pp. 1–5.
Kalinin, M., *O kommunisticheskom vospitanii* (Moscow, 1962).
Kornil'eva-Radina, M. A. and Radin, Y. P., *Novym detyam – novye igry* (Moscow, 1927).
Landar', A. M., 'Fizicheskaya kul'tura – sostavnaya chast' kul'turnoi revolyutsii na Ukraine', *Teoriya i praktika fizicheskoi kul'tury*, 1972, no. 12, pp. 12–15.
Lenin, V. I., 'Nabrosok rezolyutsii o proletarskoi kul'tury', *Leninskii sbornik*, Vol. 35, 1945, p. 148.
Lukács, G., *History and Class Consciousness* (London: Merlin Press, 1971).
Lunacharskii, A. V., 'Mysli o sporte', *Fizkul'tura i sport*, 1929, no. 17, pp. 5–22.
Lunacharskii, A. V., *Mysli o sporte* (Moscow, 1930).
Marx, K., *Capital*, Vol. 1 (Moscow: Foreign Languages Publishing House, 1961*a*).
Marx, K., *Capital*, Vol. 3 (Moscow: Foreign Languages Publishing House, 1961*b*).
Marx, K., 'Critique of the Gotha Programme', in his *Selected Works*, Vol. 11

(Moscow: Foreign Languages Publishing House, 1961c).

Marx, K. and Engels, F., *The German Ideology* (London: Lawrence & Wishart, 1965).

McIntosh, P., *Sport in Society* (London: Watts, 1966).

Mészáros, I., *Marx's Theory of Alienation* (London: Merlin Press, 1972).

'O zadachakh Partii v fizicheskoi kul'ture', *Izvestiya Tsentral'nogo Komiteta RKP(b)*, 20 July 1925.

Pantyukhov, O. I., 'Istoriya russkogo skautskogo dvizheniya. Otdel: Rossiya, 1909–1922 gody', in *Russkie skauty* (San Francisco, Cal.: Tsentral'nyi shtab Natsional'noi Organizatsii russkikh skautov, 1969), pp. 13–41.

Pavlov, S., 'Integratsiya i sport', *Teoriya i praktika fizicheskoi kul'tury i sporta*, 1971, no. 3, pp. 3–7.

Podvoiskii, N. I., *O militsionnoi organizatsii vooruzhennykh sil RSFSR* (Moscow, 1919).

'Programme of the Communist Party of the Soviet Union', in *The Road to Communism* (Moscow: Foreign Languages Publishing House, 1961).

Prokhorov, D. I., 'Nekotorye sotsial'no-eticheskie aspekty sporta', *Teoriya i praktika fizicheskoi kul'tury*, 1975, no. 9, pp. 7–11.

Prokhorov, D. I., 'Poslantsy mira', *Fizkul'tura i sport*, 1976, no. 5, pp. 5–9.

Riordan, J. 'Marx, Lenin and physical culture', *Journal of Sports History*, no. 3 (1976), pp. 152–61.

Riordan, J., 'Pyotr Franzevich Lezgaft, the founder of Russian physical education', *Journal of Sports History*, no. 4 (1977a), pp. 229–41.

Riordan, J., *Sport in Soviet Society* (Cambridge: CUP, 1977b).

Semashko, N. A., *Puti sovetskoi fizkul'tury* (Moscow, 1926).

Semashko, N. A., 'Fizicheskaya kul'tura i zdravookhranenie v SSSR', in his *Izbrannye proizvedeniya* (Moscow, 1954), pp. 263–5.

Starovoitova, Z., *Polpred zdorov'ya* (Moscow, 1969).

Sysoev, S. 'Diskussiya o laun-tennise', *Krasnyi sport*, 21 February 1924.

Tawney, R. H., *Religion and the Rise of Capitalism* (London: John Murray, 1948).

Vinnai, G., *Football Mania* (London: Orbach & Chambers, 1973).

Zigmund, A. A., 'Nauchno-metodicheskie voprosy fizicheskoi kul'tury proletariata', *Izvestiya fizicheskoi kul'tury*, 1925a, no. 3, pp. 2–4.

Zigmund, A. A., 'Fizicheskoe vospitanie i razvitie krest'yan', *Vestnik fizicheskoi kul'tury*, 1925b, no. 4, pp. 4–5.

11

Reading as a Leisure Pursuit in the USSR

JENNY BRINE

INTRODUCTION

The popularity of reading in the USSR is obvious even to the casual visitor, who sees the crowded bookstores, the clusters of people around bookstalls in the street, the travellers on buses and on the underground engrossed in books and newspapers. In Soviet works, the USSR is often described as *'samyi chitayushchii narod v mire'* (*Materialy . . .*, 1971, p. 90), which can be translated as 'the best-read people in the world' or 'the largest readership in the world'. A closer look at reading in the USSR, however, reveals many important differences in the quantity and range of reading by different socio-demographic groups, and raises questions about the reasons for the popularity of reading in the USSR.

In this chapter, two different but related approaches to the study of reading are adopted. The first is through the sociology of leisure and time-budget studies, using surveys of how different socio-demographic groups use their non-working time in order to establish how much time they have available for reading, how much time they actually spend reading, and how the introduction of television has affected reading. Secondly, use is made of studies of reading *per se* done by various agencies – newspapers' studies of their readership, libraries' studies of their members, investigations of the retail book trade and studies which treat reading as part of a more general analysis of people's spiritual and cultural needs (Maslova, 1974, p. 11).

Reading has four main prerequisites – literacy, access to reading matter, certain minimum environmental conditions, and time to read (Hatt, 1976, p. 23). In the USSR, about 70 per cent of men and women aged 47 or under were literate in 1939, and the 1959 census reported that 98·5 per cent of the population under 50 years of age were literate (Bogdanov, 1964, pp. 88–9). It is claimed that most of those who do not read nowadays are 'people who read before but cannot read now either because of old age or for reasons of health'

(Osipova, 1974, p. 143). The level of functional literacy among some rural groups and older people is still fairly low, however, but there appears to be no (publicly acknowledged) adult illiteracy among young normal adults, as there is in Britain. But to acquire the reading habit, to become a regular reader, requires more than the acquisition of literacy, and many Soviet people, including young people, appear to need guidance on reading technique and 'reading culture', for a number of texts are published to help people read more effectively. One book (Povarnin, 1974) which was first published in 1924 is still reprinted today, giving rise to doubts about the effectiveness of reading education in some schools. Access to reading matter would, at first sight, seem to be easy and cheap in the USSR. Mass libraries are freely available to all, libraries are often provided by trade unions at one's workplace, books are cheaper than in the West, and newspapers and journals are readily available on subscription. The books in the libraries are, however, not always the ones people actually want to read and there are continual complaints over the difficulties of obtaining popular fiction and books on cookery and home economics. Because of censorship, many works never reach the public at all and are available only in *samizdat* or in editions published abroad (*tamizdat*) and brought into the USSR covertly. Some of the popular writers published in the USSR appear in such small editions that they are, for all practical purposes, unavailable to most of the population even through libraries. Nevertheless, it must be acknowledged that the USSR does publish a wide range of books, newspapers and journals at prices which almost everyone can afford. The minimum environmental conditions for reading – reliable electric light, warmth and reasonable quiet – are available to many people in their own homes, but housing conditions are comparatively cramped, and public reading rooms attached to libraries are often used by people who have few facilities for study at home. Time for reading is available in differing amounts to people in various socio-demographic groups, and this prerequisite will be examined in more detail later.

THE STUDY OF FREE TIME

Serious Soviet study of leisure, mainly through workers' time-budgets, began in the early 1920s and continued until the mid-1930s. Time-budget studies were one of the first research areas to surface after the thaw in the mid-1950s (Weinberg, 1974, p. 54); since then, like so much other Soviet social science work, they have improved considerably in theoretical and methodological sophistication. They have developed against a background of the transfer to a five-day working week and shorter working hours (for most, but not all, trades and professions), and increased affluence and availability of consumer goods. Increased free time, although viewed officially as a means of encouraging people to develop all facets of their personality by devoting more time to sport, education, bringing up their children and other worthy pursuits, has also brought problems. As Hollander (1966*a*) points out, leisure is becoming more individualised and privatised as more people acquire *dachi* (small country houses), cars, television and other facilities for leisure activities based on the home and family. The 'heavy puritanical residue' in the official ideology leads to conflict with a hedonist tendency in leisure use (Hollander 1966*a*); it has also meant a low priority for the development of leisure facilities. Society's concern for the way in which people use their free time was stressed by Brezhnev (1972, p. 15) when he observed that 'a person's behaviour in everyday life is not his personal affair. Free time is not time free of responsibilities to society.' The authorities' concern is partly with obviously anti-social use of leisure, such as drunkenness and juvenile delinquency, but also with waste of free time, with people who have an 'inadequate culture of leisure'. Many people spend a great deal of their non-working time on shopping, housework and childcare, and any free time which remains is used in a 'passive-consumerist' way (Zaitsev, 1978). The increased interest in people's time-budgets and leisure activities is an expression of official concern over that part of people's lives which is not susceptible to the kind of control available in the working environment; it is also a product of the need to collect data in order to improve shopping, travel and service industries and plan leisure and cultural facilities. Time-budget studies are also valued because they reveal the cultural and spiritual profile of the modern Soviet citizen.

Soviet sociologists would generally concur with Dumazedier's identification of three functions of leisure: relaxation, entertainment, and personal development. Relaxation is mainly recovery from fatigue, entertainment is delivery from boredom and, in its function of developing the personality, 'leisure serves to liberate the individual from the daily automatism of thought and action' (Dumazedier, 1967, pp. 14–16). Not all Soviet writers, however, would agree that leisure is 'time we can use at our own discretion and according to our own choice' (Parker, 1971, p. 27), or that 'spontaneous activity and individual variation are expected in leisure activity' (Anderson, 1961, p. 34). In the traditional Soviet value system, the concept of leisure as understood in the West was given a low priority, with emphasis being placed on the socially useful aspects of free time and its effects on a person's working life (Hollander, 1966*a*). Since the early 1960s, however, there has been a considerable shift in the official view of the relationship between the workforce, its free time and production. Whereas non-working time used to be seen as a time for the reproduction of the labour force, whether directly through sleeping, eating and recovering from fatigue or indirectly through study and child-rearing, far more emphasis is now placed on the role of non-working time in the creation of the all-round developed personality (Pimenova, 1974, pp. 5–8).

Free time, leisure and non-working time are not synonymous, and these concepts are used in different ways by different Soviet writers. A category of 'occupied time' is used by Grushin (1967, p. 14), which includes: (1) travel to and from work; (2) housework and shopping; (3) basic child care; (4) personal hygiene, eating and sleeping. The time that remains is free time. Trufanov (1970, p. 137) differentiates between free time and leisure (*dosug*), arguing that the former includes 'socially necessary, creative work' such as study, self-education and voluntary work and that the term leisure should be used only for activities over which a person has a completely free choice. He notes that reading can give rise to considerable problems of definition – it may be self-education, but it can also be just 'a pleasant way of passing the time'. The term *dosug* seems to have overtones of 'doing nothing, simple passive relaxation', and does not seem to be sufficiently purposeful to cover the wide range of activities open to people once their work and obligations are behind them.

Early Soviet time-budget studies were largely quantitative in approach; Grushin (1967) was the first to pay attention to subjective factors (Weinberg, 1974, p. 94). He opposes the view that free-time activity is useful only if it contributes to the raising of labour effectiveness, and argues that labour-oriented evaluations of free time lead to the placing of too high a value on passive regenerative activities, and not enough on those which develop the personality. The goal of the all-round developed personality does not mean that the same type of free-time structure is suitable for everyone; in general, though, active forms of leisure use are preferred to passive ones (Grushin, 1967, pp. 133–41). His views are close to those of Dumazedier, who asserts that 'it is not the leisure activity itself which is active or passive, but one's attitude to it', and that the ideal leisure structure is best determined, not by identifying passive and active elements, but by looking for a dynamic approach, defined as 'a combination of physical and mental attitudes capable of ensuring the optimum growth of the personality through an optimum participation in social and cultural life' (Dumazedier, 1967, pp. 222–3).

Time-budget studies are useful in the study of reading because they show how much free time people have and how they use it. Petrosyan (1965, p. 123) concludes that 'the analysis of time-budget studies demonstrates that non-working time is actually used unequally by various members of society and various categories of workers, and that this depends upon the effect of diverse objective and subjective factors'. Basing his figures on studies done in 1959–61, before the introduction of the five-day week, he estimated that on a working day only 16·8 per cent of non-working time is free time (Petrosyan, 1965, p. 127). This average conceals a considerable difference between the sexes: men had an average of 3 hours 36 minutes free time on normal working days, whereas women had only 1 hour 57 minutes free time (Petroysan, 1965, p. 70). Gordon and Klopov (1972, p. 115), who studied the situation after the introduction of the five-day week, found that the average worker had over three hours free time on working days and over six hours free at weekends – that is, time free of travel, chores, sleep, eating, etc. However, this time is not 'free' in the sense that Parker and Anderson use the term, for, as Grushin (1967, p. 59) observes, Soviet people today are expected to read newspapers, play with their children and maintain certain standards. He stresses that most people felt that their main leisure problem was lack of sufficient free time (rather than poor facilities or inadequate financial resources). Desire for more free time did not arise simply from its actual size; dissatisfaction stemmed largely from subjective factors, that is, what people expected to be able to do with their free time. They wanted to increase their free time by reducing the time spent on housework and shopping, rather than by further reductions in the working week. He describes how people try to increase their own free time by reducing the amount of time they spend on non-work obligations, and notes that a struggle has developed between different social groups as people try to off-load their duties on to others; men try to gain free time at the expense of women, younger people at the expense of their elders (Grushin, 1967, pp. 57–61).

Education and profession affect free-time use in two ways: (1) some professional groups work longer hours than normal, notably engineering and technical personnel (ITR) who work outside industry, and female intelligentsia in education, medicine, etc.; students also work long hours (Grushin, 1967, pp. 44–5). (2) Some groups engage in evening and correspondence courses more than others. Those who already have some education are more likely to want to study further, and some professions require more attention to current developments and refresher courses than others. Time for study (apart from full-time students and young people in hostels) is usually gained by reducing the time spent on household chores and other obligations, which then fall on other members of the family (Gordon and Klopov, 1972, pp. 197–200).

THE MODEL SOVIET READER

In the previous section, some official Soviet concepts of free time and its ideal use were described. Next, we must establish the features of the ideal Soviet reader. Reading should aid the all-round development of the personality under socialism. In order to achieve this a person should have, first, a wide range of reading interests. Reading interests are divided into three groups:

(1)   Socio-political (includes international affairs, descriptions of foreign countries; the internal economic and political situation of the USSR; moral and educational problems; history; local studies).
(2)   Natural science and technology.
(3)   Belles-lettres (fiction, poetry, drama), literary criticism and the arts.

The ideal reader has a firm, continuing interest in at least one theme in each of these groups. Secondly, the reader should make use of a variety of printed sources – newspapers, periodicals and books, for each of these performs a different function. Thirdly, a person should read regularly, and spend a large part of his or her free time on reading. Fourthly, reading should be an integral part of all a person's activities in that one should turn to printed sources to satisfy various needs:

(1)   Professional (as part of one's studies; to find out more about one's job; in preparing for voluntary political and social work).
(2)   General educational (interest in world affairs; current developments in science and the arts; also reading connected with hobbies and recreation).
(3)   Aesthetic (raising one's cultural and moral standards; improving one's taste; aesthetic pleasure). (Based on *Kniga* . . ., 1973, pp. 30–42.)

Thus librarians are not content if people just read a lot; they must encourage people to deepen and broaden their reading as well.

These features of the ideal Soviet reader can be examined and analysed from survey data and other sources, and this will be done in later sections. There are, however, various factors which affect the reliability of the original data and of the conclusions that can be drawn from them. First, it is difficult to go beyond the information about what people read to discover their motives, or ascertain what satisfaction they derive from their reading. Some work is being done in this field (for example, Nikiforova, 1972), but many of the explanations and ideas which I have advanced in this study are based on hunch and supposition, rather than on methodologically sound principles. Secondly, it must be remembered that 'since the ideal citizen is supposed to be cultured and well-informed, a high consumption of reading matter is almost a political virtue' (Hollander, 1972, p. 52), and some over-reporting is likely. Time-budgets, however, may be more accurate than more specialised surveys, as a person may be willing to admit to having done little reading in the survey week, but unwilling to state his inadequacies by admitting that in general he does not read books, or reads very little (Gordon and Gruzdeva, 1975, p. 49). But time-budget studies have the disadvantage of being mainly quantitative in approach. As Rogers (1973, p. 8) observes: 'The problem is that the same amount of time spent on an activity by different people may simply mean different things. Fifteen minutes of time spent on reading a newspaper by a highly educated and purposive reader may mean coverage of a much larger amount and wider range of material than the same amount of time spent by a reader with less education and reading skill.' A further drawback of quantitative measurement is that a person who reads five light novels appears to be a more active reader than one who, in the same period of time, reads *War and Peace*. Many time-budget studies record only primary activities, and secondary activities are ignored – for example, reading while travelling to work would not appear as part of the total reading time. However, studies which focus on reading or mass communications do include such secondary reading. Finally, it must not be forgotten that averages can conceal as much as they reveal. Despite the high indicators for reading activity overall, Grushin (1967, p. 88) found that one-tenth of the population seldom, if ever, read a newspaper, a quarter seldom or never read journals, and a fifth hardly ever read books.

Each feature of the ideal Soviet reader will now be examined separately.

READING IN THE LEISURE BUDGET

How much of their free time do people spend reading? How regularly do they read? What socio-demographic factors affect reading activity? It is difficult to separate out the influence of the different variables, as they are often interdependent; thus occupation and educational level are closely linked, and age, sex and family position have to be taken together.

Education

As a general rule, the higher a person's educational level, the more he or she reads. The tables in the following pages give data for the urban employed population, based on large-scale surveys in the late 1960s and early 1970s.

In Table 11.1, the reduction in the duration of book reading by the best-educated women is surprising; this may be partly a function of more efficient reading, as Table 11.2 suggests, or result from heavier use of journal literature.

Table 11.1   *Duration of book reading, in hours and minutes per week*

Book readers	Educational level			
	4 forms or less	5–7 forms	8–10 forms	Secondary specialised and higher
Women	0·50	2·20	2·35	1·45
Men	1·05	2·05	2·10	2·45

Source: Gordon and Gruzdeva, 1975, p. 50.

Table 11.2   *Percentage of urban employed who read at least one book in the month preceding the survey*

Book readers	Educational level			
	4 forms or less	5–7 forms	8–10 forms	Secondary specialised and higher
	%	%	%	%
Women	22	45	73	74
Men	33	47	57	58

Source: Gordon and Klopov, 1975, p. 50.

The analysis of the data in these tables is complicated by the correlation between age and educational level. The majority of those who have only primary education (four forms or less) are middle-aged or elderly, but they do include some young people; a small study of workers in Ufa in the mid-1960s found that 2 per cent of young workers had only primary education (Zlotnikov, 1970, p. 118). In this educational group, two-thirds of the men and almost four-fifths of the women cannot be considered regular book readers; further, Gordon and Klopov (1972, p. 282) found that 42 per cent of urban employed people with primary education read neither journals nor books in the month preceding their survey. Their findings are confirmed by Netsenko (1975, pp. 79–80) in her study of the 'Svetlana' factory in Leningrad: the least skilled women had the most passive attitudes to cultural activities, preferring to watch television or talk to friends rather than read or study. Highly qualified women of the same age and family position spent seven times as much of their non-working time on reading and various forms of self-education as did those with primary education.

The relationship between educational level and reading is not linear, but passes through a series of thresholds. The breakthrough point seems to come after seven years of education. In Taganrog, for example, it was found that 55–60 per cent of workers with seven years' schooling were regular readers, and that the proportion of regular readers was much the same for those who left school after the eighth, ninth or tenth form (Gordon and Gruzdeva, 1975, p. 51). Specialised training and higher education provide a further encouragement to regular reading; Grushin's figures in Table 11.3 suggest that the influence is strongest in the reading of periodicals. Tables 11.1 and 11.2 may be slightly misleading in that they group together higher and

Table 11.3 *Distribution of regular reading, as a percentage of those surveyed*

	Newspapers[a] %	Periodicals[b] %	Books[b] %
Total	89·3	72·3	75·3
Sex			
Men	92·5	73·8	79·7
Women	86·5	71·0	71·2
Occupation			
Workers	90·4	67·3	74·6
Technical intelligentsia	94·4	91·2	86·5
Intelligentsia not working in industry	93·0	82·0	73·5
Employees	92·2	86·1	75·5
Students	83·0	68·7	85·0
Pensioners	83·4	65·4	68·0
Housewives	78·7	56·3	73·0
Educational level			
Primary or incomplete secondary	82·8	61·1	66·7
Secondary	94·6	75·9	81·6
Higher	94·7	90·5	82·5
Age			
16–24	91·1	76·2	88·9
25–29	98·4	89·2	86·7
30–39	78·2	63·0	66·6
40–59	75·5	59·1	58·9
60 and over	81·1	65·7	60·9

Notes:
[a] Read newspapers at least several times a week.
[b] Read periodicals and books at least several times a month.

Source: Grushin, 1967, p. 81.

secondary education, and Gordon and Gruzdeva (1975, p. 52) found that the reading of books is far more intensive among those who had a general secondary education than among those who graduated from a secondary specialised school; this may well be attributable to the more generalist and humanist emphasis of the curriculum in the general schools.

Occupation

The effect of occupation on reading can be seen in Table 11.3. The level of reading among the technical intelligentsia is particularly striking; they read journals a lot in order to keep up-to-date with their field, but the high rate of book reading is less easily explained. The low rates for reading material other than newspapers among pensioners may be largely a result of failing health and, more importantly, lower educational level. Housewives read newspapers and journals less than any other group, but read more books than the average woman. The below-average scores for students are probably due to their load of regular study – in their free time it would be natural for them to prefer sport or the cinema as a break from reading.

The effect of content of work upon a variety of free-time activities (including reading) was investigated by Trufanov in Leningrad in 1966. He studied eight large industrial enterprises and three research institutes, as shown in Table 11.4.

Table 11.4   *Time spent reading by certain professional groups, as a percentage of all free time*

	Type of work	Average %	Men %	Women %
(I)	Unskilled heavy manual labourers	11·5	13·8	9·2
(II)	Skilled heavy manual labourers, working with machinery	12·6	12·7	12·5
(III)	Skilled workers, primarily manual	11·1	15·9	6·4
(IV)	Non-manual workers, semi-skilled	15·0	18·6	11·5
(V)	Highly skilled workers, combining manual and mental work	15·8	17·7	13·9
(VI)	Skilled mental workers	14·6	16·3	13·0
(VII)	Highly qualified mental workers	17·4	17·8	17·0
(VIII)	Managers of industrial collectives	18·5	16·7	20·4

Source: Calculated from Trufanov, 1970, pp. 138–9, 146–7.

As might be expected, the highest reading levels are found amongst the most highly qualified groups. Surprisingly, skilled manual workers, especially women, appear to read less than the unskilled. Workers in group V, who would include technicians and tool-setters, read more than clerical workers in group IV.

Studies in rural Latvia convey the same impression of the relationship between content of work and reading. Data on library membership (which is one indicator of an active reader) showed that 72·5 per cent of teachers, 65·5 per cent of cultural workers, 62·5 per cent of farm managerial personnel, and 57·8 per cent of agricultural specialists were members, compared with only 32·5 per cent of construction workers and 21·8 per cent of shop and service personnel (Zepa, 1974, p. 33). In rural Belorussia, it was found that young agricultural workers, even if well qualified, were easily discouraged from library use if the opening hours were inconvenient. The high concentration of women in certain rural trades, such as animal husbandry, also affects the pattern of reading and to some extent counteracts the influence of increased education (San'ko, 1971, p. 10).

In general, however, it is education and not social position, as such, that determines reading activity, as a comparative study of workers and engineering and technical personnel (ITR) in factories in Ufa shows:

Table 11.5 *Number of books read in the month preceding the survey*

Educational level	Workers	ITR
1–4 forms	3·1	—
5–7 forms	3·2	2·0
8–9 forms	3·3	3·6
10–11 forms	3·9	4·2
Secondary technical	4·1	3·7
Incomplete higher	3·6	3·8
Higher	3·1	3·7
Average	3·4	3·6

Source: Zlotnikov, 1970, p. 127.

In several cases, workers in the survey read more than engineering and technical personnel with the same educational level. The decrease in the number of books read by the highest group may be caused partly by increased use of journals, and also by longer working hours.

Age, Sex and Family Position

These three factors are considered together because their effects are closely related. Young people have the highest rates for participation in all types of cultural activity, including reading; up to 45 per cent of young women's free time, and over 50 per cent of young men's, is spent on cultural activities; at other stages in the life-cycle, the figures are 10–20 per cent for women and 30–40 per cent for men. In addition, many young workers are studying part-time (Gordon and Klopov, 1972, p. 225). The higher level of reading among young women before marriage (compared to men in the same position) is suggested by Gordon and Gruzdeva (1975, p. 54) to be due to the generally more passive role still assigned to girls in social relationships – whereas young men learn about life and people through small groups of friends, young women are more likely to turn to vicarious sources of information.

The next stage in the life-cycle is usually marriage and the appearance of children. The impact of these events on reading and cultural activities is suggested by Table 11.6, based on the urban employed population.

The effect on women of housework is shown by the change in their leisure structure after marriage, even before any children are born. Young spouses spend less time reading after marriage than before – they may reject an individual pastime such as reading in favour of joint cultural activities, principally watching television. The amount of time women spend on study falls considerably on marriage and suffers a further reduction with the appearance of children. Reading patterns vary considerably with sex and family position. Men consistently read newspapers more than women do, but whereas there is little variation in women's newspaper reading at various stages of the life-cycle, men spend more time on reading newspapers as they get older. The amount of time that women spend on reading varies with educational level far more than it does for men. The figures in Table 11.4 show that on average men spent 16·9 per cent of their free time reading, and women 12·9 per cent. But the range was far greater for women than for men, with a difference between the most active women readers and the least active of 14 per cent, compared to a range of only 5·9 per cent for male readers. Trufanov's figures also suggest that as educational and occupational level rises, so the difference between the amount of time the sexes spend on reading decreases.

The effects of age upon reading are difficult to separate out from the effect of educational level, as a high proportion of the least-educated are over 50. Grushin's figures suggest a resurgence of interest in newspapers after the age of 60, compared to the preceding age groups; there is a slight increase in reading of books and journals, too. Table 11.6, however, shows a sharp decline in book reading among older people. Until we have data over several generations of roughly equivalent educational level, it will be difficult to carry out a

Table 11.6 *Hours and minutes per week spent on various cultural activities*

Activity	Young unmarried people		Young couples		Parents of minor children (2-parent families)		Older people	
	Men	Women	Men	Women	Men	Women	Men	Women
Reading newspapers	1·15	0·45	2·35	0·35	2·40	0·30	3·00	0·45
Reading books and journals	3·35	4·35	2·25	1·45	1·50	1·15	0·40	0·30
Television	4·35	2·15	6·40	3·00	9·25	4·15	11·55	4·00
Cinema, theatre, concerts	2·55	3·20	1·30	0·50	0·35	0·35	0·25	0·20
Hobbies	1·15	1·05	0·55	2·00	0·50	0·20	0·25	0·50
Study, self-education	10·05	9·05	7·30	3·30	3·20	1·00	—	—

Source: Gordon and Klopov, 1972, appendix, pp. 34–5.

proper analysis of reading at the different stages of the life-cycle.

Material Position

Income, as such, seems to have little effect on reading, in that libraries are free and newspapers and journals cheap. However, level of income is a determinant of the acquisition of some of the conveniences of life, through which one may gain extra free time. Housing conditions do influence reading. Gordon and Gruzdeva (1975, p. 60) found that women living in communal flats spent only half as much time reading as did similar women living in a single-family apartment. This is explained by the increase in comfort and privacy, which encourages all home-based leisure activities.

Place of Residence

Reading in rural areas is deeply affected by changes in the work pattern throughout the agricultural year; further, it must be noted that rural areas contain more older people (especially women) and fewer well-educated people than do urban areas (Rogers, 1973, p. 11). The low educational level in rural areas is suggested by calls for the provision of more books for the semi-literate ('O sotsiologiche-skikh . . .', 1967, p. 129) and the suggestion that libraries can still usefully arrange for popular journals to be read aloud to people in rural areas, especially older women and believers (Kulagina, 1967, pp. 54–5). Bachaldina and Dobrynina (1968, p. 120) studied five villages in the mid-1960s and found that 32 per cent of those surveyed never read books (41 per cent of women and 17 per cent of men). In the 1970s, about 7 per cent of rural families are made up solely of people who do not read, and a further 23 per cent of families has at least one adult member who does not read (*Kniga . . .*, 1974, p. 29). In 1978, it was claimed that 91 per cent of rural adults do read some form of printed matter sometimes (Golubtsova, 1978, p. 16); but the general picture in rural areas is probably still as reported a decade ago: 'A significant proportion of the rural population still does not have the habit of regular book use' ('O sotsiologicheskikh . . .', 1967, p. 128).

In small towns in the RSFSR (under 50,000 population), a large-scale survey in the early 1970s found that 47 per cent of the population read books 'often', 30 per cent read them rarely, 11 per cent did not read them at all, and a further 12 per cent of replies were unclassified (*Kniga . . .*, 1973, p. 283).

As well as urban/rural differences, there are also considerable variations between various areas of the USSR (see Table 11.7). Given the very low educational level of some parts of tsarist Russia, this is hardly surprising.

Obviously, lower educational level is the main reason for the low

Table 11.7 Percentage of rural inhabitants who are readers

| | USSR | RSFSR | | Other republics | |
| | | European | Siberia and Far East | European | Trans-caucasia | Central Asia and Kazakhstan |
	%	%	%	%	%	%
Adults						
Workers	91	93	92	93	89	82
Pensioners	55	56	52	67	54	28
By education						
Primary	67	69	74	73	45	45
Incomplete secondary	95	95	94	96	92	85
General secondary	94	96	94	98	94	91
Specialised secondary	98	100	96	100	97	95
Higher	98	98	100	98	98	100
Total	87	87	89	91	88	81

Source: Kniga . . ., 1974, p. 26.

average figures for Transcaucasia, Central Asia and Kazakhstan. Even people with primary or incomplete secondary education in these areas read less than their counterparts in other rural areas; presumably this is the effect of cultural traditions. It would probably have been revealing to have had separate figures for women in the traditionally muslim areas as it seems likely that they read much less than average. The influence of low educational levels is clearly visible in the difference between reading rates for pensioners and working adults in the various areas.

Television
The effects of television on reading have attracted a lot of attention in the USSR; Rogers argues that

> in the early years of the electronic media it is the more educated who register the highest exposure, be it for reasons of access (ability to afford sets, or higher concentrations in urban areas which are covered by the television network sooner than rural areas), or of motivation. But in time the pattern changes, and the middle and lower educational groups register the most frequent and heaviest use. (1973, p. 13)

This is supported by Kogan (1975, p. 112) who found that it was largely people with primary education who stopped reading when television became available. In rural areas, radio, the cinema and the club were the alternative culture and information sources which lost most adherents to television (Kogan, 1975, p. 111). Apart from the least-educated groups, it may be that it is light reading which suffers most, rather than the use of non-fiction and serious reading of novels. Table 11.6 shows how popular television is among married men with children, and older men; all age groups (except young unmarried people) appear to spend more time watching television than reading. For many people, television probably uses up time that used to be spent simply doing nothing, or in anti-social pastimes such as drinking or gambling. The relationship of reading and television is complex, and not mutually exclusive; in small towns, for instance, a third of the sample claimed to read books regularly and also to be keen television viewers (*Kniga* . . ., 1973, p. 20). Kogan (1975, p. 112) concluded that the arrival of television reduced interest in books among those groups which seldom read them, but increased it among those who already read a lot.

READING AS AN INTEGRAL PART OF LIFE

This is the fourth of the attributes of the ideal Soviet reader. It is closely linked with the regularity and duration of reading, examined in the previous section, and was analysed separately only in the small towns survey. It was found that 71 per cent of the population read for all three purposes (professional, general educational, and aesthetic); however, there are considerable differences between various social and professional groups in the amount of professional reading done. As might be expected, specialists in all fields, and people studying part-time, do far more professional reading than do unskilled workers, collective farmers or pensioners. A high proportion of all groups read for general educational purposes, but for many people this need is satisfied through newspaper reading alone (*Kniga . . .*, 1973, p. 33).

RANGE OF PRINTED SOURCES USED

Many readers read newspapers, books and journals; in small towns 79 per cent read all three forms of printed information, 9 per cent read newspapers and books, and 5 per cent read only newspapers (*Kniga . . .*, 1973, pp. 284–5). Newspapers and journals have been discussed in some detail by Hollander (1972) and Rogers (1973), and so only a brief survey will be provided here.

Newspapers

Table 11.3 shows that a high proportion of the population claims to read a newspaper regularly; many people read several different newspapers. Newspaper sales in the USSR are lower than in Britain – 388 per 1,000 inhabitants as opposed to 443 in the UK (*Social trends*, 1978, p. 187). The newspapers people read in the USSR include the weighty dailies well known in the West, such as *Pravda* and *Izvestiya*, but local newspapers are very popular. In small towns, 35 per cent of newspaper readers read only the local newspaper, 80 per cent read local and central newspapers, and 16 per cent read only the central press (*Kniga . . .*, 1973, p. 35). In general, local papers contain more 'human interest' stories and more features of immediate concern to their readers; they also carry some local 'small-ads'. In non-Russian areas, the high level of interest in local newspapers is further explained by their being in the local language. Of the central newspapers, *Sel'skaya zhizn'* (Rural Life) is probably the lightest in content. This is confirmed by one report that under a third of collective-farm women read a newspaper, and of them over a half read *Sel'skaya zhizn'* and over three-quarters read the local (*raion*) newspaper (Levykin and Kharitonova, 1975, p. 70). By contrast, of the specialists living in small towns, only 1 per cent did not subscribe to a newspaper, and 77 per cent took three or more (*Kniga . . .*, 1973, p. 279). Hollander believes that the popularity of weeklies such as *Nedelya* and *Krokodil* is due largely to their satires and short stories.

She concludes her discussion of what people look for in their newspaper with the observation: 'The audience surveys leave us with the impression that the most popular rubrics are international news, family circle topics and news about accidents and crime (to which newspapers devote very little space even now), and satirical features. Economic news and political resolutions are considered boring and uninteresting by most readers' (1972, p. 74).

Periodicals
Like newspapers, periodicals are widely available on subscription; indeed, during the 1960s and early 1970s they were given priority over books in the allocation of paper (Walker, 1978, p. 15). Table 11.3 shows that nearly three-quarters of the adult population reads a journal regularly. Much of the reading of journals is, however, confined to popular magazines, such as *Roman-gazeta*, which publishes novels in serial form. Gordon and Klopov (1972, p. 169) found that 40 per cent of all the women who subscribe to any journal take *Rabotnitsa* (Working Woman – a popular journal for women) and that over 20 per cent of the urban workers who subscribe to any journal take one of the popular scientific journals such as *Nauka i zhizn'* (Science and Life). Overall, they concluded that about 80 per cent of all urban workers' journal subscriptions were for entertainment and general-interest magazines (*zanimatel'no-razvlekatel'nye zhurnaly*). Only 5–6 per cent took a 'thick' literary periodical such as *Novyi mir* or *Ogonek*. In small towns, specialists accounted for most of the reading of technical journals, and almost a third of the survey read only the general-interest journals. Only 11 per cent read political journals (*Kniga* . . ., 1973, p. 281).

Reading of newspapers and journals, although widespread, varies considerably in range and content among different groups, with a significant number of people confining their reading of journals and newspapers to popular magazines and the local press. The subject range and depth of reading of newspapers, magazines and books will be discussed further in the next section, which analyses the variety of reading interests.

VARIETY OF READING INTEREST

Studies of readers suggest that many have a wide range of reading interests. A large-scale study in urban areas found that 42 per cent of workers and 55 per cent of ITR read material about art, socio-political affairs and their profession, as well as popular science and fiction. As a rule, the higher a person's education level, the more varied his or her reading interests; however, young people (up to age 28) generally had wider reading interests than older people of the same educational level

(Smirnova, 1968, p. 36). In a study of rural areas all over the USSR, only 26 per cent of the population were found to have a full range of reading interests; here, too, education seemed to be the deciding factor (*Kniga* . . ., 1978, p. 165). Each of the three subject groups – socio-political, science and technology, belles-lettres – will be examined in more detail, to see what kind of material people actually read.

Socio-Political Literature

Socio-political literature covers a wide range of subjects, including history and current affairs. In a large study of small towns in the RSFSR, 93 per cent of the population claimed to be interested in it (*Kniga* . . ., 1973, p. 286). But 43 per cent of them satisfy this interest just from newspapers, and only 47 per cent read books on socio-political themes. Party and Komsomol activists, and others with a 'professional' concern for social and political developments have a deeper interest in this type of material than the average reader, and pay far more attention to journals and books (*Kniga* . . ., 1973, p. 50). In rural areas, nearly two-thirds of those surveyed read books in this subject area, a surprisingly high proportion when compared to small towns where the educational level is generally higher (*Kniga* . . ., 1978, p. 166). Newspaper reading is mainly to keep up-to-date with current affairs; journals in this subject are divided between popular mass journals such as *Rabotnitsa* (Working Woman) and *Krest'yanka* (The Peasant Woman), on the one hand, and on the other, political journals such as *Agitator* (The Agitator) and *Politicheskoe samoobrazovanie* (Political Self-education). The difference between the two groups is suggested by the following quotations. The first is by a working woman with incomplete secondary education: 'I read *Krest'yanka* and *Rabotnitsa*. I am a woman, and so it is always interesting and useful to read my own journal. There are a lot of interesting articles about everyday life, moral questions, the family and bringing up children.' The second is from the reading diary of a 'propagandist' with higher education: 'I read in *Politicheskoe samoobrazovanie* an article about the economic laws of capitalism. Interesting new material. Good statistical data demonstrating various facets of the problem' (*Kniga* . . ., 1973, pp. 52–3). Thus, if a similar classification of reading were applied in Britain, those who read only *The Sun*, *Titbits* and *Woman's Own* would be classified as readers of socio-political literature, alongside people who read *New Society*.

Books are read far less than magazines and journals; most people's interest in current affairs, politics, education and the family is satisfied without consulting books. Library statistics suggest that up to a fifth of all library issues are for socio-political books (Sultanov, 1978); this has apparently doubled over the last decade, as a result of ideological and educational measures by librarians (Golubtsova, 1978). Such measures are part of the reading guidance practised by Soviet librarians, particularly in mass libraries (for more details, see Burnett, 1977). Increases in the issue of socio-political literature are a major part of libraries' plans, and levels of use clearly fall short of what is considered desirable. Indeed, it is admitted that average figures for issues hide the fact that very many readers do not use socio-political literature at all (San'ko, 1971, p. 14). In many rural libraries, the socio-political section is the least used of all; in one library in Belorussia it was over a quarter of the total stock, but only 9 per cent of the issue (Savitskaya, 1971, p. 49). The books that people do borrow seem to be largely in the areas of history, biography and travellers' tales. In small towns, over three-quarters of the socio-political books borrowed from the mass libraries were on history, and the bulk of them were about the Second World War. Series of military memoirs, regimental histories and semi-documentary spy and adventure books are popular, and are obviously very popular among young people as well as veterans (*Kniga* . . ., 1973, pp. 46–8). Steady interest in foreign countries and international affairs among urban workers and engineering and technical personnel was shown in a study in the early 1960s; about a quarter of them read books in this field (Smirnova, 1968, p. 85). In rural Latvia, nearly a third of library users read travel books and material about other countries (Aishpure, 1974, p. 26). In small towns, though, only 7 per cent of books borrowed from libraries were in this area (*Kniga* . . ., 1973, p. 57); this may be due to poor supplies of books to the libraries.

The study of Marxist–Leninist literature and books about ideological problems is officially encouraged; one study reports that as a result of positive action by library staff, issues of this type of material have increased four-fold over the last four years (Sultanov, 1978). About half the urban workers and ITR who use libraries read books on philosophy, religion and atheism, according to a survey in the early 1960s (Smirnova, 1968, p. 50). Here again, one must allow for the effect of reading guidance.

Most people who have an interest in socio-political literature seem to satisfy it by reading newspapers and journals, and some historical and travel books. The interest in the latter may contain a good deal of escapism, because of the appeal of a good story or an adventure, often related in fairly simple, direct language with plenty of action. Reading political literature, narrowly defined, seems to be limited to Party and Komsomol activists, and those obliged to read it to fulfil other commitments.

Science and Technology

This group of interests includes medicine, gardening, cooking and fishing as well as popular scientific literature and specialist material about one's trade or profession. In small towns, three-quarters of the population took an interest in this area (*Kniga* . . ., 1973, p. 59); in rural areas, 65 per cent did (*Kniga* . . ., 1978, p. 166). Newspapers do publish some articles in this subject area, but apparently only one person in three reads them; about two-thirds of the people with interests in these topics are satisfied by reading journals. These include the mass medical journal *Zdorov'e* (Health) which is read by about half the people who subscribe to scientific and technical journals; it is especially popular among women. Other journals read by significant numbers include *Nauka i zhizn'* (Science and Life) and *Vokrug sveta* (Around the World) (*Kniga* . . ., 1973, pp. 61–4).

The USSR produces a wide range of popular scientific books, which set out information about various topics, often fairly complex, in a form that is accessible to the interested general reader, or to a specialist from another discipline. The more intellectually demanding a person's work, the more he or she reads popular scientific literature (*Kniga* . . ., 1973, p. 60). People read it out of general interest in recent developments in science and technology, or out of a desire to learn about a subject in general – nature perhaps. Many consult it for utilitarian purposes, such as improving the cultivation of their garden, or finding out more about fishing.

Reading literature about one's job, trade or profession is considered to be an indication of a positive and socialist attitude towards work. In small towns, 92 per cent of specialists, 58 per cent of employees, 42 per cent of workers and 26 per cent of collective farmers read work-related literature; among workers there was a range of from 7 per cent of unskilled labourers to 75 per cent of skilled workers. Of the specialists, teachers and medical personnel did most work-related reading; this is partly because of their high educational level, but also because they are thought to have most opportunity to apply new ideas and new methods in their work (*Kniga* . . ., 1973, pp. 100–1). Another study of urban workers found that the majority of those who read work-related literature had the aim of raising their skill level (and hence their pay), or of learning a new skill and changing jobs. Much of the other reading of work-related literature was limited to consulting reference works to answer specific queries; only about a quarter of the workers in the survey read the special journals about their branch of industry or their trade (Smirnova, 1968, pp. 39–49). In rural areas, the use of work-related literature is clearly affected by the wide range of educational levels; there may also be a shortage of suitable pamphlets and books for some groups of farm workers. A study in rural Belorussia found that even among the younger workers, a third of those who were library members did not read any material about agriculture or their profession (Kravtsevich, 1971, p. 49). There is, however, considerable interest in rural areas in books about subjects other than paid employment – books on gardening are very popular, as are books on household management and amateur mechanics (Osipova, 1978, p. 64).

As with socio-political literature, reading scientific, technical and work-related literature covers a wide range of subjects. Interests seem to be divided into three groups (1) general interest in new achievements in science and technology; (2) reading in order to improve one's daily life or increase the enjoyment of a hobby; (3) use of literature to help in one's work. The second type of reading seems to be most widespread, with general interest in new achievements and specialist reading being mainly the concern of the better-educated sections of the population.

Belles-Lettres

The most widespread type of reading is belles-lettres (fiction, poetry, drama); it is read by 93 per cent of readers in rural areas (*Kniga . . .*, 1978, p. 166), 95 per cent of readers in small towns (*Kniga . . .*, 1973, p. 74) and 98 per cent of urban workers and ITR (Smirnova, 1968, p. 92). Stel'makh (1974, p. 6) argues that the reading of belles-lettres deserves especially detailed study not just because it is so widespread, but also because it is disinterested, having no utilitarian goals (apart from pupils or students reading it as part of a syllabus) and is a means of emotional and aesthetic experience. Therefore, she argues, it can be used as an indication of the level of development of a person's whole personality, because it involves feelings, imagination, fantasy, ideals and general view of life.

Newspapers publish some fiction, in the form of short stories, and over two-thirds of all readers read them; 4 per cent of readers of fiction satisfy themselves with these newspaper stories alone. Ninety-two per cent of people interested in belles-lettres read books, and 62 per cent also read poetry and fiction in journals (*Kniga . . .*, 1973, p. 291). In rural areas, a similar proportion read books, but only 18 per cent read poetry and fiction in the newspapers, and about a third, in journals (*Kniga . . .*, 1978, p. 166). General journals such as *Rabotnitsa* are one element in the journal reading, but the most important journal is *Roman-gazeta*. It is reported to publish quite a lot of material 'of little worth', too often undemanding, requiring 'neither literary education nor aesthetic taste' (*Kniga . . .*, 1973, p. 77).

Some information is available on the type of novels people like to read, and is shown in Table 11.8. In small towns, only 17 per cent of those surveyed read all five categories of literature, and 35 per cent read only Soviet literature (*Kniga . . .*, 1973, p. 80).

In Table 11.8, there is a striking difference between the amount of pre-revolutionary literature read in small towns and the figures given

Table 11.8 *Percentage of people in each survey who read each type of novel*

Type of literature	Small towns[a] %	Rural areas[b] %	Urban workers[c] %	Urban ITR[c] %
Pre-revolutionary Russian	10	} 73	70	70
Soviet Russian	63		} 77	} 72
Other Soviet peoples	9	21		
Foreign classics	12	} 19	60	63
Modern foreign	6		39	39

Notes:

[a] From *Kniga . . .*, 1973, p. 78 (100% = all books actually being read at the time of the survey).

[b] From *Kniga . . .*, 1978, p. 166.

[c] From Smirnova, 1968, p. 93.

for urban workers and ITR. However, library data for the same people showed that only 22 per cent of workers and 16 per cent of ITR had borrowed books in this area during the previous eight months (Smirnova, 1968, p. 93). The data provided on rural reading do not give sufficient detail, but it seems likely that much of the Russian literature read is from the Soviet period. The inconsistency between reported and actual reading of the classics was discussed in the small towns survey. They found that up to 80 per cent of readers said they read the Russian classics if asked directly if they did, although only 10 per cent were actually reading it at the time; people also tended to respond using stereotyped answers based on school work on the classics. This is an example of the 'halo effect' – people do not want to appear uncultured, for the Russian classics enjoy high prestige. People may also feel that, as the classics will always be there, keeping up with the latest fiction is more pressing (*Kniga . . .*, 1973, pp. 79–80). The figures for reading foreign books also show some inconsistencies; again, the library issue statistics for urban workers and ITR show they borrowed far fewer foreign classics and rather more modern foreign novels than the questionnaire responses suggest (Smirnova, 1968, p. 93). It seems likely that a lot of the foreign literature read is detective and adventure stories. In general, however, readers in small towns found foreign names and concepts difficult to grasp, and some claimed to be discouraged by the different worldview of non-socialist authors (*Kniga . . .*, 1973, p. 79). In rural areas, Jack London, Alexandre Dumas, Georges Sand and Theodore

Dreiser were the most popular foreign writers (Dobrynina, 1978, p. 39). Lack of interest in foreign writers may also result from difficulties in obtaining translated literature outside the big towns, and the dearth of foreign literature translated into languages other than Russian.

Some comment is also necessary on the reading of novels by Soviet writers, other than Russians. This covers two phenomena (1) reading of literature in one's own mother-tongue by writers of the same nationality; (2) reading the literature of other Soviet peoples, usually translated into one's own mother-tongue or into Russian. The popularity of one's own national literature varies considerably according to the strength of the literary tradition and the degree of assimilation to another language (usually Russian). In Belorussia, only 10 per cent of library users read Belorussian literature (San'ko, 1971, p. 21), whereas in rural Lithuania, which is far less russified, over a third of the books borrowed were by Lithuanian authors (Dobrynina, 1978, p. 37). In Central Asia and Transcaucasia, between a half and three-quarters of rural readers read only 'their own' writers (Dobrynina, 1978, p. 32). The small towns survey was based on the RSFSR, and the level of reading non-Russian Soviet literature is much lower than in the multi-national rural survey. Here we are dealing with literature translated into Russian from other languages; the most popular authors include Chingiz Aitmatov (Kazakh), V. Lacis (Latvian) and the Ukrainian O. Gonchar. Reading literature by writers of other nationalities in the USSR is seen officially as one way of encouraging the peoples of the USSR to grow together. In rural areas (excluding the RSFSR) 39 per cent of readers actually read Russian novels, or wanted to; but only 6 per cent actually read or wanted to read novels by writers of other nationalities except their own or Russians (calculated from Dobrynina, 1978, pp. 34–5). This suggests the pressure of russification in the non-Russian areas, not matched by a similar pressure on Russians to take an interest in the literature of other nationalities. This is perhaps inevitable, as Russian is the working language of the USSR.

Some information is available on what people read in terms of subject and genre, and is shown in Table 11.9. In small towns, at the time of the survey, 10 per cent were reading detective stories, 10 per cent were reading historical novels, 9 per cent were reading about the Revolution and civil war, 24 per cent were reading novels about the Second World War, 2 per cent were reading poetry, and 3 per cent, science fiction (*Kniga* . . ., 1973, p. 82).

The interest in documentary accounts about the last war has already been noted, and the popularity of fictional works is to be expected. For some people, it is an opportunity to re-live their own experiences; young people are supposed to see in war stories models of courage,

Table 11.9   *Proportion of rural inhabitants who mentioned an interest in a particular subject or genre*

Subject	% of rural readers who mentioned it	As % of total replies
Second World War	52	22
Revolution and Civil War	18	7
Historical	26	11
Detective stories	26	11
Rural life	28	12
Youth	21	8
Love	34	14
Science fiction	12	5
Humour	14	6
Poetry	10	4

Source: Calculated from Dubin, 1978, p. 55.

determination and high moral principle, but for many the attraction is a fast-moving story with plenty of action and drama. Despite efforts to discourage them, detective stories are still very popular; the small town study attributes their continued popularity to the intellectual challenge and the appeal of solving a problem, and calls on librarians and publishing houses to discourage 'bad' detective stories and encourage the fans to read better-written detective stories. Librarians approve of Agatha Christie, and the series *Zarubezhnyi detektiv* (Foreign Detective Stories) includes writers such as Ngaio Marsh and Erle Stanley Gardner.

The figures for reading science fiction are surprisingly low, as one has the impression that science fiction is very popular in the USSR. However, it may be concentrated in particular groups – particularly younger people, the better educated, and people with a training in science and technology. High levels of public demand are, however, indicated by the edition size planned for novels in the series *Biblioteka otechestvennoi fantastiki* (Library of Soviet Science Fiction), and the annual anthology of short stories *Fantastika-79* which has a huge edition planned – 200,000 copies (*Novye . . .*, 1979, pp. 43–4). Perhaps it is being encouraged officially in order to foster an interest in science and technology, especially among young people.

The information on rural areas shows the interest in novels which touch on moral and ethical problems, and on rural life. People often read in order to learn more about life, to acquire vicarious experience, and so choose books about topics close to their own hearts. This is particularly true of the less-educated – in Latvia, for instance, over four-fifths of field-workers preferred novels on everyday themes (*bytovoi roman*) (Sardyko, 1974, p. 21). Women are probably the main consumers of this type of literature, with men preferring war stories and detective stories. Humour and poetry seem to be mainly the preserve of the better educated. However, the survey of urban workers and ITR found a high level of interest in poetry, especially Soviet poetry (Smirnova, 1968, p. 102); however, some of this may be due to the 'halo effect' mentioned earlier – what Russian could admit to not reading Pushkin, Esenin and Mayakovskii?

In the library literature there are frequent calls for efforts to raise the level of 'reading culture' (*kul'tura chteniya*). Symptoms of an inadequate level of reading culture include the frequent inability of readers to recall either the author or the title of the book they are currently reading, and the tendency to ignore style and other aesthetic features in evaluating a book, preferring to concentrate on the story alone. Few readers apparently know how to judge a book on anything other than its subject matter and story line. Many people simply read whatever happens to be at hand – for instance, books brought home by children or grandchildren (*Kniga* . . ., 1973, pp. 95–6). In the small town study, it was found that many people selected books mainly on the recommendation of their friends, which would tend to encourage the reading of familiar or fashionable works, rather than more challenging literature which might be recommended by a librarian (*Kniga* . . ., 1973, p. 85). Few people read literary criticism. An interesting comment on the effects of censorship appears in one person's criterion for assessing books – 'If it was issued by the publishing house, then it must be good' (*Kniga* . . ., 1973, p. 90).

People do read a lot of fiction, but much of it seems to be read fairly superficially, involving minimal intellectual effort and little apprecia-tion of style. There is a strong recreational and amusement element in the reading of novels, rather than a desire for aesthetic and cultural development, at least among many mass readers. Hollander (1966*a*) stresses the escapist element in science fiction, detective and adven-ture stories, and sees a strong nostalgia for the past in the affection for pre-revolutionary Russian literature among older collective-farm peasants. Friedberg (1962, p. 62) argues that, because Soviet litera-ture is so dull, serious readers often prefer translated literature of no great literary merit, or turn back to the Russian classics. He believes that pre-revolutionary literature is read partly for its sheer artistic quality, but also because its moral values contradict the Soviet spirit. Some readers may find parallels between criticisms of tsarist Russia and the USSR today, and he describes Russian classics as 'the spiritual mainstay of the more disaffected segments of the population' (Fried-berg, 1962, p. 173). We have no way of testing his opinion against survey data of the type available for the broad mass of the population. The small town survey did show, however, that people with higher education read the same amount of pre-revolutionary literature as the average person; people with primary education read rather more of it than average (*Kniga* . . ., 1973, p. 292). This would be consistent with Hollander's suggestion that it is the preferred reading of the older and less-educated people. Personal observation suggests a great interest among intellectuals in older Russian literature, but this would include early Soviet writers such as Bulgakov, Pilnyak and Zamyatin as well as pre-revolutionary writers not included in the school syllabus.

Discussion of the reading of novels must always take place in the context of the chronic shortage of fiction in the USSR, due largely to paper allocation. But over the last year or so, it seems that the edition size of fiction published has increased, but prices have increased too. There are reports that the market for some standard works has been glutted (Walker, 1978, p. 105), but multi-volume sets of the classics are generally only available on subscription, and in an attempt to ensure that libraries get sufficient supplies of new books, special library editions are now being published of some popular works. Copies of the works of some of the most desirable authors are available only in exchange for coupons earned by collecting waste paper. In Moscow or Leningrad, queues for new novels are a common sight, and high prices are paid on the black market for most publications in series such as the *Biblioteka poeta*, or for any works by writers such as Tsvetaeva or Mandel'shtam, who have been published in the USSR since the Thaw of the 1950s, but only in small editions. Books have apparently become something of a status symbol, and there is increasing official concern about the mere collecting of books, although the building of home libraries is generally encouraged. It seems likely, however, that willingness to pay black-market prices and to stand all night in a queue for books is limited to a small group, largely made up of urban intellectuals. They are probably the main consumers of *samizdat* and *tamizdat*.

CONCLUSIONS

A detailed study of reading thus confirms the general impression that the Soviet people read a lot. Whereas in the USSR, only a fifth of the population do not read books, in the UK a quarter seldom or never read them (*Social Trends*, 1978, p. 184). As in Britain, the quality of what Soviet people read varies considerably. It is the most educated sections which most closely match the model of the ideal reader, and unskilled women in rural areas who are furthest from it. For urban workers, reading books has been a mass activity for only a few decades, and has not yet become an integral part of their daily life. Many people appear to have wide-ranging interests, but these are sometimes superficial. Novels are indeed tremendously popular, but are read mainly for relaxation and enjoyment, for the pleasure of a story, rather than with any deep cultural or aesthetic interest. Yet reading enjoys considerable prestige among all groups; this is partly because of official encouragement and cultural traditions, but also because education is the key to social status. As in many developing countries, books and reading are seen as a way of advancement open to everyone.

The official policy of encouraging books and reading is made up of several factors. First, reading is essential in building up a skilled labour force, able to adapt to new technology and bring in new ideas. Reading is also seen as an essential part of forming the all-round developed personality, of building the 'new Soviet person' who is as essential a prerequisite for full communism as the material and technical base. Culture is generally considered to be a 'good thing', a source of prestige for socialism, showing its advantages over capitalism. Reading matter is comparatively cheap and easy to provide, and is a channel of political socialisation (although to a lesser extent than radio and television). It is also an essentially home-based pastime, and thus fits well with the official concern for strengthening the family. Reading is often advanced as one remedy for anti-social leisure pursuits.

To the people, reading offers a far wider choice than is possible from radio, television or the cinema. One can read at one's own pace, selecting the information required. Books are portable, convenient and cheap. Reading demands more concentration and imagination than audio-visual entertainment, but is far more rewarding. It can also be far more apolitical and escapist, offering, as Hollander (1966*b*) puts it, 'an irreproachably legitimate escape from the unpleasant realities of life'. Reading is essentially individual, not shared with other people. As a privatised and solitary act it can conflict with the collectivist principle in official ideology – hence the official concern with what material is available and how to guide people's reading.

Despite the impact of censorship, small editions and supply difficulties on what is practically available to them, people do still have the opportunity to exercise considerable choice over their reading matter. Our study shows that there is still a significant gap between their choice and the official recommendations.

BIBLIOGRAPHY

Aishpure, A. 'Otraslevaya literatura i ee chitatel'', in *Kniga i chtenie na sele: nauchnaya konferentsiya* (Riga, 1974), pp. 25–8.

Anderson, N., *Work and Leisure* (London: Routledge & Kegan Paul, 1961).

Bachaldina, S. P. and Dobrynina, N. E., 'Kniga v zhizni sovremennogo seia', in *Sovetskii chitatel'*: *opyt konkretno-sotsiologicheskogo issledovaniya* (Moscow, 1968), pp. 116–56.

Bogdanov, I. M., *Gramotnost' i obrazovanie v dorevolyutsionnoi Rossii i v SSSR* (Moscow, 1964).

Brezhnev, L. I., 'Resheniya XXIV s''ezda – boevaya programma deyatel'nosti sovetskikh profsoyuzov', in *Materialy XV s''ezda professional'nykh soyuzov SSSR* (Moscow, 1972).

Burnett, P., 'Reading guidance and recommendatory bibliography in Soviet libraries', in *Four Studies in Soviet Librarianship*, ed. G. Harris (London: Library Association, 1977), pp. 32–51.

Dobrynina, N. E., 'Internatsionalizatsiya chteniya na sele', in *Kniga i chtenie v zhizni sovetskogo sela: problemy i tendentsii* (Moscow, 1978), pp. 19–46.

Dubin, B. V., 'Chtenie i vsestoronnee razvitie lichnosti v usloviyakh sela', in *Kniga i chtenie v zhizni sovetskogo sela: problemy i tendentsii* (Moscow, 1978), pp. 47–58.

Dumazedier, J., *Towards a Society of Leisure* (New York: Free Press, 1967).

Friedberg, M., *Russian Classics in Soviet Jackets* (New York: Columbia University Press, 1962).

Golubtsova, T., 'Po leninskim zavetam', *Bibliotekar'*, 1978, no. 1, pp. 13–17.

Gordon, L. A. and Gruzdeva, E. B., 'Rasprostranennost' i intensivnost' chteniya v gorodskoi rabochei srede', in *Problemy sotsiologii i psikhologii chteniya* (Moscow, 1975), pp. 47–64.

Gordon, L. A. and Klopov, E. V., *Chelovek posle raboty: sotsial'nye problemy byta* (Moscow, 1972).

Grushin, B., *Svobodnoe vremya: aktual'nye problemy* (Moscow, 1967).

Hatt, F., *The Reading Process: a Framework for Analysis and Description* (London: C. Bingley, 1976).

Hollander, G. D., *Soviet Political Indoctrination: Developments in Mass Media and Propaganda since Stalin* (New York: Praeger, 1972).

Hollander, P., 'Leisure as an American and Soviet value', *Social Problems*, vol. 14, no. 2 (1966a), pp. 179–88.

Hollander, P., 'The uses of leisure', *Survey*, no. 60 (1966b), pp. 40–50.

Kniga i chtenie v zhizni nebol'shikh gorodov: po materialam issledovaniya chteniya i chitatel'skikh interesov (Moscow, 1973).

Kniga i chtenie v zhizni sovetskogo sela. Vyp. 4. Rasprostranennost' chteniya i pechatnykh istochnikov na sele (Moscow, 1974).

Kniga i chtenie v zhizni sovetskogo sela: problemy i tendentsii (Moscow, 1978).

Kogan, L. N., 'Kniga i sovremennoe televidenie', in *Problemy sotsiologii i psikhologii chteniya* (Moscow, 1975), pp. 103–16.

Kravtsevich, E., 'Chitatel' – rabochaya molodezh'', in *Kniga v zhizni molodezhi; izuchenie rabochei i sel'skoi molodezhi* . . . (Minsk, 1971), pp. 28–41.

Kulagina, R., 'Formirovanie raznostoronnikh chitatel'skikh interesov u zhenshchin', in *Materyyaly trokhdzennykh haradskikh i raennykh seminaraw kul'tasvetrabotnikaw i saktarow kamsamol'skikh arhanizatsyi* . . . (Minsk, 1967), pp. 54–64.

Levykin, I. T. and Kharitonova, O. V., 'Poznavatel'nye interesy sovremennogo kolkhoznogo krest'yanstva i chtenie', in *Problemy sotsiologii i psikhologii chteniya* (Moscow, 1975), pp. 65–74.

Maslova, O. M., *Metodicheskie problemy izucheniya chitatel'skoi auditorii v SSSR* . . . *avtoreferat dissertatsii* (Moscow, 1974).

Materialy XXIV s"ezda KPSS (Moscow, 1971).

Netsenko, A. V., *Sotsial'no-ekonomicheskie problemy svobodnogo vremeni pri sotsializme* (Leningrad, 1975).

Nikiforova, O. I., *Psikhologiya vospriyatiya khudozhestvennoi literatury* (Moscow, 1972).

Novye knigi SSSR, 1979, no. 1.

'O sotsiologicheskikh issledovaniyakh v bibliotechnom dele', *Biblioteki SSSR*, 1967, no. 34, pp. 124–32.

Osipova, I. P., 'Prevalence of reading and study of readers' interests in the USSR', in *Books in the Service of Society*, ed. A. N. Efimova, V. V. Serov and O. S. Chubaryan (Moscow: Ministry of Culture of the USSR, 1974), pp. 138–56.

Osipova, I. P., 'Chtenie zhitelei sela v pomosch' popolneniyu professional'nykh znanii', in *Kniga i chtenie v zhizni sovetskogo sela: problemy i tendentsii* (Moscow, 1978), pp. 59–70.

Parker, S., *The Future of Work and Leisure* (London: Macgibbon & Kee, 1971).

Petrosyan, G. S., *Vnerabochee vremya trudyashchikhsya v SSSR* (Moscow, 1965).

Pimenova, V. N., *Svobodnoe vremya v sotsialisticheskom obshchestve* (Moscow, 1974).

Povarnin, S. I., *Kak chitat' knigu* (Moscow, 1974).

Rogers, R., *Media Receptivity in the USSR* (Cambridge, Mass.: MIT Center for International Studies, 1973).

San'ko, K., 'Sel'skaya molodezh' i kniga', in *Kniga v zhizni molodezhi; izuchenie rabochei i sel'skoi molodezhi* . . . : (Minsk, 1971), pp. 5–27.

Sardyko, S., 'Chtenie khudozhestvennoi literatury na sele', in *Kniga i chtenie na sele: nauchnaya konferentsiya* (Riga, 1974), pp. 20–5.

Savitskaya, L. 'Izuchenie chteniya molodezhi v Taimonovskoi sel'skoi biblioteke', in *Kniga v zhizni molodezhi: izuchenie rabochei i sel'skoi molodezhi* . . . (Minsk, 1971), pp. 49–55.

Smirnova, S. M., Osipova, I. P. and Smirnova, O. M., 'Chitatel'-rabochii i chitatel'-inzhener', in *Sovetskii chitatel': opyt konkretno-sotsiologicheskogo issledovaniya* (Moscow, 1968), pp. 29–115.

Social Trends, vol. 8 (London: HMSO, 1978).

Stel'makh, V. D., *Literaturno-khudozhestvennye interesy chitatelei i osobennosti ikh issledovaniya* . . . *avtoreferat dissertatsii* (Leningrad, 1974).

Sultanov, F., 'Mestnye sovety i biblioteki', *Bibliotekar'*, 1978, no. 11, pp. 4–6, 9.

Trufanov, I. P., 'Byudzhety vremeni kak instrument issledovaniya byta trudyashchikhsya', *Sotsial'nye issledovaniya*, vol. 6, 1970, pp. 128–49.

Walker, G. P. M., *Soviet Book Publishing Policy* (Cambridge: CUP, 1978).
Weinberg, E. A., *The Development of Sociology in the Soviet Union* (London: Routledge & Kegan Paul, 1974).
Zaitsev, V., 'Biblioteka i svobodnoe vremya', *Bibliotekar'*, 1978, no. 2, pp. 19–22.
Zepa, B., 'Sotsial'nye portret chitatelei, pol'zuyushchikhsya i ne pol'zuyushchikhsya bibliotekoi', in *Kniga i chtenie na sele: nauchnaya konferentsiya* (Riga, 1974), pp. 31–5.
Zlotnikov, R. A., 'Svobodnoe vremya i obrazovanie', *Sotsial'nye issledovaniya* vol. 6, 1970, pp. 111–27.

Geoffrey Barker, 1923–77

by R. W. DAVIES and JAMES RIORDAN

Geoffrey Russell Barker studied economics and Russian at Cambridge, where he was a pupil of Maurice Dobb. Like Dobb, he was one of the very few scholars in this country who attempted, in years of Cold War, a sympathetic Marxist analysis of Soviet economic development. In the 1950s, his main academic interest was in Soviet labour problems; and he contributed articles on this subject to the Birmingham *Bulletins on Soviet Economic Development*. His *Bulletin* no. 6 (1951), 'Soviet Labour', remains an indispensable study of its period; this was followed by a monograph, *Some Problems of Incentives and Labour Productivity in Soviet Industry* (Oxford: Blackwell, 1955).

He found an academic foothold in the Department of Economics and Institutions of the USSR at the University of Birmingham under Alexander Baykov, where he was successively research student, research associate and lecturer. Apart from Glasgow, Birmingham was perhaps the only university where someone with Geoffrey Barker's approach to Soviet studies could have found a home at that time. Baykov was amused by what he saw as Barker's political naïveté; but world economic developments in the 1930s had convinced Baykov that planning was essential to world progress, and this conviction, reinforced by Soviet victories in the Second World War, was, of course, shared by Geoffrey Barker.

With the end of the Cold War, and the trauma of the 20th Soviet Party Congress in February 1956, Geoff, like other left intellectuals of his generation, was impelled to re-examine his political views fundamentally. The process of rethinking continued to the end of his life. His socialism and his Marxism emerged stronger than ever, though he never resolved to his own satisfaction the basic problem of applying Marxism to an analysis of Soviet developments.

When the Department of Economics and Institutions of the USSR at Birmingham was incorporated into the new Centre for Russian and East European Studies in 1963, Geoff was one of its four founder members. He played a very full part in the life of the Centre: promoted to a senior lectureship in 1967, he served as acting director on many occasions. These years saw a marked shift in his academic interests. Profoundly convinced that social equality and social justice should be the overriding goals of mankind, Geoff turned his attention, in both research and teaching, to social developments in the USSR. He continued his work on Soviet labour: in 1965 his study of Soviet research and development manpower was published by the Organisation for Economic Co-operation and Development (in *The Research and Development Effort in Europe, North America and the USSR*, ed. by C. Freeman and A. Young, Paris: OECD, 1965). Geoff's paper on women in the USSR, delivered at the 12th International Seminar on Family Research in Moscow in 1972 (published in *Sociologie et sociétés*, vol. 4, no. 2, November 1972), created a minor sensation. It was strongly criticised by some Soviet scholars, on rather flimsy grounds; but his vast knowledge of the subject, and his evident honesty and objectivity, eventually won their respect. He undertook a massive compilation of Soviet social statistics, which was unfinished at the time of his death.

It must be unusual for a book to be composed in memory of someone who left so little in terms of scholarly publications. His list of publications does not reflect his contribution to the subject. Many students and scholars owe much to his assistance. He was an infuriating supervisor. Manuscripts were returned only after immense delays; and, when they were returned, duly embellished with cigarette burns and coffee stains, his pedantic comments on such matters as punctuation (Geoff was very fond of unnecessary commas) and his obsession with minor details sometimes failed to please the budding or more senior author. But most of his advice was pertinent and helpful; and his enthusiasm for the subject, his appreciation of work well done and his sympathetic understanding overcame deficiencies. A multitude of books, articles and theses by students and colleagues owe much to his guidance.

But, above all, it is the deep affection he inspired as a man which has determined his friends, colleagues and students to prepare the present book. This enduring affection is difficult to convey to those who did not know him. His life was badly organised, even chaotic. His car was never washed, his hedge never cut, his trousers never ironed and his bank account never in the black. A lift in Geoff's car, always generously offered, frequently resulted in a long wait while he set off on foot with a petrol can to the nearest garage to fill his empty tank. Somehow the day was always too fleeting: he rarely found time to go to bed before 2 or 3 a.m. Consequently he was always tired: he fell asleep in seminars (sometimes stretched out to his full, not inconsiderable, length on the floor) and even in the middle of a conversation. He ate irregularly and smoked incessantly.

Why, then, did Geoffrey Barker matter so much to all of us? He was an utterly honest man, gentle, sensitive to the feelings of others and always generous of time and material goods; only under the most extreme provocation could he bring himself to say a bad word about anyone. He could always be relied upon for advice and ready assistance in times of trouble. Above all, we remember him as a man of principle, who could be trusted for his frank and independent judgement, entirely uninfluenced by his personal interests.

Index